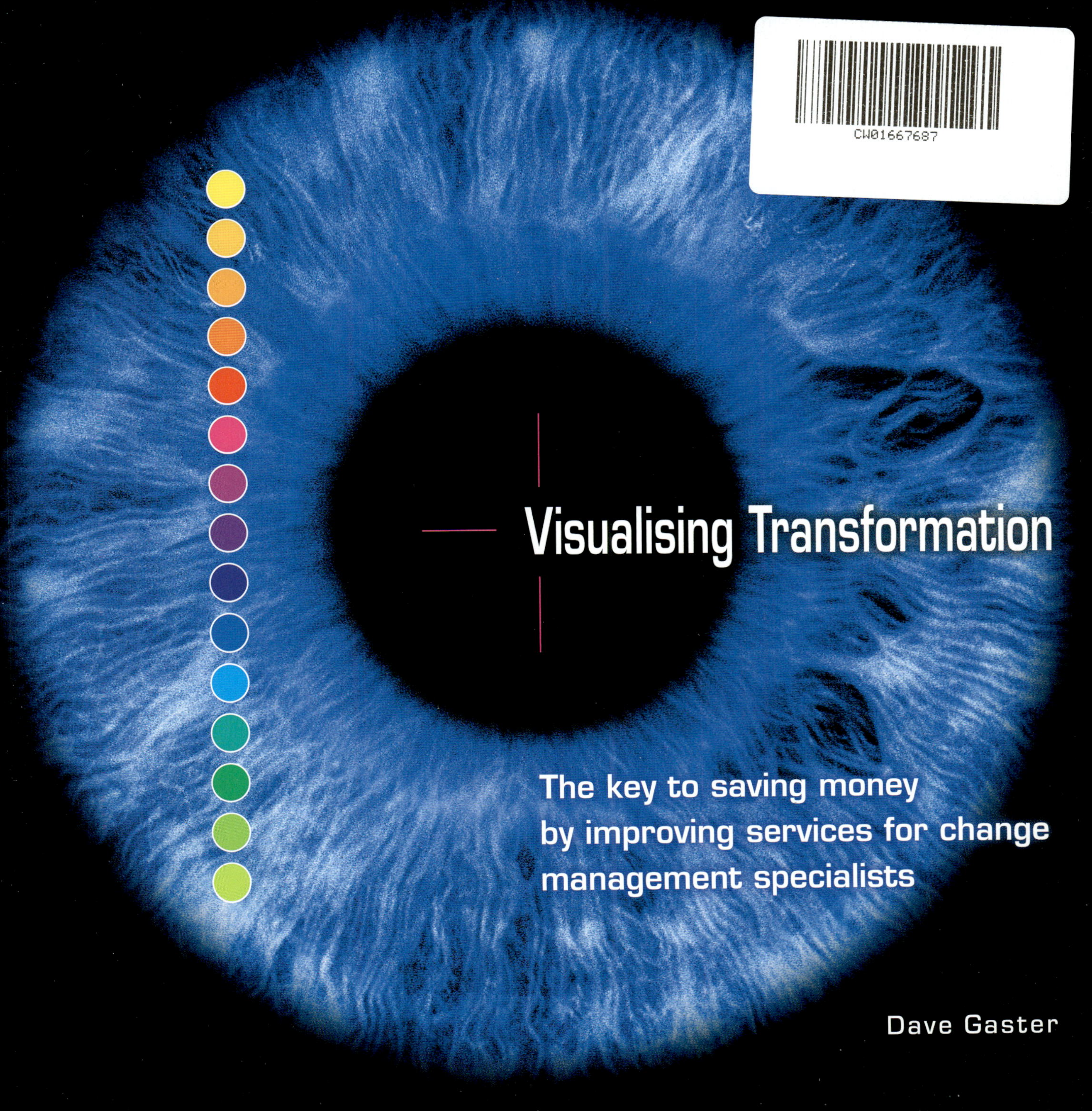

Visualising Transformation

The key to saving money by improving services for change management specialists

Dave Gaster

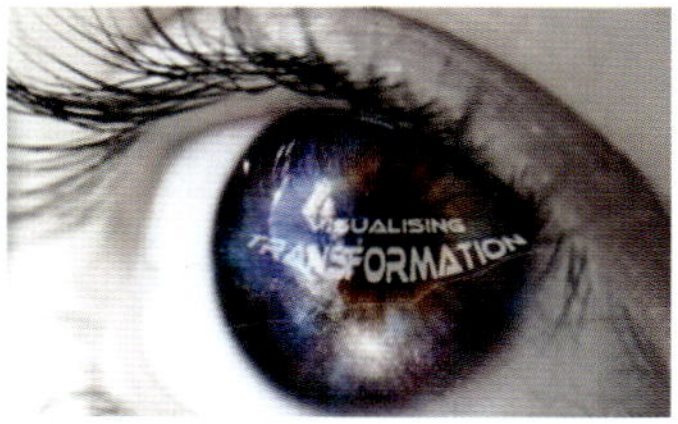

Visualising Transformation™ is registered to Support Services Direct

ISBN 978-1-906316-52-5

Published in 2010 by HotHive Books
www.thehothive.com

A CIP record of this book is available from the British Library.

Printed in the UK by Cambrian Printers, Aberystwyth

hothivebooks

FSC
Mixed Sources
Product group from well-managed forests and other controlled sources
www.fsc.org Cert no. TT-COC-2200
© 1996 Forest Stewardship Council

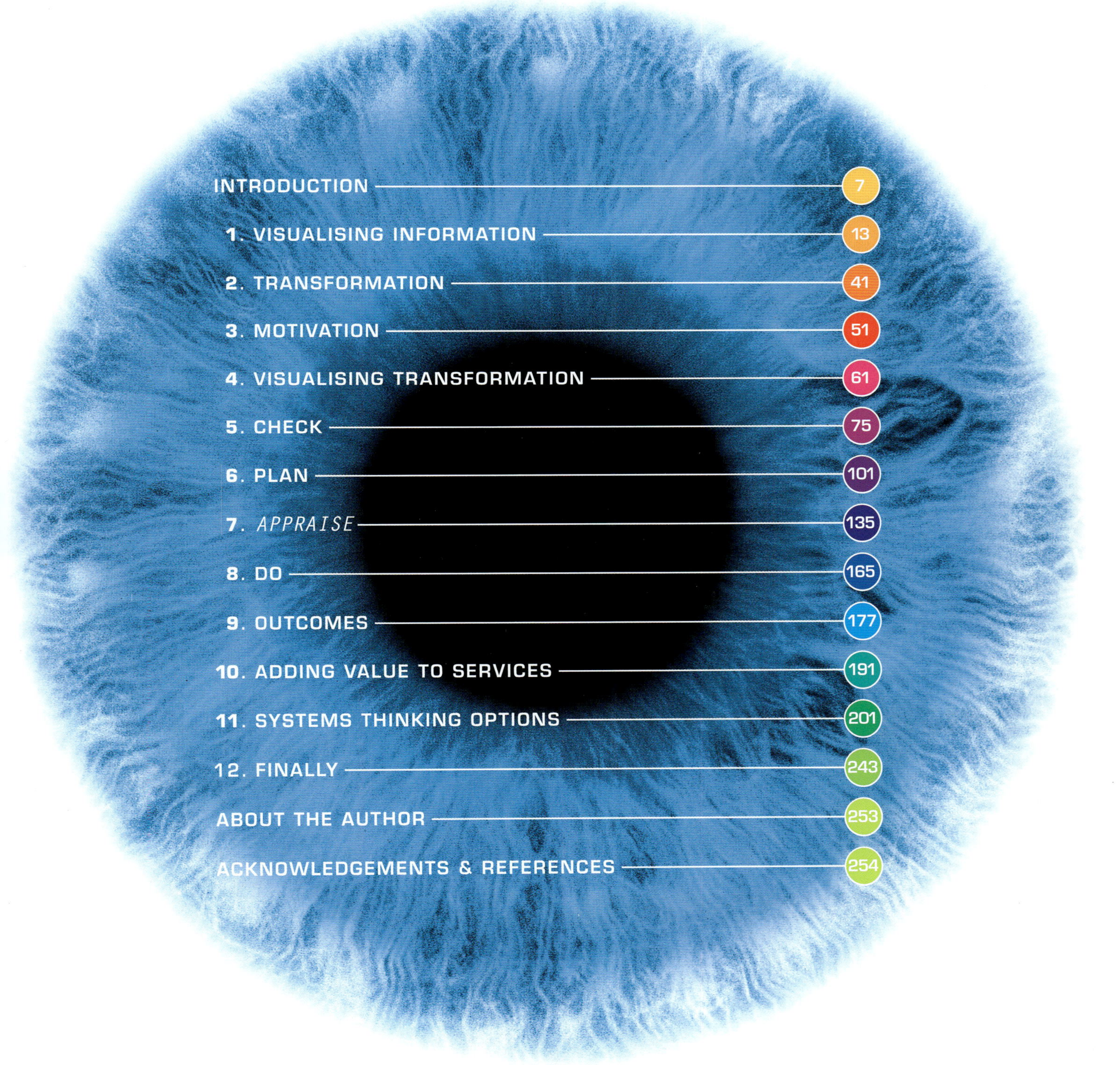

REGISTER OF GRAPHS, PICTURES & ILLUSTRATIONS

REGISTER OF GRAPHS, PICTURES & ILLUSTRATIONS

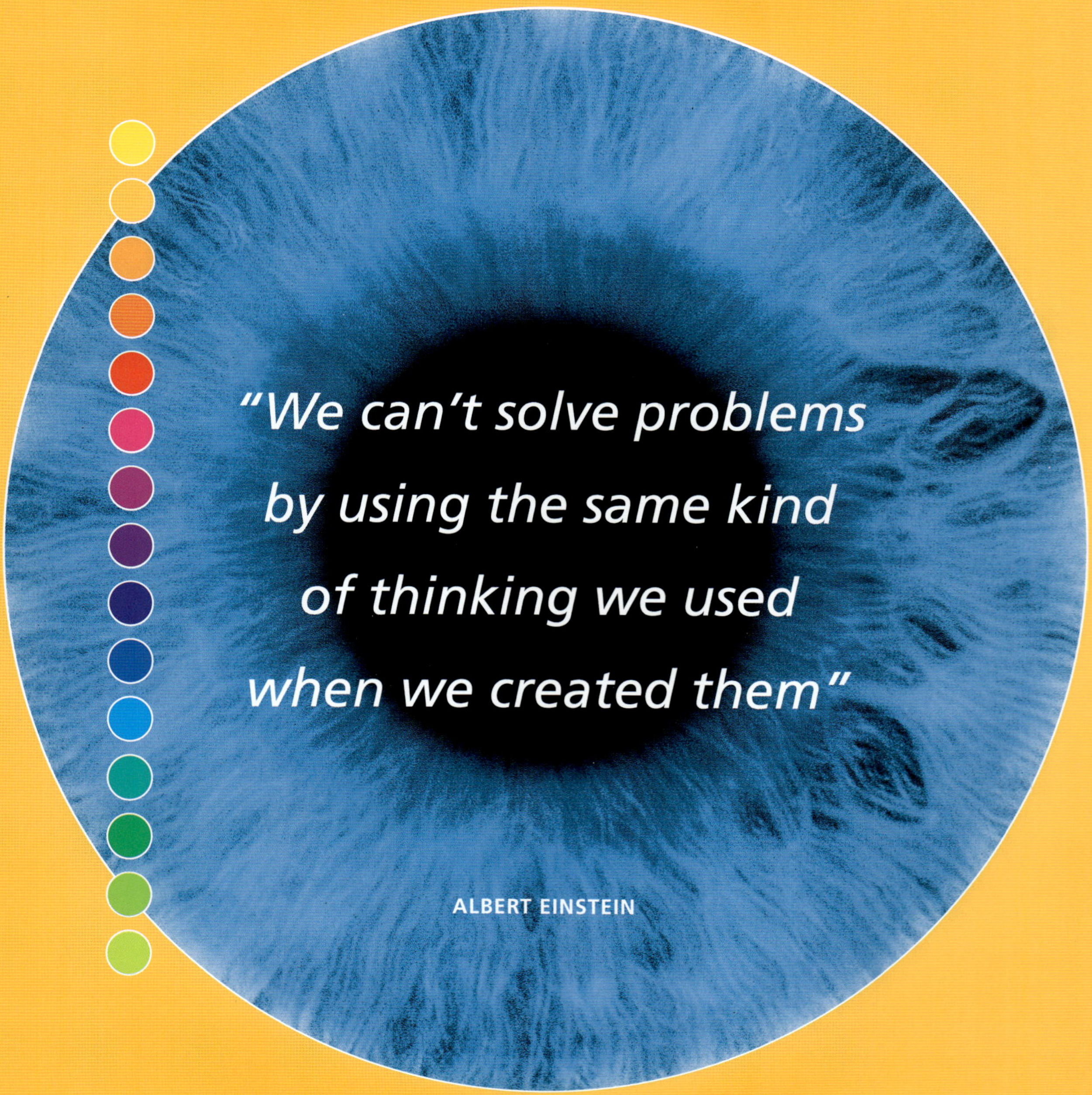
"We can't solve problems
by using the same kind
of thinking we used
when we created them"
ALBERT EINSTEIN

INTRODUCTION

Visualising Transformation is a system integrating a number of approaches from both traditional and scientific change management techniques to enable the host organisation to adopt characteristics which complement its current ethos, with a view to adopting and adapting to 'Transform' into a more effective efficient organisation in the future.

This book is written as a guide mainly for the public sector with a view to enabling other books to follow for other sectors.

Visualising Transformation should be applied in a wide array of services addressing both strategy and operations, preferably together so as to maximise the impact of step change and continuous improvement thereafter. This is based on an approach most recently devised by John Seddon, known as Systems Thinking, adding an *Appraise* element to considerably improve value-for-money.

In the last seven years I have helped my employers save over £2M capital costs and improved revenues by around £11M per annum. The prime tasks of improving customer services and service delivery, reducing complaints and response times, delivering safer services and better environmental outcomes have all exceeded expectations, with no redundancies required.

This book will help support people who are starting on a 'Transformation' for the first time, together with experienced practitioners. It will help people who are very 'operations' minded, 'strategists' and 'academics'.

I have applied the Check Plan *Appraise* Do process to both design this book, and then add value for the readers. The concept is to create a new pull to use this design, rather than it being pushed on anyone.

There are endnotes in each chapter to enable more experienced readers to have continuity of message, unencumbered by background notes, while those on a steeper learning curve will be able to cross reference.

As this book is written in modern times, it will be possible to gain further insight from supporting documents; thus links to the Support Services Direct website together with other key references will be included on a page by page basis. This enables the book to be relatively wide and generic, while detailed case studies, PowerPoint presentations, links to other systems thinking based providers and further visual information can be collected electronically.

As is inferred by the title, this intervention methodology is very graphical in nature. The old Chinese proverb that 'a picture paints a thousand words' comes to mind. In all my assignments, whether they were as an interim manager or as a consultant, I have given back to the host information which had so much impact and insight that they have been stunned that they had no idea of what was really happening, or indeed, how easy positive change could be from that new insight.

Each chapter will enable the broadening of understanding, dealing initially with concepts and narrow applications, gradually showing how from small beginnings, that Transformation can evolve.

I will draw on various real interventions from the last few years in support of this new integrated approach to change. For instance – in a waste management intervention, an organisation that was seeking to increase recycling from just under 40% to around 60% for a few hundred thousand pounds extra, are now well on their way to delivering 68% recycling for *two million pounds a year less* than their original budget.

A highways authority was looking to improve its legal position for 'trips and falls' and save £25,000 per annum as well. The initial stages of the operation originally cost £300,000 a year, with 21 people involved, taking on average 90 days to achieve completed incident reports. After the intervention there were 2.5 people involved, claims took an average of 2.65 days to complete, claims were 100% accurate first time and the costs reduced to £67,000 a year.

Lastly a council was failing in its review of parking services, seeking to achieve 'decriminalisation of parking', that is taking 'on street' parking enforcement from the police to the council. It also had a number of operational and financial issues. The main decriminalisation project was being controlled via a PRINCE2[1] methodology, with many disparate parties meeting fortnightly to ensure delivery. The project was floundering and had no chance to be delivered on time. The council's service director also reduced staffing levels during this period; income was behind profile and essential information not to hand.

The project management was transferred to a 'Mind map[2]' with a simple bar chart of key stage times to achieve (we used the term of 'drop dead dates' for these). Significant financial improvements were achieved via a new tactical pricing change, agreed with two other partners, plus a review of the fine appeal methodology.

Inside eleven weeks the main contract was back on schedule, pricing was agreed and implemented without complaint and refuted appeals went from 20% successful to 80% successful. The budget *improved by £400,000 a year* prior to the further improvements gained from decriminalisation.

The core approaches to all three interventions were the same, using workshops, appropriate information and creating positive energy between all parties involved. It is because of these successful outcomes that I have absolute confidence in the approaches described in this book. I can think of no other intervention methods where Transformation of these magnitudes would be discussed at outset.

This doesn't mean that every part of every organisation in the public sector could achieve this magnitude of improvement; however, there will always be huge opportunities that can be tapped if only the employees are given the chance.

Visualising Transformation is a new way to address Systems Thinking[3] building on the work of Deming[4] and Ohno[5] whose production model is sometimes known as the Toyota Production System (TPS). In general these systems are referred to as closed systems; they tend to be of a repetitive nature where standardisation of approach is beneficial.

It also incorporates concepts from Checkland (soft systems) and Buzan (mind maps). Soft systems tend to be more abstract in style, where several parties may be working on wide issues, or a strategy is to be developed. In these areas variation[6] needs to be embraced so as to fully understand all aspects within the area of interest so that boundary conditions[7] and controls[8] can be designed. All these terms and concepts are discussed later in this book.

The development of greatly improved Information Technology (IT) systems is a mixed blessing now. Far too often people hide behind 'computer errors', 'that's call centres for you' and 'too complex for me!' There are growing trends for people to have no ownership of the information and as a direct result are unable to tell whether data[9] is correct or not.

Visualising Transformation makes considerable use of data within various systems, often integrating data from several sources to create new insight. There is also a conscious borrowing of concepts from one area to another, for example databases are often linked to GIS[10] and spreadsheets are worked hard to interpret database information. Aged debtor styles[11] of bottom harvesting worst issues enable people to see the prime cause of system failure. I will also address how to make best use of both the left and right sides of the brain and how to multi-task and ensure you don't lose great ideas.

Collecting meaningful data is a primary step to being able to visualise current performances.The following chapters will clarify the process from having data, to creating information to visualising it in very meaningful ways. Information should also include being able to understand how work occurs now perhaps seeing the true reality of services through the eyes of the customer.

The English language is a very powerful tool for managing and running businesses. It's interesting to see instructions in four European languages; invariably English is the shortest column, or it will be placed in a narrower column to hide the effect. The richness of English can also hide issues where several people can all discuss an issue and have different concepts in their brains. That is part of the reason why Visualising Transformation is so rich in pictorial images.

For example simple terms such as 'fly-tip and side-waste' were being used in an authority in very different ways across the four sections of one department plus the customer call centre. By simply conducting two workshops involving all five sections together, customer complaints were reduced from 200 a month to less than 80 in three months for the whole service, not just for the subject in hand. Basically every section had flow-charts for how work would be done, but nobody had checked how the work flowed through the whole service.

A 60% reduction in complaints creates capacity to add value or resolve the other issues. Doing work better reduces costs and makes it easier to work. This is a key learning point; ***improving service delivery will reduce costs or release capacity to do more work.***

In addition to bringing greater technology use into reviews, Visualising Transformation adds a new step to current approaches, '***appraise***'. In this context *appraise* is a review of aspirations and business opportunities that are possible if capacity to achieve them can be created. It is this final wash which can massively alter outcomes, creating genuine innovation for the host, employees and their customers.

It is intended that this book will be used extensively to help with the start-up, running and development of interventions in the public sector and service industries. It will work very well where people relate to pictorial information. It will create capacity in many obvious and subtle ways. It will also help to eradicate an array of non-value adding work that currently gets in the way of service delivery.

The mind map on the following page gives an overview of Visualising Transformation, in some ways this is 'too much information, too quick', it is here to help initial thoughts, and to be referred back to as you read through the whole book.

Endnotes

1 PRINCE2 is a project control methodology which evolved from IT systems implementation. It is often specified for project managers or companies. It is one of a very select few methods which has rigour and control, Visualising Transformation seeks to replace this as an industry standard.

2 A Mind map is a simple diagram showing all the related aspects of quite complex issues on a single page. The use of colours and images sometimes will add to the speed of understanding. They can be used for planning projects, such as the writing of this book, for brainstorming concepts alone or in small groups, or indeed for discussing complex issues so people can assimilate their own position in a wider project.

3 The term Systems Thinking here is generic in meaning taking in both Continuous Improvement and Soft Systems which are discussed in Chapter 11.

4 W Edwards Deming was a statistician who worked extensively in Japan from 1950, helping to transform a decimated economy to become a world leader. He continued to develop his theories until his death at the age of 93. The three most notable areas of inclusion within Visualising Transformation are the Plan Do Check Act cycle, the 14 points of management and the system of profound knowledge.

5 Taiichi Ohno helped develop the 'Toyota Production System' (TPS), which revolutionised the quality of the final product enabling more reliable cars to be built for far less money than originally. There are a number of operational developments from Deming and Ohno including: Statistical Process Control (SPC), employee ability to stop production to resolve a new issue, supplier involvement and 'Continuous Improvement'.

VISUALISING TRANSFORMATION: SUMMARY

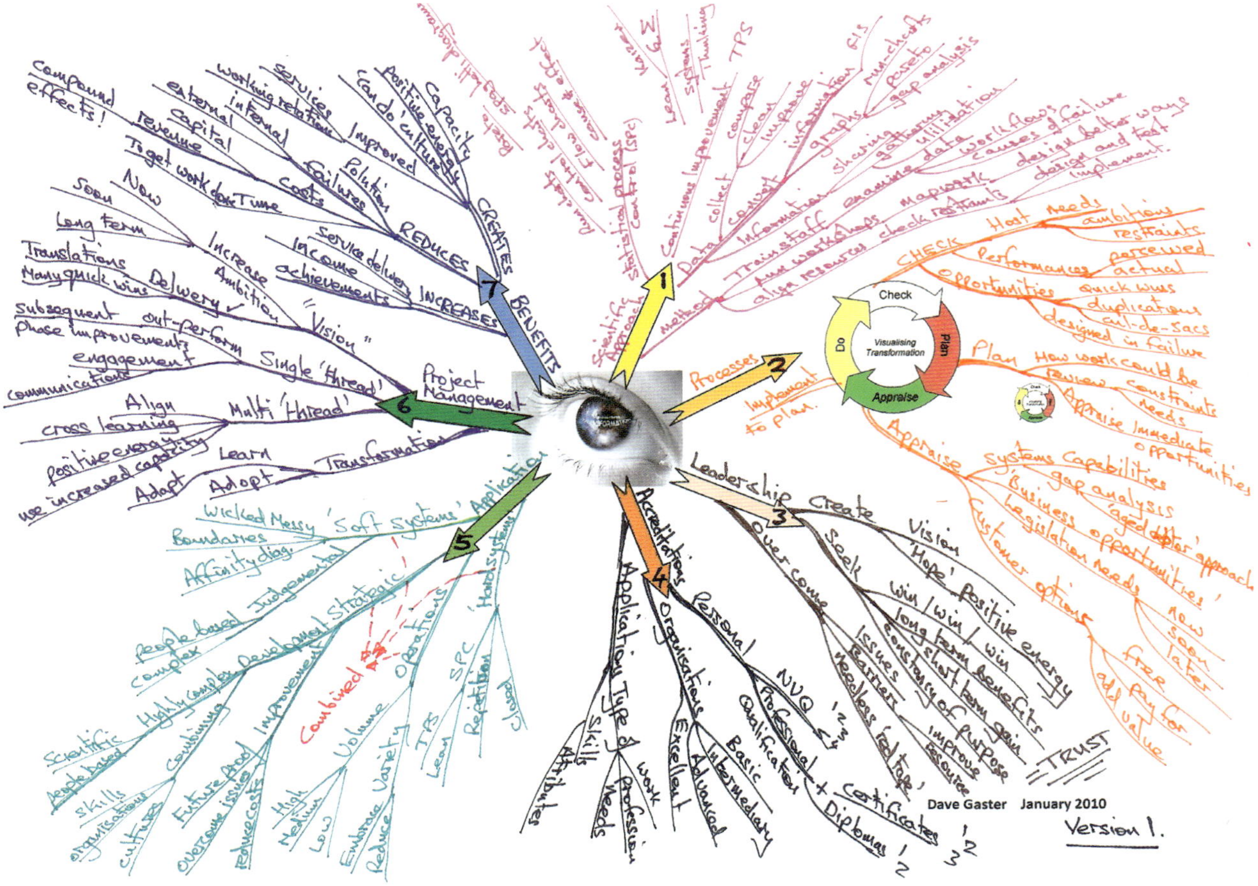

6 Variation is a statistical term with much of its development of thought coming from Walter A. Shewhart. Within the development of Visualising Transformation relatively lower case attention is applied to data, in that run charts, control charts and Pareto analysis will suffice in most cases.

7 Boundary conditions, for ease at this point, are used to define what is in or not in the review in question, again these are discussed in chapter 11.

8 Controls will refer to methods of working, processes and procedures on a day to day basis.

9 Many organisations have masses of data; very few have good, sound, reliable, accurate information. The cleaning of data and production of stunning information is key to progress.

10 Geographical Information Systems have an enormous potential to enable improved strategic and operational planning and monitoring. GIS links powerful databases with map based plans. Too often opportunities to sprint forward are missed because of short sighted managers.

11 I use the term aged debtor style for any table of data sorted to place the oldest data at the bottom, largest schemes, most complex jobs, most difficult customers, heaviest loads. By sorting data via several filters trends can be seen and dealt with.

"Our task is not to fix the blame for the past, but to fix the course for the future"

JOHN F KENNEDY

Following on from the introduction; information is far more than simple data. To achieve useful information data needs to be: accurate, reliable, in a timely manner and well presented. I am yet to find an organisation which truly has developed information systems to such a point that everything adds value, can be used first time and cross relates to every other function correctly.

Most organisations have plenty of data, although that data is rarely joined up. Even where good central systems exist, there will be a plethora of sub-systems run off-line so as to enable those vital, or occasionally, not so important operations to run. The maturity of an organisation can be measured via the CMMI approach, which expresses the current position as to data use and availability on a 1 to 5 scale, where 1 is the worst. Many well performing organisations only score a 1 or 2 initially (see Chapter 11).

Had you ever considered how many separate spreadsheets, databases and systems you routinely push information into and then take information from? Try counting them up, if you've got less than twenty I'd be surprised. Now consider how much of what you are doing off-line is replicated by others in your team, then in accounts, payroll and purchasing. If all information was held reliably in a central system, in the way that you need it held, shared with all others in your operation, how much time would you save a week? This should be considered as the second key learning point, ***good information systems may cost more to set up, but will create capacity.***

When you carry out routines for regular monthly accounts, weights analysis, jobs on time, complaints and so forth, are you sure you have ***all*** the information, could some be delayed elsewhere? When you pass on that information, do you have to create different reports about the same information for several people? Do National Indicators or Key Performance Indicators[1] need information in several different formats?

Having created this raft of data for 'monitoring', how much time is actually spent on thinking about what that data tells you? What is missing, what is implied, where could you close a gap on a service issue or increase the yield to improve something? Has the value increased somewhere which would create a value for money change that wasn't cost effective last time it was reviewed? Senior managers spend most of their time in meetings and preparing for them, they rarely have time for work, yet the most valuable time that they should lever into their diaries is time to think.

Designing information systems so that they add value to the work being done takes time. Some of that time is because there is no 'corporate style', so several individuals who demand information need different approaches. Even worse is when the corporate style doesn't allow the information to be a by-product of work, so you do the work and monitor it, and then create the corporate monitoring reports for others who may well be happy to accept routine reports if they knew the true costs of meeting their current styles.

So I'll try to describe what good information looks like and how that is different to data. I'll also describe the process to initially develop information and give examples of information evolving from OK to stunning.

Data: is in the background of everything we see and do. Our whole waking life consists of picking up data, evaluating it and reacting to it. When we sleep our brain reassembles today's data; it files some for future use and lets most data disappear into oblivion. Part of the beauty of Visualising Transformation is that it enables and develops the conscious use of both sides of the brain. While data in tables works for some people, the mixture of graphs, pictorials, colours and structure in a knowledge system wakens up the creative and analytical processes that simple data reporting cannot achieve.

In business or service terms we are receiving and sending e-mails, attending or running meetings, writing or reading reports, having ad hoc discussions and trying to understand irregularities in accounts and performances. All the time we are bombarded with data, but how much of that data adds value to your business or service from a customer point of view?

Consider also how you work, do you use your brain to anywhere near its natural capacity? If you could absorb far more information via pictures, graphs and charts, what else can you do?

Modern banter states that men cannot multi-task while women can. However, I can prove that all people can multi-task far more than they suspect, and that practise and training will help improve this further.

Consider the process of learning to drive; at first it's very difficult and stressful, getting the biting point right on the clutch, the right weight on the accelerator and brakes, not over-steering round corners, getting the right revs on the engine for gear changing; then the use of mirrors and watching out for danger. It was a huge learning task, which was full of stress and using all your brain power.

Then as a mature driver you do all those things without conscious thought, while navigating a new route and being word perfect while you sing along to a song from 30 years ago. Multi-tasking is natural and very easy, so why shouldn't this be the same in the office?

In the same way that learning to drive and add skills took a lot of effort, multi-task skilling[2] in the office is also worth time and effort, as is speed reading. Once you believe that different parts of your brain can work at the same time, or even more interestingly, that different word related elements can work together, keeping up with work-loads gets easier. For instance I'm very relaxed about having a phone conversation with a person while I'm typing a report. It's very rare that the caller is aware that I'm still working and even rarer that I need to stop one process to concentrate on the other.

This applies also to taking part in meetings for instance. Speed reading a report while a meeting is taking place is quite easy, enabling context to be added to conversations where preparation time was tight. Where appropriate queuing ideas for later in the meeting is also useful, I always keep lots of notes in meetings and queue ideas in the top right hand corner of my page.

Sometimes, using mind maps as a note-taking process also aids adding value to the meeting. Even in saying this, make sure you are aware of the meeting, and don't miss out on the subtleties of body language and communications or opportunities to add value.

In a standard eight hour day, how many minutes do you do something which 'absolutely makes a positive difference to your customers?' If you had totally reliable information that met every need you have, would those minutes translate into hours? *(I'll return to this for audits and central services)*

Consider virtually any form of service carried out; the actual working tasks to do that work probably take minutes, and yet those tasks take weeks to achieve, such as: Planning applications, invoice payments, housing benefits claims, fly-tip removal and door repairs.

So why do operations that take minutes to do in real work time, fail to be routinely complete in: six weeks, 30 days, 56 days, etc.? The main causes of delay are waiting for the right information or the work is in an in-tray or queuing for the next available person.

So if waiting for the right information is so critical to work, why are organisations routinely 'data rich–information poor'? Well the main reason is the fascination with targets and benchmarks. If 98% of invoices are paid within 30 days, and that is upper quartile there isn't a problem, is there? Our priorities are most often dominated by 'doing the wrong things better'.

What difference would excellent information make to you? *Inside a relatively small council we established genuine partnering with our suppliers and contractors, by ensuring better sharing of information and faster communications we managed to pay 100% of invoices on time. That is, if they were invoiced correctly by Monday at noon, they were paid by Thursday morning.*

So the council lose out on the interest from slower cash flow achieved by deliberately holding back payments until day 30? Accountants and economists have many interesting ideas that may improve elements of costs, but in many instances the process of delaying invoices to the last day adds to costs. However, by establishing lasting partnerships founded on trust and knowledge, we went on to reduce overall service delivery costs by 14%, improving the suppliers' profitability as well. Our customers gained faster, more reliable services and tenant satisfaction rocketed, while re-let times for voids were halved.

At the core of all this were information systems that added value every minute of the day. Our computer system cost us £18,000 plus a data abstraction tool for about £1,000. We created an array of meaningful reports and graphs, some of which ran overnight, e-mailed to us every morning. We regularly provided housing stats to our Client who had a £1/4M system which gave them little knowledge[3].

'Dirty data' is information which contains errors, these can be errors of: omission, facts, figures, trends, interpretation.... We've recently seen parallel reports being sent to three different moderating bodies as the official quarterly waste and recyclates weight submission for a district council. As those reports needed to be made into three quite different formats, they are completed over a number of days. In the intervening time, some additional weight tickets were added to last month so the numbers change.

Even more interesting, were the huge great spreadsheets created over time by a succession of officers. I've seen instances where the same three reports are created virtually together from the same massive spreadsheet, where the three answers should be the same, but are not. No one was aware that three 'official reports' were all wrong. No one had ever carried out some very basic maths to compare them.

In one council a totally inappropriate computer system had been installed to run the biggest service in the council, which also had the most amount of customer contact. As the system couldn't address the business needs, 90% of the business was run on spreadsheets or by word of mouth. The system didn't produce management reports, the IT section used to design and run enquiries from the database. I was examining customer complaints and needed to compare one set of data to another, they didn't match at all, with a 60% error between two quite large reports; both of these should have been the same.

I then ran reports to produce several months of information, where I had previously ran these reports every month and stored the results, random returns started to arise. It turned out that not only was the computer system inappropriate for the business need, but also the reporting fields were so complex, that two attempts to gain the same data rarely would provide the same results.

Lastly in a quite progressive Housing Association the 'Performance Manager' created a really appealing monthly performance journal, with snippets of information in a very classy, stylised booklet. I started working through the booklet with great interest, then realised that there were two pieces of data that were mutually impossible. So I read with increased awareness and found three pairs of data that simply couldn't all be right. I then also discovered that a huge slice of her benchmarking report which she was praising as being of great value had transposed data, such that answers were missing for three questions, with data entered at position 21 instead of 24.

All answers after that point were wrong, some showing tens instead of thousands. She hadn't even got beyond the third page of the returns and she was more likely to look at it than anyone else in the organisation. Effectively the whole cast (Senior Management Team and Board) were going through the motions of monitor and sign off without ever switching their brains on. The host was paying around ten thousand pounds a year for a system that added no value other than a tick in the box from the BV Auditor.

So if we are to move out of the current paradigm[4] of checking the checker and never having meaningful information, how can we achieve that? We have already shown that it is not expensive to have better information! If you can stop having lots of wrong information, lots of people will also have additional time to produce continuously improving information and indeed provide better services for the public.

There's a useful quote by someone in the Deming movement: "The more we know about what's wrong with a piece of data, the more useful it is." Simply recognising the wrongness of information should enable the start of making it better. Accounts are often a scary combination of right information, almost right, pure guesses, with a series of totally unknowns. Yet you never get a quarterly report which states this.

The data collection systems need a degree of self honesty and introspection. If in every quarter review process there was a method to eliminate causes of error based on a Pareto[5] approach, the accuracy of accounts would improve massively in a relatively short time.

Thus within a 'Check[6]' process to start a review of all information available helps: who has what, where, when and how? Duplications and paradoxes can be identified. Next, if we could provide better information, would this help? Look at the way work is carried out, if an activity creates information, do we harvest it, or can we harvest it in a smarter way for several purposes?

Examine data via a trained business analyst, ask them to dig out more information, see where errors occur, and then dig back to find out why. While there will be far more information regarding process within the 'Check' chapter, a useful process for getting to good information is to use the five whys[7] technique. Also seek out information and data that are recorded and then never used. I've frequently found data being recorded for many years, but never used by the organisation.

The five whys is a very simple and powerful way to discover underlying issues and via that discovery to ensure adequate business processes are put in place to prevent problems rather than working round them.

Seek to show various people in the service *true information* in various formats based on their current systems, seek to deliver high level meaningful information as a by-product of simply doing the job. Find errors in existing systems with a view to having them corrected. Set up shared systems where possible as a short-term fix. Also look for evidence of batch updates and trends. Current management thinking believes that 'economy of scale' reduces costs, so work is often batched or driven to achieve monthly targets.

However, batching work and information in this way is often a significant cause of both additional costs and reduced income and indeed, wrong decisions. Practicable examples will later expand upon this position.

Use the evolving information packages to ask more meaningful questions. What happened to Round One missed collections on Tuesday last week? Why have recyclates tonnages dropped off so much on week two for Round C? Why do 90% of planning applications take eight weeks when most can be resolved in less than two weeks? Would it be cheaper to resolve these in two weeks? Would there be less need for workload control? Would there be fewer calls to the call centre and enquiry team? In an era where stimulating the economy is so important are such delays a cause of recession lasting longer?

Let's show a typical evolution from data to information:

1. Work is carried out and a paper record is written after completion
2. The paperwork is returned to the head office at the end of day or at week-end
3. Information is typed into a database or spreadsheet to show what was done with values
4. Weekly or monthly summaries are prepared
5. Late arriving data is posted into the following month
6. Supervisors may examine data regarding future work allocation or for performance awareness
7. Data may be compared to invoices or supporting information from third parties
8. Performance management information is prepared in corporate style for senior use
9. Trends, comparisons to target and failures are examined
10. Some graphs may be prepared if it's the norm.

Note, that within the ten stages above, there is no real attention to validating data, unless a third party supplier is involved, watching for duplications or decimal point errors may not be culturally wanted. Even under a 'Systems Thinking regime' data checking is an issue, on one hand there should be no mass inspection and on the other, learning curves would need to be achieved for new employees.

Having a fully inter-connected database can make some issues far easier, if the workers carry out their work and then as an automated end of that work process, relevant data is harvested, then related suppliers electronically send their data / invoices, any error, gap or duplication can be flagged from the system.

In addition reasonable maximum and minimum levels for certain processes can be entered into the system (ones based on the findings from a control chart[8] will not be arbitrary), such that a flag will show immediately if the value is outside those parameters. There would be no need for a hand-off from the worker to administration and data can be transformed into information as an immediate by-product. The creation of information would then look like this:

1. Work is carried out and completed electronically
2. Data is automatically collected to various tables and graphs plus monitoring dashboard, including gap analysis
3. Supporting information from suppliers or material purchasers is received electronically and auto-compared
4. Anomalies between data are auto-flagged to supervisors for remedial action
5. All data is available in needed formats between any pair of dates as well as the standard months and quarters. Graphs, run charts, bell charts, process control charts, Pareto analysis and similar output visualisation methods can all be updated automatically.

TABLE 1

	Paper			
	00/01	99/2000	98/99	97/98
APRIL	397	415	280	267
MAY	414	365	280	274
JUNE	427	419	319	238
JULY	395	405	342	273
AUG	407	344	315	216
SEP	370	431	391	289
OCT	499	425	421	310
NOV	483	412	429	269
DEC	366	387	355	276
JAN	472	431	403	255
FEB	423	442	414	272
MAR		431	445	281
Av. Sum	423	409	366	268

TABLE 2

	Cans and Plastics		
	00/01	99/2000	98/99
APRIL	63	67	8
MAY	71	65	13
JUNE	72	76	38
JULY	67	74	49
AUG	68	76	50
SEP	62	77	61
OCT	73	67	66
NOV	69	57	61
DEC	54	66	55
JAN	70	74	80
FEB	65	70	64
MAR		63	75
Total	**733**	**831**	**620**
Average	**67**	**69**	**52**

The tables above were generated to monitor the sale of recyclates from a small district council. Data was collected daily and summarised at the end of each month. This was then presented to a management team on a monthly basis using the graphs as below.

Most tables tended to be basic as a data capture and simple presentation format only. It's only now looking back at these that I've noticed the average tonnes per month for cans and plastics started to reduce.

GRAPH 1

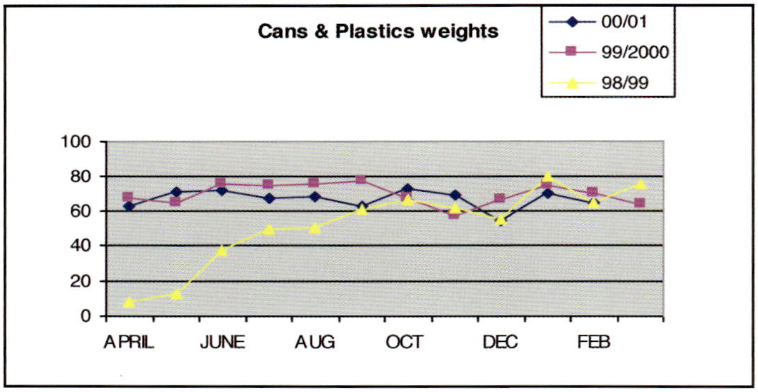

GRAPH 2

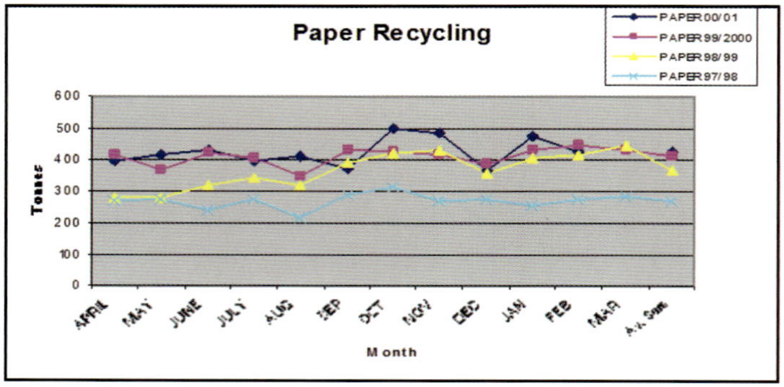

You'll note that we viewed the graphs as Excel produced them. They were small with very little graphic area showing.

We accepted the size of margins around the graphs and the description block without question.

This shows that for cans and plastics there was a rapid start up of the service in 1998 and a relative plateauing off thereafter.

For residual waste we also monitored quarter on quarter to map trends.

Door to door paper recycling started two years prior to plastics, again we had seen a build up and plateau of the service.

Other than this basic monitoring we carried out no further interrogation of the data. We had taken the council from under 4% recycling to around 15%, and were ahead of most other councils at that time. Thus we had no drive to do better.

As time has progressed we have recognised the importance of good information to enable improved performances. The culture at the turn of the century was to improve, benchmark and meet targets. As recycling was relatively in an infancy stage, the concept of trying to squeeze more from the area was not prevalent. In addition, corporate pressures were being exerted in other areas.

The pressures ***now*** are to achieve far higher recycling rates with reducing budgets and the threat of significant financial penalties for failure looming, so the culture of process has become more sophisticated together with a far higher acceptance and awareness of environmental matters for the public. The next graph shows the difference that using space, scale, colour and boldness of lines can add to what was before a simple diagrammatic representation of data.

GRAPH 3

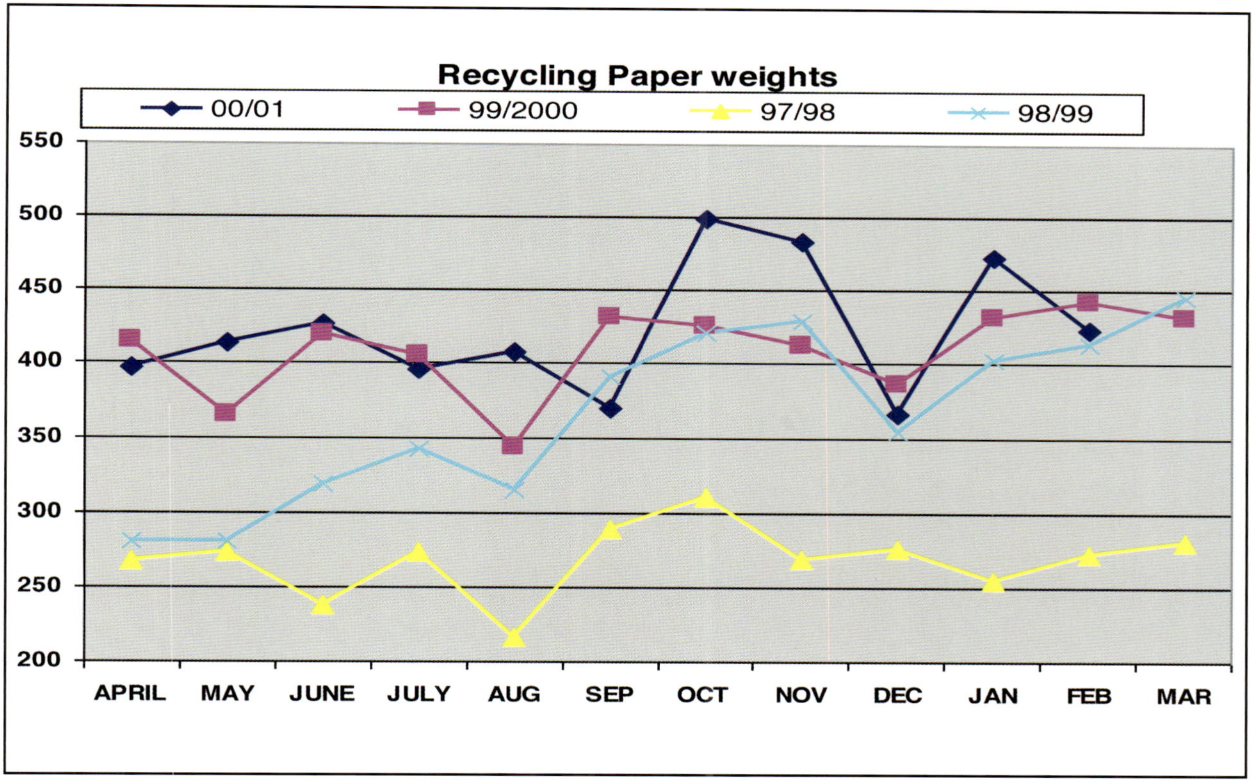

Suddenly there is far more information to hand, the rapid growth during 1998/99 is clearer, then the plateau effect in 1999/00. But what had been missed at the time was that having achieved around 425 tonnes per month this then reduces down to around 380 tonnes.

I've not kept notes relating to the reasons for the low tonnages in September and December 2000, although I do recall issues with the paper loading machine. Later graphs will show how annotation against data enables a cause and effect retention.

Run Chart 1 shows the same data as in the previous graphs but now shown in a run chart format. The initial service achievement stays level then increases quite rapidly in 1998, but now quite clearly shows a slight trend down late in 2000 prior to some other effects being realised. The saw-tooth affect makes it quite difficult to see any trends. While excessive scale on some graphs can lead to a degree of over reaction, maximising the awareness of what your data can tell you is very important.

Just compare the original 'automatic small graph generation' above to these last two graphs, to me, there is far more information available which I will demonstrate in the run charts below.

RUN CHART 1

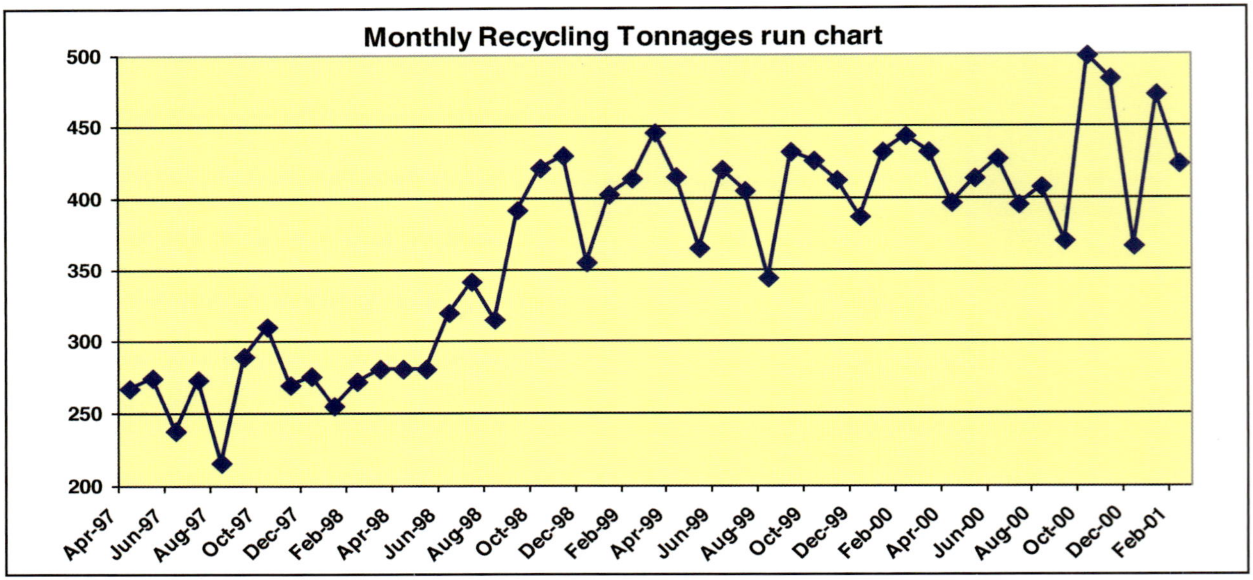

The additions of a trend-line and comments start to create corporate knowledge, passing through operational details to the management areas. The 'late info from weighbridge' would then explain the saw-tooth pattern through early 1999. The 'shovel breakdown' comment would then also explain a low December high January 2001 tonnage. This style of information would work well at the boardroom level, reducing the need to explain a relatively stable operation with operational, or simple data entry delays.

The trend-line choice should be used in consideration of the type of information in question, to add to the above diagram, a moving four month average was later introduced. This is particularly useful where data lags occur causing the saw-tooth pattern above, as it flattens out the information.

However, even with a four month moving average, the reduction in materials in mid 1999 and in mid 2000 becomes clearer. During this whole period there were increases in housing and population across the whole district and a gradual increase in the percentage of households included in the scheme. At that time we did not monitor the collection of paper per household. Had we done that, we would have seen a clearer loss of materials captured, which may have informed us that something extra was needed.

RUN CHART 2

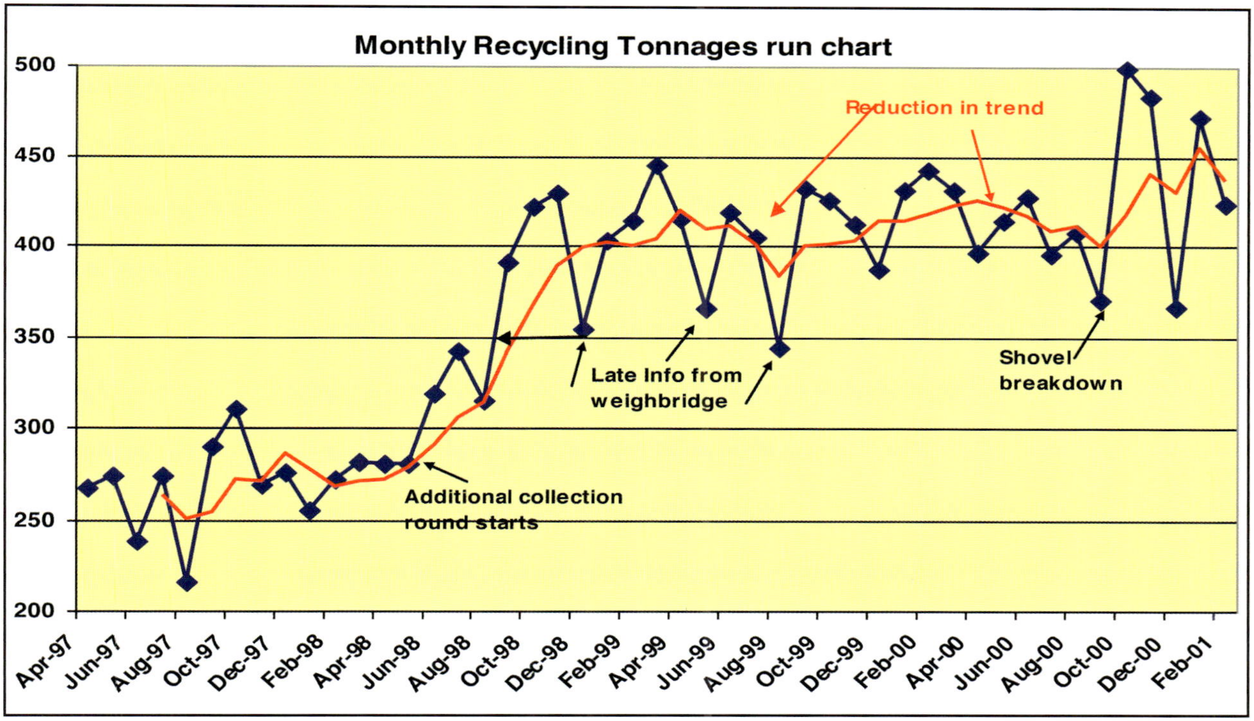

The role of the supervisor or manager within 'performance management' should be to question unusual data. Saw-tooth error rates can evolve from two individuals carrying out work, or the difference from shift one to shift two. It's quite common for the method of work to determine the quality of outcome. It's also quite common for results to be entered into systems well after the due date, causing the following month to include the prior month's data. If two sets of data have different lead time, current performance managers may be inventing interesting concepts to explain the patterns which are not based on facts.

BAR CHART 1

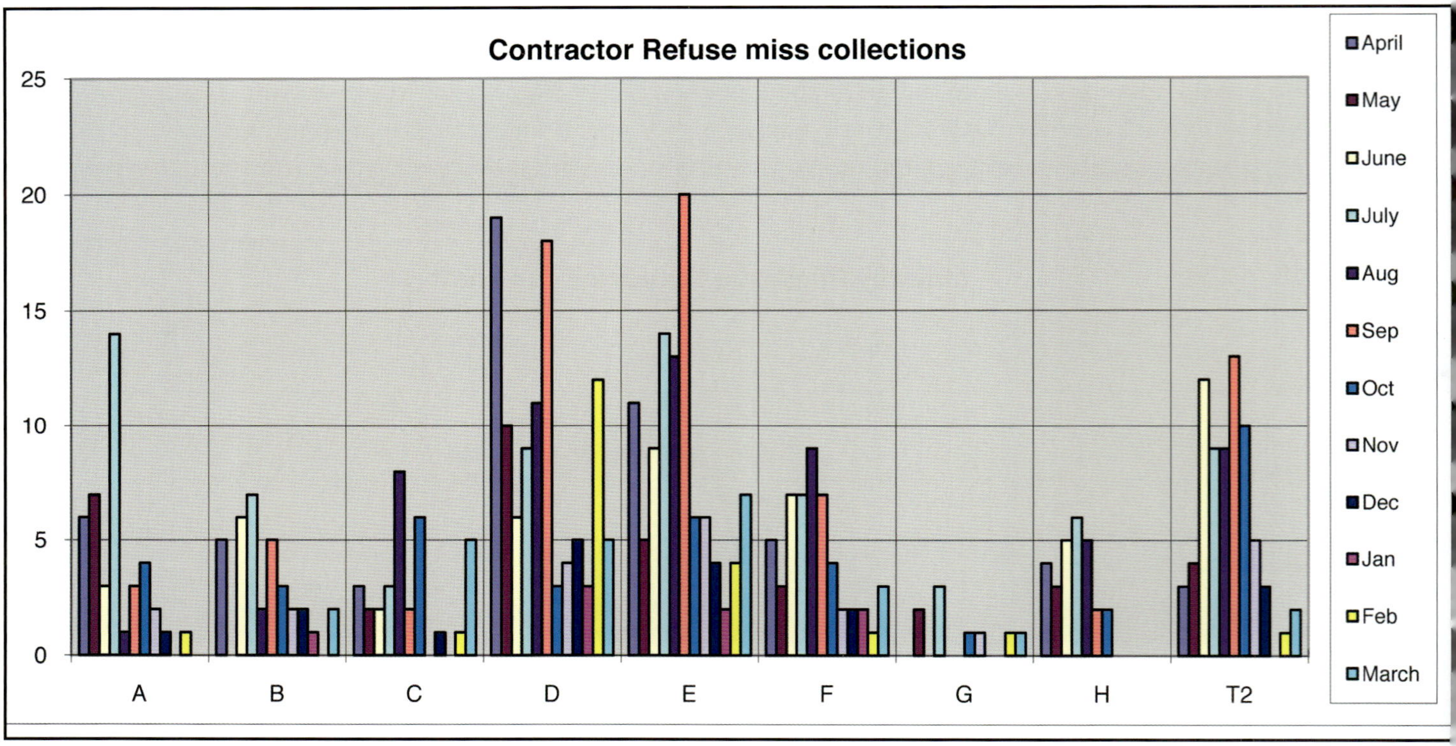

At the same time that we missed so many chances to improve recycling performance, we had addressed customer satisfaction and service improvement for waste collection. The bar chart above shows a use of Excel where each crew's failures (missed collections) were plotted this was compiled and displayed for all crews every month. Rounds A to F had about the same amount of customers, while G to T2 had fewer.

Crew A gradually became the most effective crew overall, extremely well led by their driver, even though one of the loaders was far from ideal as a team member. The run chart below will help to identify why refuse collection services improved so well to the expense of recyclate improvements. We focused on the issues that increased income, recycling wasn't a prime area.

A sizeable 'Incentive Payment' was made to the DSO (Direct Services Organisation) against a series of parameters including: missed collections, addressing defaults quickly, improving recycling tonnages and similar concepts. This helped focus the mind on dealing with *those issues*.

RUN CHART 3

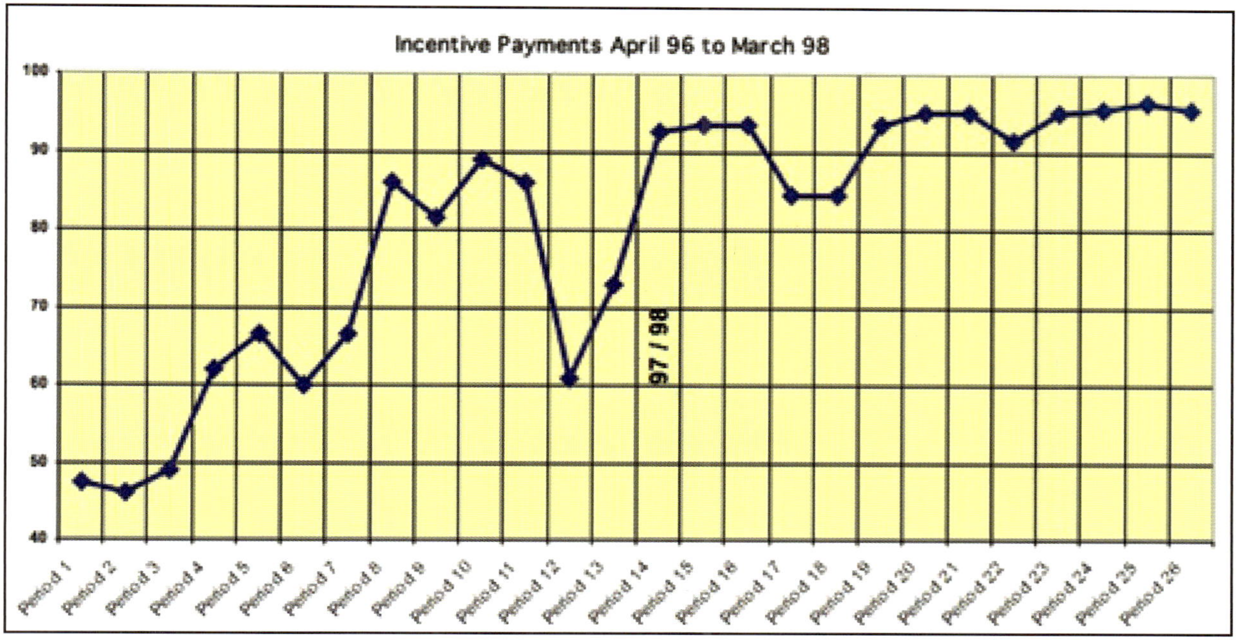

The tables and graphs used so far have been fairly routine for all business other than the annotated run chart, which was created entirely within Excel. Now I will introduce a few more helpful charts which will help with decisions for prioritising what to address, and in some cases how to address these issues when a Transformation process starts, some of these will be used now without realising their wider potentials.

Pareto was an Italian economist who introduced the 80/20 rule stating that 80% of problems were caused by 20% of the issues. Within the service above we used Pareto analysis a great deal recognising month of year variations relating to agency staff, differences between crews and as below the cause of issue.

Overall customer complaints were reduced by more than a factor of three in two years, a MORI Poll had shown this was the most admired waste collection service in the country the year prior to starting this improvement.

Note the significant reductions over an eighteen months period from around 370 missed collections in a year, to just over 100. The complaints caused were invariably missed collections initially, as that aspect improved, other issues started to become relatively more important.

PARETO CHART 1

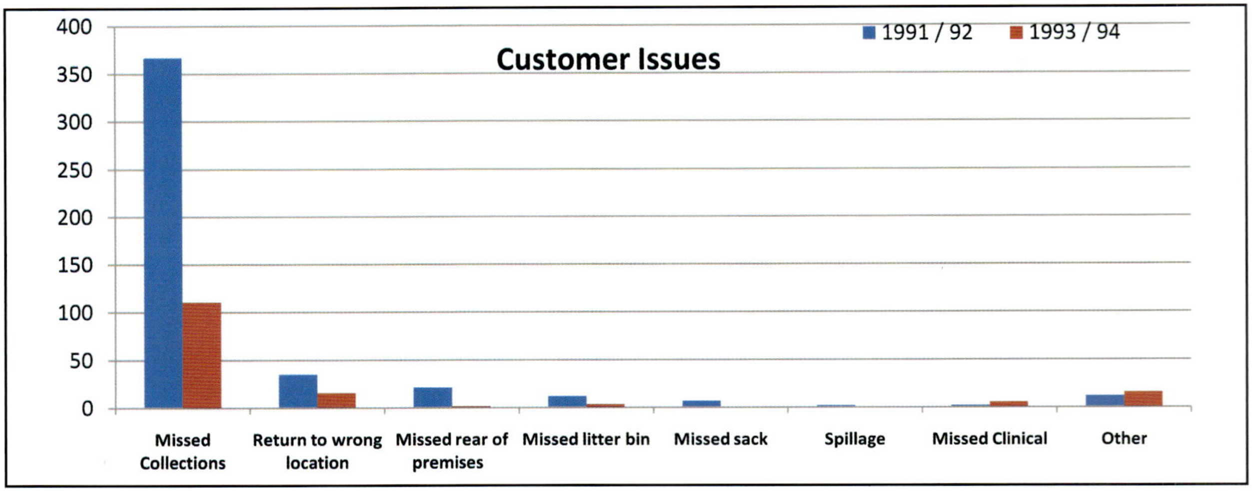

These uses of Pareto diagrams were for two prime purposes, the first to show how many free type options (this is the ability to type people's names, addresses and details slightly different on each occasion instead of using a drop down menu) were being used in the customer call centre to identify reasons for claim, and secondly to show again that very few types of issues cause most problems.

PARETO CHART 2

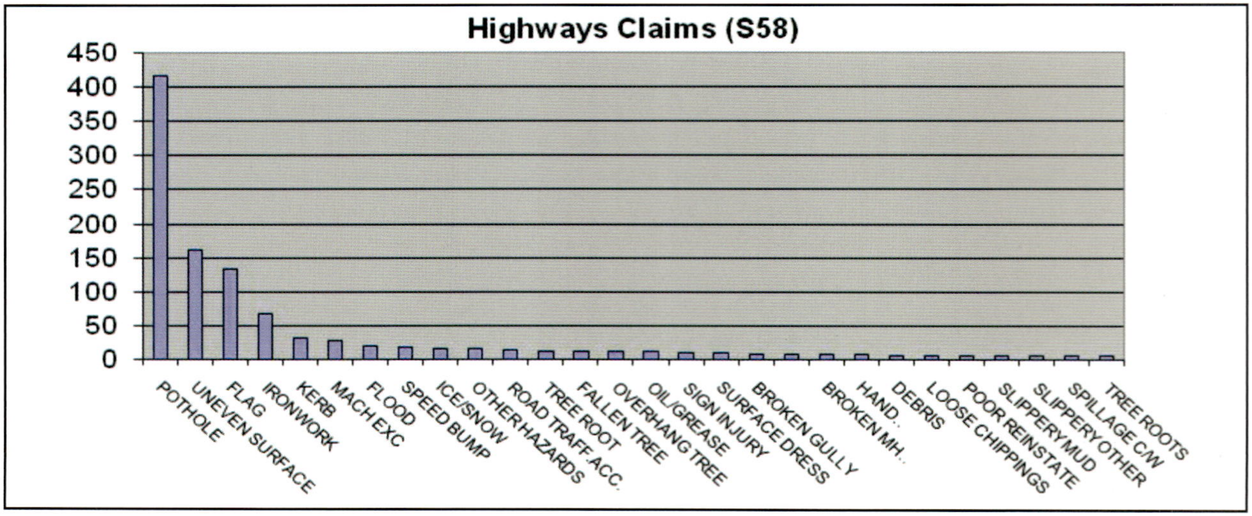

When we used this information with some other graphical representations the staff working in the trips and falls system were surprised how little effort was placed in trying to identify cause in the reduction of issues. Nearly all their efforts were placed in heading off possible legal claims.

The later introduction of a cause and effect chart plus mind map for trips and falls, started to enable all the interested participants to understand why certain information was more useful than others. You will be able to see that Tree Root and Tree Roots are both entered, with four types of slippery surface. Analysis is impeded by inconsistent definitions.

SPAGHETTI DIAGRAM 1

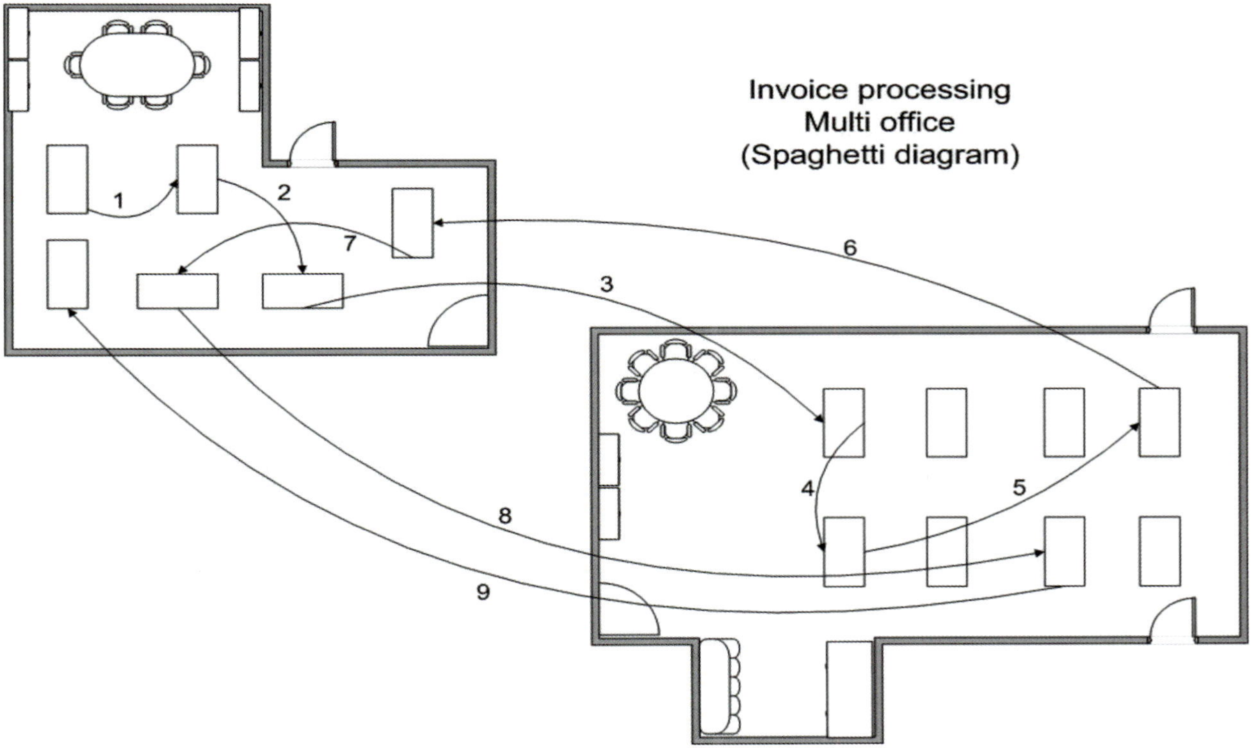

This spaghetti diagram was used to help the understanding of a paper flow between two buildings, the original issue wasn't quite this bad. This style of a process illustration helped reduce the defensiveness of the staff and teams within the process to achieve a reduction in time to pay to three days without fail.

A Control Chart is very much like a run chart, except that the upper and lower limits are calculated using standard deviation applied to the data. In the case below the upper and lower limits have had a split applied to the calculations, before and after a change of service design in September 2008.

Any points occurring above the upper control limit are probably due to a 'Special Cause'. In the case below 'Christmas' is a special cause. (The lower control limit above is mainly zero.) Again, the control chart becomes more informative with annotated comments. The Systems Thinking based quick intervention started with a cause and effect analysis together with Pareto to eradicate some design problems and to give better information to the teams carrying out the work.

CONTROL CHART 1

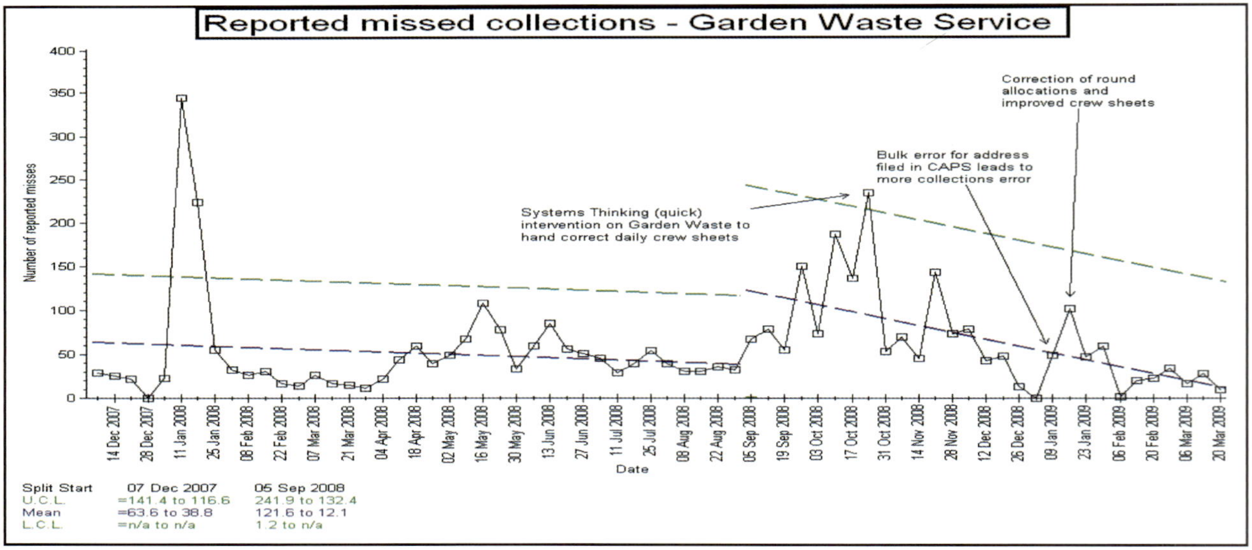

Repetition of quick redesigns transformed the service blighted by catastrophic implementation errors in October 2008 to a highly effective one by February 2009. The volume of work more than doubled from August 2008 to February 2009 while the numbers of complaints were halved.

A second part of investigating 'Special Cause' for the above piece of work was to consider the reasons for the 'saw-tooth' patterns with far more complaints in week 1 collections than for week 2. As we increased the focus on data analysis we found that data for round collection routes had been polluted for a round for week one[9], and that by repairing that information, errors greatly reduced (a mixture of the five why's and Pareto analysis was applied). Consider the power of using control charts for '*Performance Managing*'.

The two diagrams shown below are clearly both hand drawn. While there are IT systems that allow these to be developed, including a form of cause and effect via Excel, drawing them first in rough in pencil and then using iterations and sharing, in order to produce a final colour version always helps with my mental focus to broaden thinking rather than simply create an appealing drawing. These were both used to help identify the issues for highways claims and supported massive service step changes from: £300,000 to £67,000 per annum and from 90 days to process to 2.65 days.

CAUSE AND EFFECT CHART 1 (ISHIKAWA OR 'FISHBONE' DIAGRAM)

MIND MAP 1

TRIPS & FALLS
Section 58 H.Act
Circa £1.3 M P.A. – Increasing
Finances
Claims handling
Legal
Risk... Admin
Env. Mgt Admin
Overheads
£288,000 Inspections
£520,000 Claims
Reducing? No!
£250000 Insurances
FRAUD
Colleagues
Solicitors
Encouraged
Considered
accurate? report
Time
Hole nearby
'tripped?'
opportunistic
Inspectors
Acceptance
Links
Risk based
Slow
over tolerant
reduced risks
Adoptions
Designs
control
S.38
24 months NRSWA
History
condition
use
frequency
Asset Management Plan.... No Links!
claims handling
Parties
County Solicitors
Finance
Legal
Contractors
Risk
HiWay H.Q.
Hi way areas
Inspectors x 6
'Perhaps'? Add value?
complex
inconsistent
not effective
costly!!
whole! part ownership
inspect administration
slow
several in system parallel
repair rapid action
Projects
secondary claims
Cross overs
Maintained?
Inspected?
Interfaces
Boundary
Back of path
Paving types
Trenches
Design
Repair
Long term failure
Heavy vehicles
Exceed designs
rapid damage
Face drivers
un-authorised
informal
temporary
responsibility
Pot Holes
Carriageways 'Poor' construction
S.38
L.T.P.
Reinstatement NRSWA
county
contractors
Footways construction
Edges
Design
ISSUES
Design - initial
Repair / alter
getting worse
Adoption
spec
control
cost-cutting
Desire lines obstructions
Hedges / trees
Bus shelters
Street furniture
Parking?
Routes
mis-match
usage change
predictable?
Drives
X-overs
ambiguity?
adopted?
Kerbs
Tactiles
missing
eroded
replaced
Channels
fragmented
holed
weed-embedded
Damaged
slip
staggered
Too-Low
Trip
ineffective
Poor materials - disappear... no or little warning?
- carriageway overlays reduce kerb height. Easy for cars to mount footways - causes much damage!
Slabs (A.S.P.)
Vehicle damage
Low kerbs
Parking
Easy mount
Low damage to wheels
High damage to A.S.P.
Half on - obstruct
Enforce - TRO's
Enforcement
Concordat?
Corners
Desire lines
Bollards?
more damage
1/2 off road parking
C Way narrow
Loose
grids
lift
distort
Trees
roots
lift paving
damage property
Stones significant...
Dave Gaster... 2008

The concept with each of these is to get as many issues on a single page, with no hindrance from thousands of words getting in the way of meaningful discussions while helping to recognise the relationships between various elements, systems and teams. Later methodologies will cover the concept of using a single A3 sheet of paper to guide a whole meeting.

GIS DIAGRAM 1 (GEOGRAPHICAL INFORMATION SYSTEM)

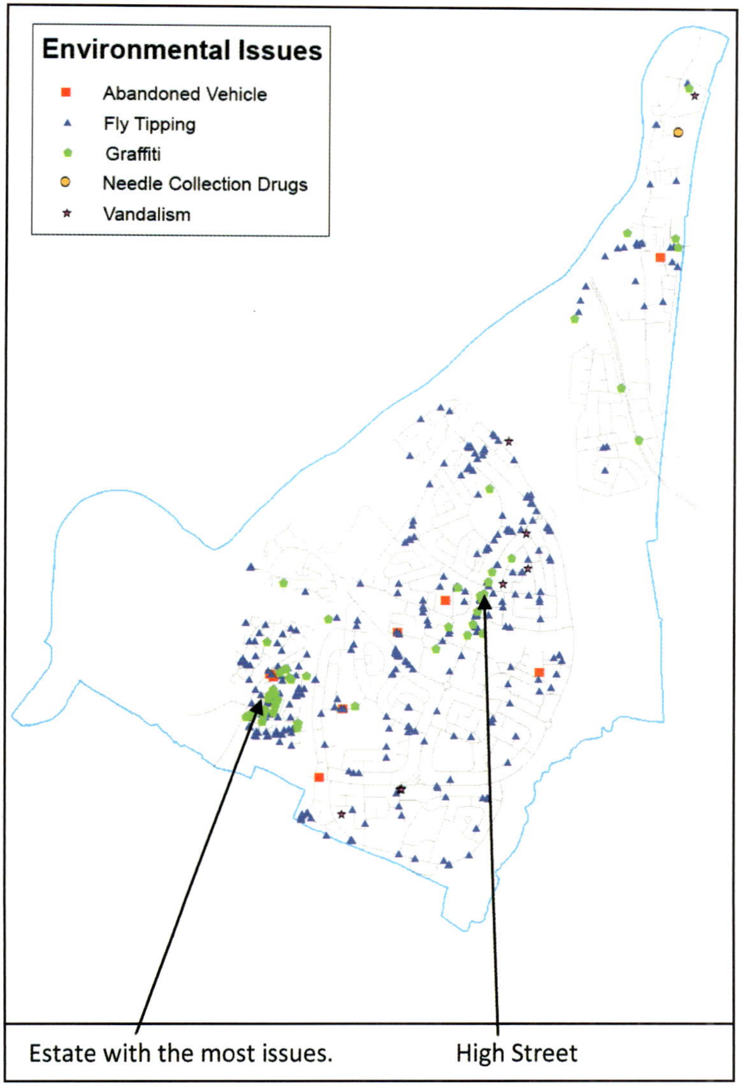

The GIS map for a portion of a city council shows all the minor ASB (Anti-social behaviour) which is plotted out over a basic line drawing showing only boundaries and roads.

With no knowledge of the area it's easy to see where the 'problem estate' and the High Street locations are situated.

A single map for each of the nine city areas was produced on a quarterly basis replacing five data sets which had variable delay periods associated with them.

The discussions within the management boards became far more pro-active and focused. The deployment of the rapid response teams also improved with some routine operational redesigns to further reduce the number of incidents.

The true power of GIS is much more evident when the data is shown for Friday and Saturday evenings only, or individual tagging signatures are given different codes.

We also used GIS to show how socio-economic mapping can be quickly visualised or indeed how an area with previously unexplained high mortality rates for cardio-vascular problems was diagnosed and greatly improved.

Later examples of visualising information will pick up on RAG (Red Amber Green) reports, direction of travel, dashboards and single A3 page centric meetings.

The next important aspect in this introduction to visualising information is to actually go to where the work is and actually watch what is done, keeping the brain in gear, asking a mixture of probing and 'idiot' questions.

Many years ago I was taught the art of managing by walking about, but at that time more often than not I would not understand what was happening and was seen for the sake of being seen. Going walkabout and meddling in the work is even more harmful. If you don't understand why things are done a certain way, instructing a change can simply cause it to become less effective.

If it's impossible to go to the work, have some pictures or video taken to look at examples of the issues and some of the approaches to overcome them. A workshop ran by my employees had a break-out session where we all viewed a series of pictures with side waste, littering and fly-tip. We were asked to define which category of waste each picture centred on. We were mainly waste experts, with differing backgrounds, we had a wide array of ideas about what we were looking at which in turn led to differing ideas of how to deal with the issues. If professionals can see the same issues differently, how hard is it for the public to report?

This had led to hand-offs, indecision and delays. What it also brought home was how difficult our existing systems made it for customers and the call centre staff to get reporting right.

PICTURE 1

PICTURE 2

Picture 1 shows a mixture of side waste heaped around a single bin, if the initial order was to collect side waste and the refuse crew reports it as fly-tip another instruction is given out. Delays occur and customers get annoyed, as time goes on more waste is tipped and the issues get worse.

Picture 2 is quite typical where a bad landlord finds their property vacated but full of old unusable furniture. They then may either throw it in the backyard or have a firm collect it, who if they are not reputable and licensed may then simply tip it around the corner.

PICTURE 3

This back alley had been as bad as the two previous pictures. Successive clean-ups, education and enforcement in a genuinely joined up way can lead to this sort of outcome.

However, these pictures are not placed here to remind people how the real world can look, but more to remind you that discussing tangible, irrefutable issues can resolve differences where several people are using exactly the same words, but have different mental images tied to those.

Just to finish off I have three diagrams, two of which are standard for project management and the second starts to show the difference between Visualising Transformation and normal project management.

Project planning is an inexact science for many organisations, with a great deal of detail placed in a project plan such as the one below, often prior to any knowledge of parameters being created. This abstract from a far larger project plan was built in Excel 2007 which can cope with most of the characteristics that MS Project would have been needed for only a short while ago.

PROJECT PLAN 1

ID	Project Name	Owner	Days	Start	End	1-Apr	7-Apr	14-Apr	21-Apr	28-Apr	5-May	12-May
1.0	**Strategic Waste Plan**	**Peter Smith**	**180**	**1-Apr**	**28-Sep**	■	■	■	■	■	■	■
1.1	**Validate Scope concept**	**Dave Gaster**	15	**1-Apr**	**16-Apr**	■	■	■				
1.1.1	Confirm broad objectives	D Gaster	3	1-Apr	4-Apr	■						
1.1.2	Design an achievable outcome	D Gaster	7	7-Apr	14-Apr	■	■	■				
1.1.3	Test design with waste team and PS	D Gaster	4	14-Apr	18-Apr		■	■				
1.2	**Carry out options appraisal**	**Dave Gaster**	110	**14-Apr**	**2-Aug**		■	■	■	■	■	■
1.2.1	Design questionnaire	D Gaster	3	14-Apr	17-Apr		■	■				
1.2.2	Test Questionnaire	D Gaster	2	21-Apr	23-Apr			■	■			
1.2.3	Create Q're in Excel	D Gaster	2	23-Apr	25-Apr				■			
1.2.4	Send Q're out/ await returns	D Gaster	21	28-Apr	19-May				■	■	■	■
1.2.5	Evaluate feedback / summarise	D Gaster	18	12-May	30-May						■	■
1.2.6	Discuss Issues … @waste exec	P Smith	1	8-May	9-May						■	
1.2.7	Create portfolio of options	D Gaster	20	14-May	3-Jun							■
1.2.8	Evaluate via agreed process	P Smith	15	9-Jun	24-Jun							
1.2.9	Reduce to four favoured options	D Gaster	22	7-Jul	29-Jul							
1.3	**Elemental designs**	**Peter Smith**	**192**	**21-Apr**	**30-Oct**			■	■	■	■	■
1.3.1	Start evaluation of management structure	D Gaster	5	21-Apr	26-Apr			■	■			
1.3.2	Phased approach to structure?	D Gaster	10	28-Apr	8-May				■	■	■	
1.3.3	Interface Waste structure with wider structures	D Gaster	10	12-May	22-May						■	■
1.3.4	Implement waste structure	P Smith	150	2-Jun	30-Oct							
1.3.5	Options paper for trade recycling	D Gaster	10	21-Apr	1-May			■	■	■		
1.3.6	Forecast plan for trade recycling	D Gaster	15	5-May	20-May					■	■	■
1.3.7	Action plan for trade recycling	D Gaster	10	12-May	22-May						■	■
1.3.8	IT systems review and options	D Gaster	20	14-Apr	4-May		■	■	■	■		
1.3.9	Incremental improvements to IT	D Gaster	120	21-Apr	19-Aug			■	■	■	■	■
1.3.10	Operational changes to best use IT	D Gaster	120	5-May	2-Sep					■	■	■
1.3.11	Consider best recyclate options	D Gaster	60	14-Apr	13-Jun		■	■	■	■	■	■

The next diagram attempts to compare traditional project management systems to those within Visualising Transformation. Most major schemes create a PiD (Project Implementation Document), project plan and forecast benefits from or for a project, prior to gaining much knowledge of the actual core work.

While I have a natural dislike of PRINCE2 outcomes, I have been assured by some PRINCE2 accredited managers (who also were trained in Systems Thinking) that, when it is used correctly, it is useful. I have been involved in three projects managed under PRINCE2 by fairly regimental officers, dealing with work packages and PiD compliance in such a way that adding value was virtually impossible.

My main messages within this comparative diagram are that a project shouldn't (or doesn't need to) start with a PiD, project plan and detailed outcomes. The methodology on the left can typically take three months before any actual intervention work commences. With PRINCE2 methodology running several inter-related interventions concurrently would be very difficult.

Whereas within the methods on the right, the initial activities will include forming and training the Transformation Team, but by the third week some quick wins could easily be emerging. As will be seen through this book, Visualising Transformation will always reflect and work with the current ethos and methodologies of the host. If the host is willing to learn and adapt to faster change options, with more leadership and empowerment as time goes on, more will be achieved.

This is one of a few diagrams which will be returned to later in this book.

The final part of this chapter deals with the implementation of the designed works. As far as your customers and stakeholders are concerned, this is the most important part to address. What will come from the workshops, designs and review processes are a host of great ideas which will work most of the time and a series of issues which need specific designs of their own. All ideas and issues are noted at every discussion.

The penultimate stage is to draft implementation plans, again mirroring corporate styles as far as possible, repeatedly checking for better designs, clarity of information and compelling reasoning for taking the next step.

Bringing this all together is the final art; most pressures in the public sector will be to address two issues: reduce costs and improve services. To hit deadlines when implementing the final designs, make sure either a project plan as shown on page 34 is completed and, or, introduce a critical path analysis.

Over the page attempts to visualise a traditional project which may take three months from inception to actually starting any work, to work under a Visualising Transformation approach. The 'squiggles' on the right hand graphs indicate the levels of work activity. Quick wins could occur within days of starting.

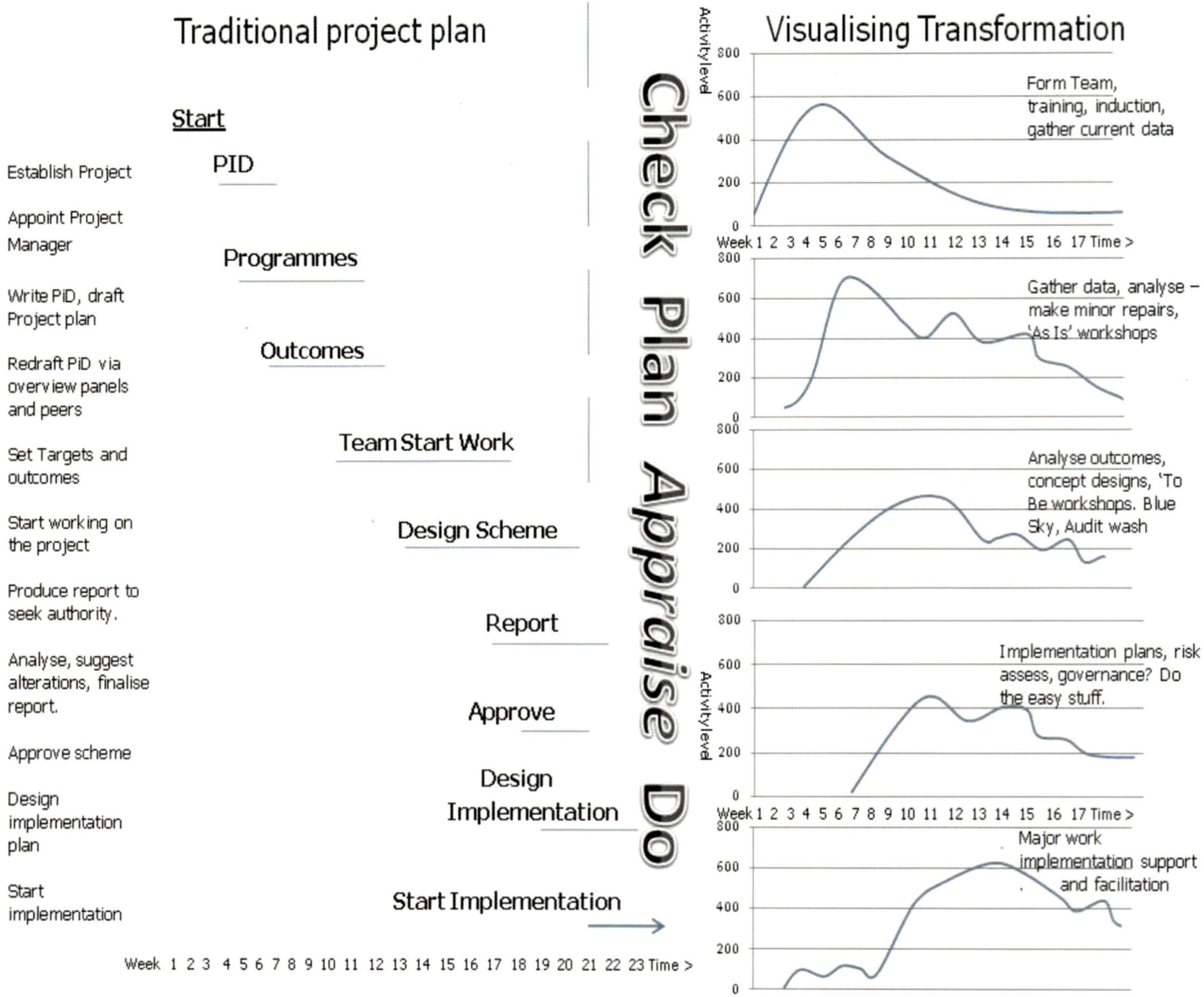
Traditional project plan
Start
Establish Project
PID
Appoint Project Manager
Programmes
Write PiD, draft Project plan
Outcomes
Redraft PiD via overview panels and peers
Team Start Work
Set Targets and outcomes
Start working on the project
Design Scheme
Produce report to seek authority.
Report
Analyse, suggest alterations, finalise report.
Approve
Approve scheme
Design Implementation
Design implementation plan
Start implementation
Start Implementation
Week 1 2 3 4 5 6 7 8 9 10 11 12 13 14 15 16 17 18 19 20 21 22 23 Time >
Check Plan Appraise Do
Visualising Transformation
Activity level
800
600
400
200
0
Form Team, training, induction, gather current data
Week 1 2 3 4 5 6 7 8 9 10 11 12 13 14 15 16 17 Time >
Gather data, analyse – make minor repairs, 'As Is' workshops
Analyse outcomes, concept designs, 'To Be workshops. Blue Sky, Audit wash
Implementation plans, risk assess, governance? Do the easy stuff.
Major work implementation support and facilitation

CRITICAL PATH ANALYSIS 1 FOR IMPLEMENTING THE DESIGN

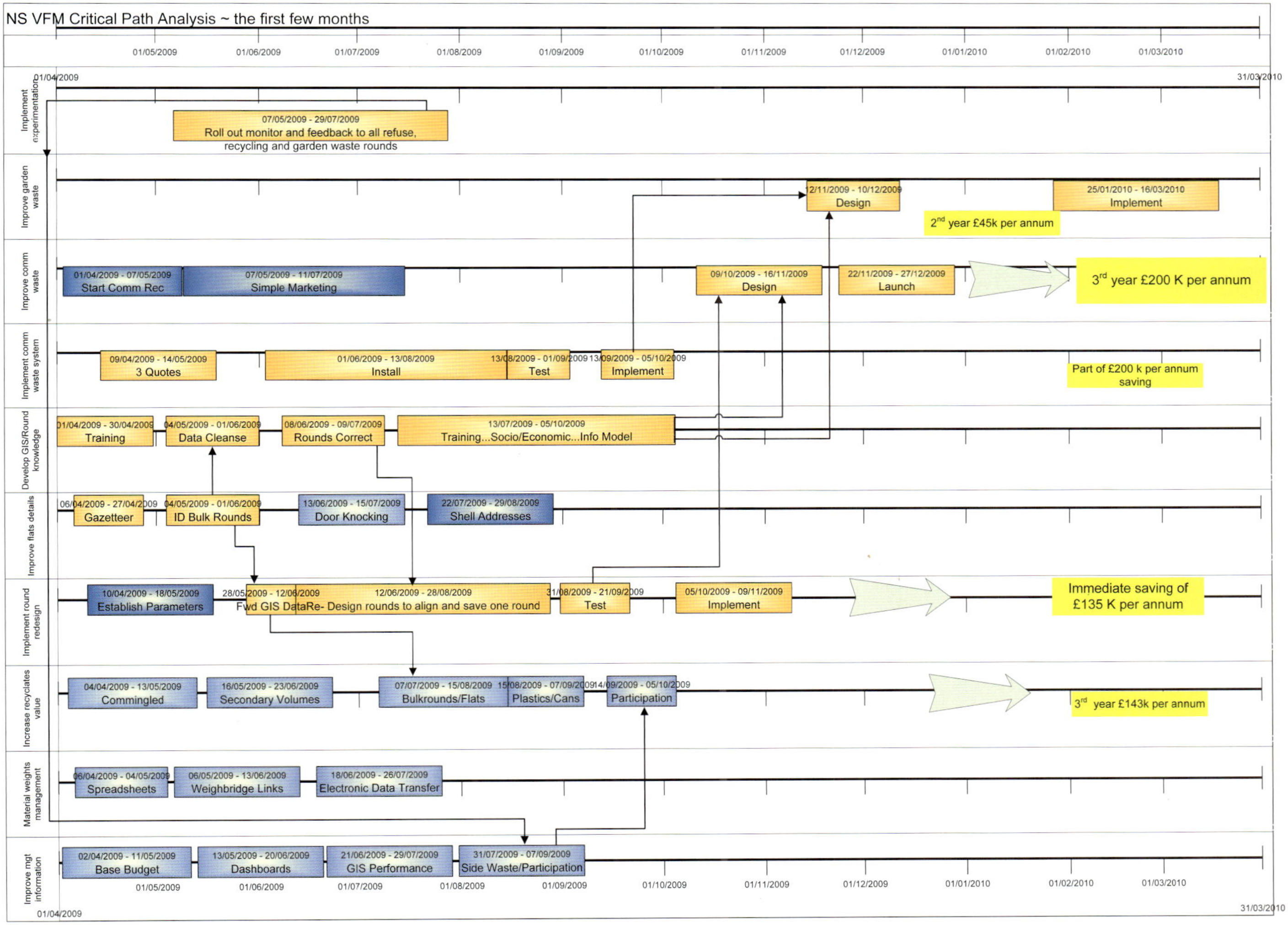

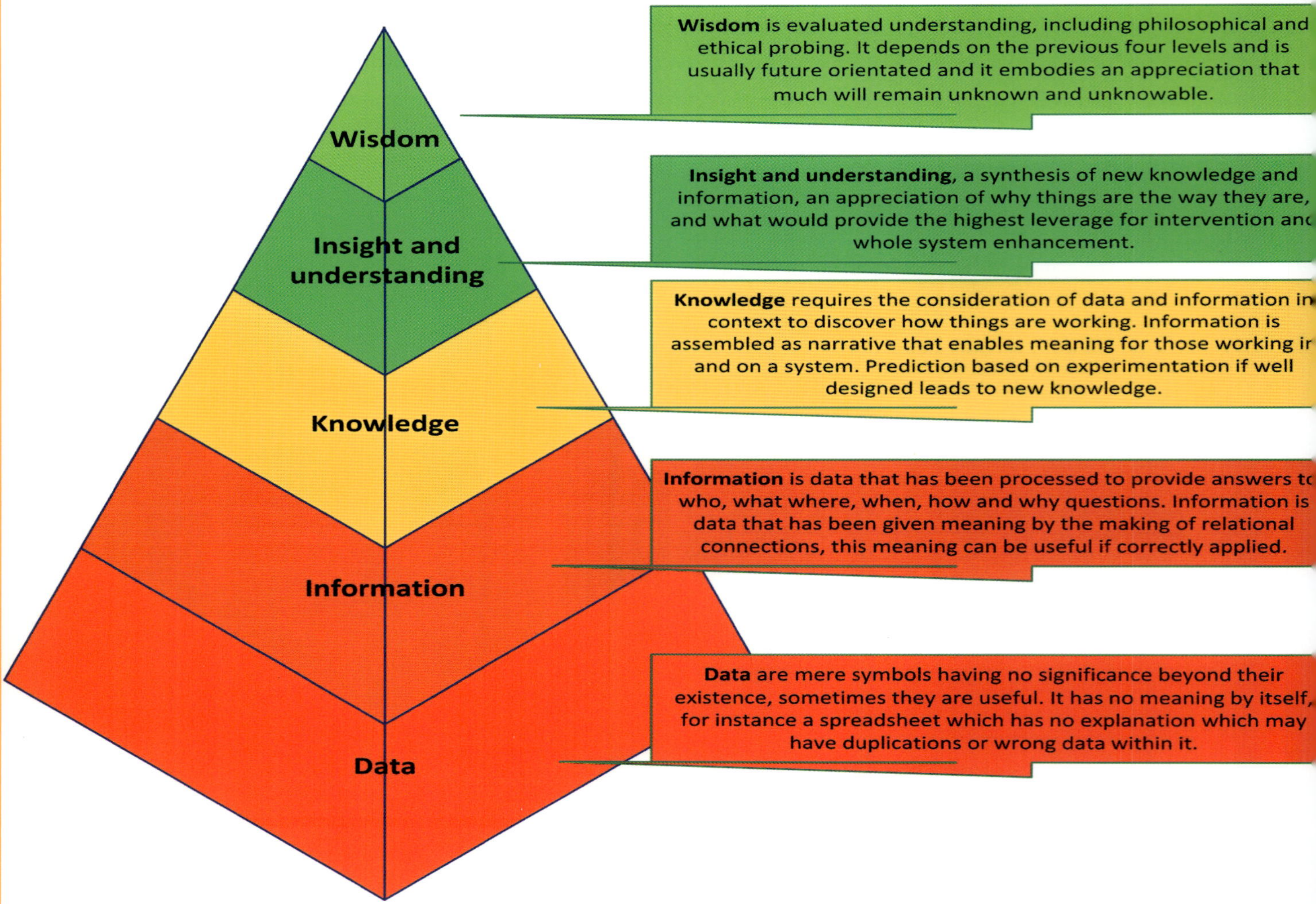

A hierarchy of profound knowledge, based on Russell Ackoff

The critical path analysis shows how a number of work threads have interdependencies, the golden thread in this case being the areas that are critical. Within the electronic version a number of comments were embedded so that cross referenced detail was retained. This was used to good effect to radically change round structures when there was least impact on the public, with the most amount of time to bed in between Bank Holidays. The preparation time was used to ready service expansion, to utilise released capacity. Lastly the differences between data, information through to wisdom are shown here.

Endnotes

1 NI's and KPI's are currently thought to add a great deal of value to organisation management. Invariably these are translated into RAG reports (Red Amber Green), with a direction of travel indicator (getting better or getting worse) and lastly is the annual target going to be achieved? Monitoring is key to Visualising Transformation and will be extensively addressed later. However, the current trend is also to only focus on the red, failures, when over 90% of the work is in the green and perhaps amber. Celebrate success, create positive energy with a view to positively encouraging the elimination of reds, some of which may be the result of arbitrary targets that the system cannot achieve.

2 I suggest that you should read, *Harnessing the ParaBrain* by Tony Buzan, BCA books, 1993

3 Russell Ackoff showed a hierarchy from: Data, through 'Information and Evidence', Knowledge, Insight and finally wisdom. So where is the wisdom in ignoring incorrect data? A diagram for this is on the facing page.

4 A paradigm is the way of working, the ethos and methodology of your current existence. Thus a paradigm change is part of the process of Transformation. Having information which you instantly can understand and work with would be a considerable shift for most people.

5 Pareto was an Italian economist who first postulated that 80% of issues arise from 20% of causes, the oft quoted 80/20 rule. By analysing data and showing it in a simple bar chart, weighted to the left hand side as largest issue, either by value or number of errors, and addressing the largest cause, data cleansing can be achieved very quickly.

6 Check is the starting position for any review or simple work placement. It's about finding out where an organisation is and where it would like to be. There is a whole chapter on this later in this book.

7 The five whys is a digging method simply trying to sort the root cause of in issue. 1. Why is there an error in the spreadsheet? Those items were posted on late. 2. Why were they posted on late? Because they were correcting some information from the supplier. 3. Why was there incorrect information? We were using different vehicles and didn't use the right numbers. 4. Why did we get the numbers wrong? Operations didn't tell us they were using hired vehicles. 5. Why were we using hired vehicles? Because we'd had so many breakdowns.

8 A control chart is a run chart of work results over time with upper and lower control limits added based on statistical probabilities for special cause being the likely reason for a change. There is much more information on this later.

9 This was a fortnightly collection, week one collection structures were set up incorrectly, while the week two information was correct.

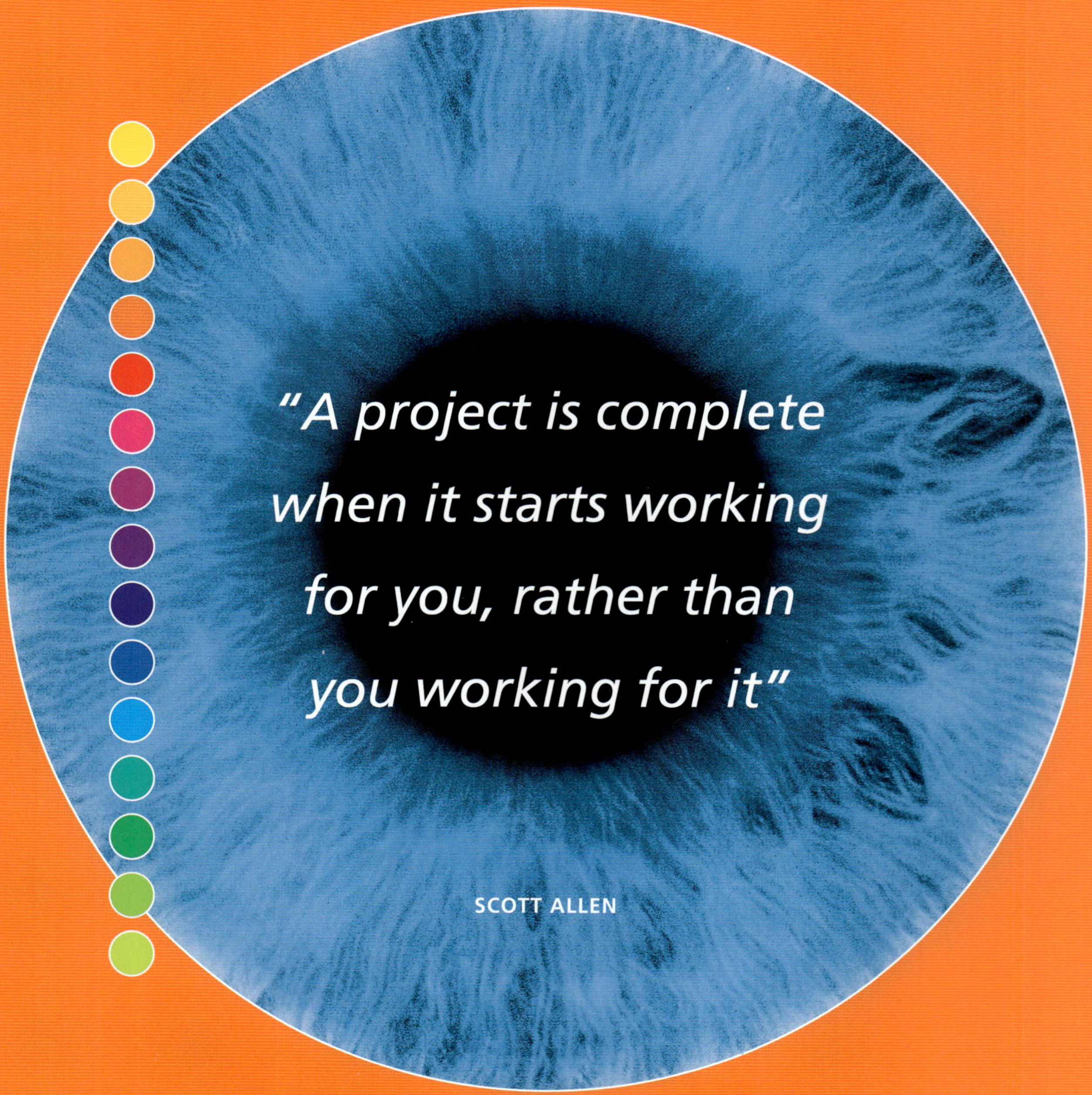
“A project is complete when it starts working for you, rather than you working for it”
SCOTT ALLEN

2. TRANSFORMATION

Like so many words in the English Language Transformation can mean many things to many people. The Oxford short dictionary defines it as: "***noun*** – a marked change in nature, form, or appearance" and in Wikipedia: "***Transformation*** – design, a human-centred, interdisciplinary process that seeks to create desirable and sustainable changes in behaviour and form – of individuals, systems and organisations – often for socially progressive ends."

Chapter one dealt with some forms of information visualisation, hopefully showing the difference between basic data and information and then how to grow existing systems to add more useful information to make decisions.

This chapter seeks to clarify the difference between narrow silo-orientated improvements to working methods which are often conducted under a 'Lean' banner, compared to much more holistic paradigm shifts from one culture of working to a far more customer-centric, efficient and effective way of working.

The two definitions above are both useful in that they describe a 'marked change in nature' and more helpfully in the Wikipedia definition as Visualising Transformation encompasses a wide array of factors that is 'human-centred' for both customers and staff, must be 'inter-disciplinary', for organisations seeking to improve socially progressive ends.

However, this approach is also very much based on an awareness that cultural shift cannot be achieved over-night nor to a culture which is strong, or determined enough, not to change much. Referring to the Beckhard change equation where $D \times V \times N > R$, for change to occur, the product of Dissatisfaction with the current state, a Vision how things might be better, and a Next Steps plan must be greater than the organisation's inertial Resistance to change. So if any of dissatisfaction, vision, or a plan are zero, then change won't happen.

Thus Visualising Transformation accepts the current paradigm as being useful or essential to the host, with certain aspects sacrosanct while other service areas may be willing to learn and modify where clarity of advantage can be achieved. There should never be a 'Marmite' reaction where people either love it or hate it, there should be a constant direction of travel with a growing insight that value is added, costs are reduced and services are better.

So 'Transformation' in this context will not necessarily be a process where a caterpillar pupates and several weeks later a beautiful butterfly emerges. For a start, there will never be a loss from current service delivery capability as a direct result of the review starting, a number of small 'eureka moments' will occur, with an array of quick wins adding value and capacity to do even more. The 'big bang effect' will possibly occur once there are sufficient people bought into the new ways of working, or the impact from design is really understood.

In many instances staff will accept that their systems are actually detrimental to effective work and be willing to change for mutual improvement. People will examine how they interact with others, how information could flow better and how by a series of small changes considerable step changes will occur. All the way through the early days of a process there will be new learning, insight and sharing of information, as work becomes easier and more effective, people and teams will become happier to do their work, to voice opinions to contribute to the corporate whole.

What will happen with the right training, leadership and nurturing is an increasing momentum to embrace change in a very positive manner. The involvement and commitment from decision makers is imperative for genuine Transformation, all the lower case[1] benefits described above will cascade out from the people initially involved, but it's the most senior, most influential people in the organisation who will eventually either enable total Transformation rather than significant improvement.

This can be achieved in a number of ways, most often it will come from curiosity: 'How can the backlog have reduced from 2,000 to 250 in three weeks?', 'Why have customer complaints reduced by 60% in three months?' , 'How have we quadrupled the number of pothole repairs with no extra budget?' To some extent this is how the host will wish to pull[2] the new way of working for the future, rather than being pushed into it.

When a number of operational step improvements occur at the same time, people will want to become part of that; however, the current ways of working have been learned over many years, the challenge to unlearn some of that and take on a new paradigm is far more difficult for experienced managers and directors than it is for people who can see the change far more tangibly. That is why Visualising Transformation[3] does not assume a step change in culture as a prerequisite of a package. At no time will there be a statement that, 'either you do it this way, or we won't work with you!'

However, the very heart of this is about 'Visualisation', if we take information which is compelling or often quite stunning to an executive board, decisions can be made on a rational basis, to draw people into the concept that something far better is happening and perhaps we should also learn more about it.

So let's go back a little into the core design principles. Visualising Transformation has at its heart a system of Continuous Improvement as articulated by W. Edwards Deming[4]. There are three key elements to this which will be expanded on a little here and in later chapters. These are:

▷ The PDSA (Plan Do Study Act) cycle of continuous improvement

▷ Deming's 14 points for management

▷ The System of Profound Knowledge.

NORMAL PDSA DIAGRAM

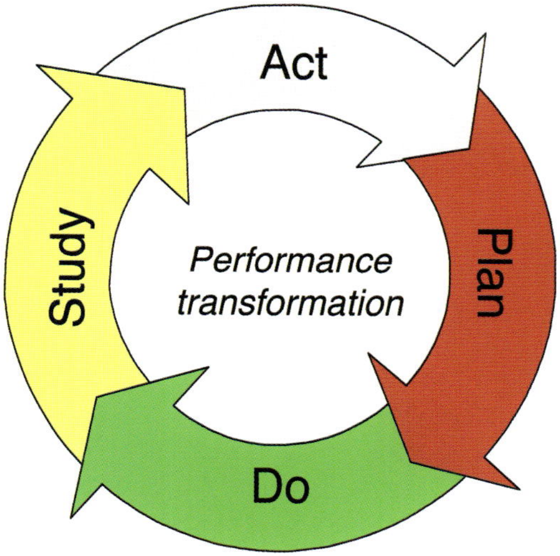

VISUALISING TRANSFORMATION CPAD DIAGRAM

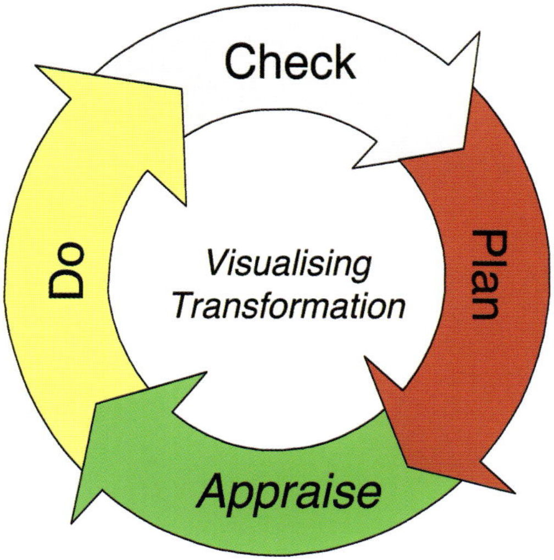

PDSA is often represented as a circle of events, each one feeding into the next, never stopping the process of continually improving.

When this was devised by Deming it was aimed at guiding self fulfilling teams within an organisation to look at how they are working with a view to working better in the future. It was at a period in time where change traditionally was slow and technology evolved over generations rather than months.

Today most change is generated from the outside, whether that is via an external consultancy or via an internal change team. The twin forces of risk management and governance generally stifle change leading to a greater dependence on central services and directors to allow change to occur. This in turn may potentially cause interventions to create less improvement than was actually possible.

As an interim or consultant the 'Study Act' aspects are better when rolled in together or in fact the process can often start best from 'Check'. Check allows a briefing, data gathering and reality checks to inform a planning stage. So 'Check, Plan Do' has become quite popular within Lean-Systems Thinking reviews.

Visualising Transformation adds in an *Appraise* stage partly at the end of Check, but strongly at the end of Plan, the basic idea is to understand what desires there are in the host and their customers for service improvement, additional services and value added, then to seek how to achieve those ambitions using the capacity that a redesigned service will achieve.

Previous applications of this have enabled a three to one benefits improvement compared to harvesting a capacity reduction alone.

Deming's 14 points of management were extensively covered in my previous book, *Quality or Politics/ Politics or Quality*. The concepts and arguments raised by Deming 20 years ago are as pertinent now as they were then.

1. Create constancy of purpose toward improvement of product and service, with the aim to become competitive and to stay in business, and to provide jobs.
2. Adopt the new philosophy. We are in a new economic age. Western management must awaken to the challenge, must learn their responsibilities, and take on leadership for change.
3. Cease dependence on inspection to achieve quality. Eliminate the need for inspection on a mass basis by building quality into the product or service in the first place.
4. End the practice of awarding business on the basis of price tag. Instead, minimise total cost. Move toward a single supplier for any one item, on a long-term relationship of loyalty and trust.
5. Improve constantly and forever the system of production and service, to improve quality and productivity, and thus constantly decrease costs.
6. Institute training on the job.
7. Institute leadership. The aim of supervision should be to help people and machines and gadgets to do a better job. Supervision of management is in need of overhaul as well as supervision of production workers.
8. Drive out fear, so that everyone may work effectively for the company.
9. Break down barriers between departments. People in research, design, sales, and production must work as a team, to foresee problems of production and in use that may be encountered with the product or service.
10. Eliminate slogans, exhortations, and targets for the work force asking for zero defects and new levels of productivity. Such exhortations only create adversarial relationships, as the bulk of the causes of low quality and low productivity belong to the system and thus lie beyond the power of the work force.
11. a. Eliminate work standards (quotas) on the factory floor. Substitute leadership.
    b. Eliminate management by objective. Eliminate management by numbers, numerical goals. Substitute leadership.

12. a. Remove barriers that rob the hourly worker of his right to pride of workmanship. The responsibility of supervisors must be changed from sheer numbers to quality.
    b. Remove barriers that rob people in management and in engineering of their right to pride of workmanship. This means, *inter alia*, abolishment of the annual merit rating and of management by objective.

13. Institute a vigorous program of education and self-improvement.

14. Put everybody in the company to work to accomplish the transformation. The transformation is everybody's job.

This approaches leadership, empowerment, pride in work, fun to work and unifying everyone into an smooth running organisation that sees 'Transformation' being everyone's job. It will also push back against arbitrary targets. Too often targets set are based on no knowledge of the capacity of neither a process nor the underlying issues that will determine outcomes.

Also consider how stretch targets work or don't work, there's probably a 50/50 success rate. I've been involved in interventions where the traditional PiD based objective was to save £25,000 out of £300,000 and then saved £230,000. No stretch target would ever start with that magnitude of saving, yet by enabling these opportunities that magnitude of improvement can frequently be achieved.

Point 11 b. above says eliminate 'management by numbers', seeking leadership instead. If a project is to enable improvement, what benefit does an arbitrary number inserted in a PiD add to the start?

I've talked to chief executives and directors about 'a leap of faith', they usually prefer the PiD based 'guess' as that has some form of predictability and comfort factor. However, by shaping broad aspirations as a lead in to Check, then using the Check process to inform potential capacity gives a far more realistic potential to Benefits Realisation which can evolve as work proceeds and knowledge replaces data.

Once a Transformation process truly starts to gain pace the concept of allowing Check to frame potential benefits rather than pre-guessing outcomes will become far more useful and inspirational. Within a large organisation the momentum of change processes will create an ever increasing capacity to change. This is again counter-intuitive, but so long as the cultural change improves, the corporate ability to get even better with less effort will also improve. As time goes on the need for extensive work to create a PiD will reduce.

Deming talked about a chain reaction; this applies just as well to the public sector as to a mass producer of cars. The example provides one quick pen picture; a later chapter starts to give many possibilities.

Start for example at 'improve quality' and you apply it to refuse collection, street light repairs, housing benefit processing, or report writing. If all work is done correctly to a good standard first time, you will have less cost from: Going back to do it again, complaints management, version control, or even needing a call centre.

DEMING'S CHAIN REACTION

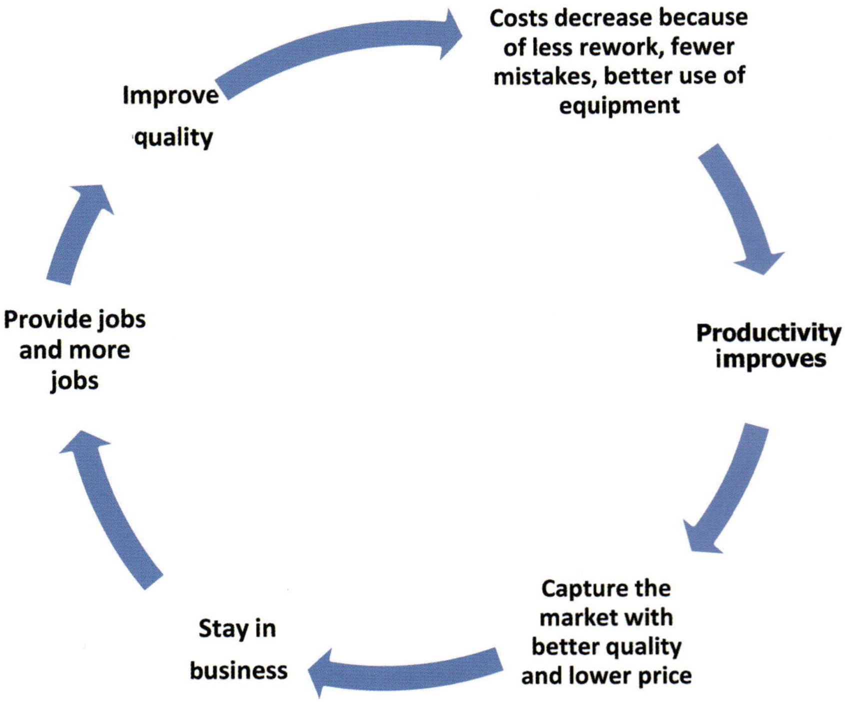

So the spare capacity to do a mix of good work and then repair bad work is less than to do good work only, so productivity improves. If you carry out domestic recycling collection and you create capacity, you could apply that to commercial recycling, starting it as an additional service with 'free' labour and vehicles released from domestic areas.

Commercial recycling then adds to profit, thus enables more publicity for domestic recycling which captures more materials at the same costs. Thus more jobs can be created and still have lower costs.

The pen-picture above shows that as capacity is released it is then re-used, staff are able to provide improving services at lower prices, the customers gain, the staff feel more fulfilled and the organisation finishes up with better services at lower costs, thus the willingness of staff to go even further next time increases, there is no trade union relationship problems, and in the widest sense, the authority can contribute to far wider socio-economic benefits than any traditional plan would allow with a reducing budget. Key learning point: ***reinvesting released capacity into additional work creates massive positive energy.***

This is an extremely important aspect of this methodology, the traditional project plan will devise outcomes that meet reducing budget issues, then have to force through those changes on the staff and perhaps the public. Most performance managers use the term 'efficiencies' as a code word for service cuts, they don't even consciously realise that a service cut has nothing to do with efficiency, it's just a handy disguise.

It's also well known that the implementation stage of a project will involve a reduction in morale, service achievements and customer satisfaction. This is not because that has to be, it's because the design and methodology are not good enough to achieve objectives.

The system of profound knowledge[5] leads onto an array of better management concepts, taking those out of specialist silos and into routine ways of working.

SYSTEM OF PROFOUND KNOWLEDGE

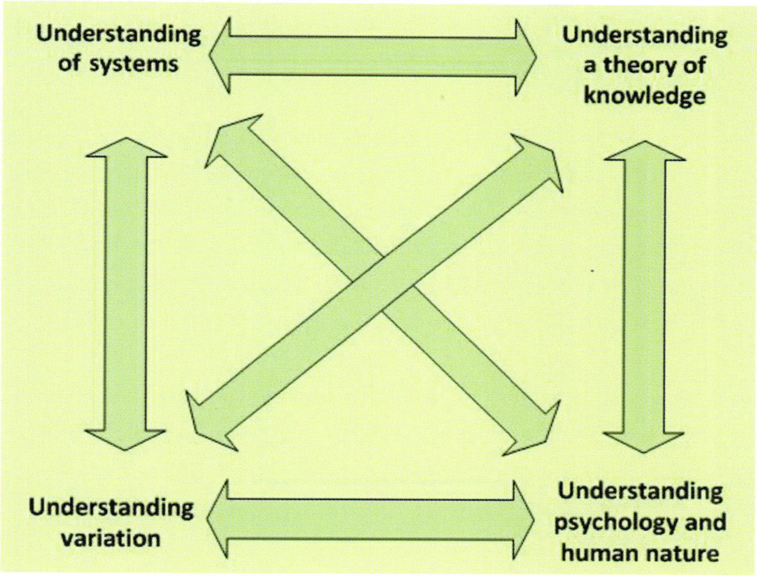

The system of profound knowledge is worth researching in its own right, what Deming tried to teach was that to manage people and processes you had to take a rounded view of all aspects.

Understanding systems is not just aimed at processes and procedures, but also how people and teams become motivated to do work.

I will later introduce more about 'knowledge', I've already discussed the difference between data and information, but knowledge, insight and wisdom are dimensions beyond information.

As a statistician Deming had a brilliant insight for variation, by simply adding the upper and lower control limits to a run chart obviates the need to describe common cause variation.

Deming used to use the term 'willing workers' a great deal, most workers are bright, intelligent and full of great ideas, and then we suppress every desire to improve, managers don't listen to supervisors who agree with front line staff that things could be better, if only they would listen.

The Visualising Transformation processes make people listen, and encourage people to contribute. As a result you get lots of ideas that will add value. When you get to a final design it has been worked on by all the people (or their representatives) who will be working on the new systems, they are eager and ready to do better work, reducing their stress and serving their customers better.

The quality and quantity of work done will usually improve significantly even before authority for major change is granted and will further 'step improve' as soon as permission is in place.

So if all is well at the coal face, how will this get translated through the organisation? Leadership is key to true Transformation, without leadership the work will be far more of an uphill struggle, an effective struggle, but sub-optimised by bureaucracy and well intentioned officers.

At a very large Transformation intervention for a county council progress was good but often in sudden surges, partly due to being inhibited by the central control systems dominated by 'Risk and Audit' officers. The most senior manager was intrigued about a number of steps forward; they were totally counter-intuitive to him. I had two lunch-time coffee sessions with him in order to support his personal learning opportunities.

In one very difficult area of work we were seeking 'a leap of faith' to use technology bought for a purpose but unused for three years due to legal and audit concerns. So I had a discussion with this Manager for him to talk with his team members prior to meeting with me and a technical officer. I had said to him that if they were instructed to not tell us what we can't do, but to jointly address how we could use the technology, that it would take 40 minutes to design a method that we were all happy with. Strangely it took us 40 minutes to gain approval to that usage, which in turn aided a step change in insurance repudiations.

I've worked with some excellent leaders over the years, and it's a pleasure to see the highest ranked officers still actively listening to quite junior staff. Excellent leaders will enable the generation of vision, team-working, empowerment and a natural ability for effective communications. These elements will not all be tied up neatly in their little silos; they will all be part of their natural working day.

Good leaders create positive energy around them; it becomes addictive and self perpetuating. Positive energy is also extremely useful for motivation, if people trust and are inspired by a leader who listens, there will be little need for the negative energy of certain types of appraisals and stretch targets that abound.

Good leaders will also be more human with their staff, rather than be mechanistic. Most officers I've worked with, work far more hours than they are paid for, starting early, finishing late and picking up e-mails from home in the evening and weekends. With those sorts of employees, if they need to suddenly take a couple of hours off to help a relative, should they be made to feel guilty about that? No, in a world of give and take, support the givers as much as possible.

Transformation is also a journey, from one paradigm to another. The bigger the organisation the more emphasis will have to be placed on communications as so many teams will be at different stages of the journey.

Mature organisations will have both formal and networked based information streams, so all information should be good and accurate; false claims are very quickly exposed and can be very damaging for overall credibility. Case studies[6] often are brilliant pen pictures, enabling a celebration of Transformation with the involved team's part of that delivery. It's good to keep a simple record of all improvements made as it helps to support a positive feel good energy. This could also be used as part of 'target setting' (if still needed), 'achieve 100 positive improvements per annum for customer service and effectiveness of service delivery'.

The use of social media options, with blog sites and short videos may help transmit the positive energy genuinely exuding from some of the early teams. The intra-net is an ideal repository for case studies and to share methods that could be used elsewhere.

The emphasis here must not only be about achieving positive improvements quickly – it must also address sustainability and continuous improvement. There are many organisations which were best in class only a few years ago who are now needing to create a new way forward. The Royal Bank of Scotland could be an example of that positioning. RBS has many units which created brilliant short term results but have led to long term problems.

For Transformation to genuinely work there will need to be that continuity of purpose, to continually improve. Thus all aspect of how work is carried out will need to be reviewed. When recruiting people in the future, take on people with big ideas, but make sure they will genuinely fit in with a naturally harmonious team.

Endnotes

1 Lower case in this terminology means the small wins or gradual increase in insight as to the larger picture as the review goes on.

2 It is always best to deal with pro-active people, if they can see the benefits of working in a different way; then there will be more positive energy, and a greater likelihood of success. The term pull is often used in systems thinking to represent the natural flow of work, or responding to desires, as opposed to pushing someone to do something. This would then flow to the concepts of intrinsic motivation rather than extrinsic motivation.

3 Visualising Transformation creates a new way of working both instantly for some quick wins and for the corporate whole as time goes on. The training will enable new discussions to emerge and will enable the host to agree a set of agreed elements to embrace change in a methodical way. The adoption of host tools to maintain and develop controls will support the new ways, using the risk register to show critical support to the way forward will help show the impact of promising certain outcomes but failing to deliver for instance, or an early insistence that certain current aspects of work are sacrosanct will show when proposed work methods have considerable amounts of non-value work elements built in from the outset.

4 Deming learned his statistics, PDCA cycle and work orientation of that knowledge from Walter A. Shewhart.

5 The system of profound knowledge is described by W. Edwards Deming in Chapter 4 of ***The New Economics***, and is also covered in *Quality or Politics/Politics or Quality*.

6 Part of the qualification process for Visualising Transformation will be the generation of a case study regarding the process being addressed.

"The job of a leader is to accomplish transformation of his organisation. Possessing knowledge, personality and persuasive power"

W. EDWARDS DEMING

There will be many motivational forces to start a transformation of an organisation. The most basic motivator is simple survival. Deming wrote to the effect in *Out of the Crisis* that many people don't realise that there is a crisis until it's too late. In some ways the recession which started in 2008 could come into that category, although two years prior there were grave warning about the housing market in the USA, and yet our wonderful investment bankers were picking up toxic debt with gay abandon only days before the writing on the wall was understood.

I was fortunate to listen to a latter day economist Arie P de Geus discussing world affairs at the Deming Forum in 2009; one very resounding observation was that no one should become a CEO of a bank if they have never made a significant loan[1]. In effect the concept that a good manager has an automatic right to manage anything is fundamentally flawed.

So I've considered that position for change managers – should a project manager have control of a project when they have no basic instinct of that service area? Simple qualifications in PRINCE2 or Six Sigma for instance shouldn't enable the total power for moving a project forward. Thus I propose that under the banner of Visualising Transformation the project leader should have some fundamental grounding in the service area if there isn't a strong subject-knowledgeable sponsor leadership from the host.

GDP GROWTH (NATIONAL STATISTICS OFFICE 121109)

The above graph is taken straight off a Government website. It shows quarter on quarter growth as a bar chart and year on year as a line. What it shows is an extremely stable position in statistical terms until the economists and free press scared themselves.

If the same data were expressed as a run chart, with 100% representing the initial position as below, with the plotting shown as would be the case for most data series, then the graph would look like the one as shown below. There are lots of causes for recessions, the two greatest are probably the press and economists. If they didn't shout so loudly about doom and gloom, the self fulfilling destiny wouldn't be any where near as severe.

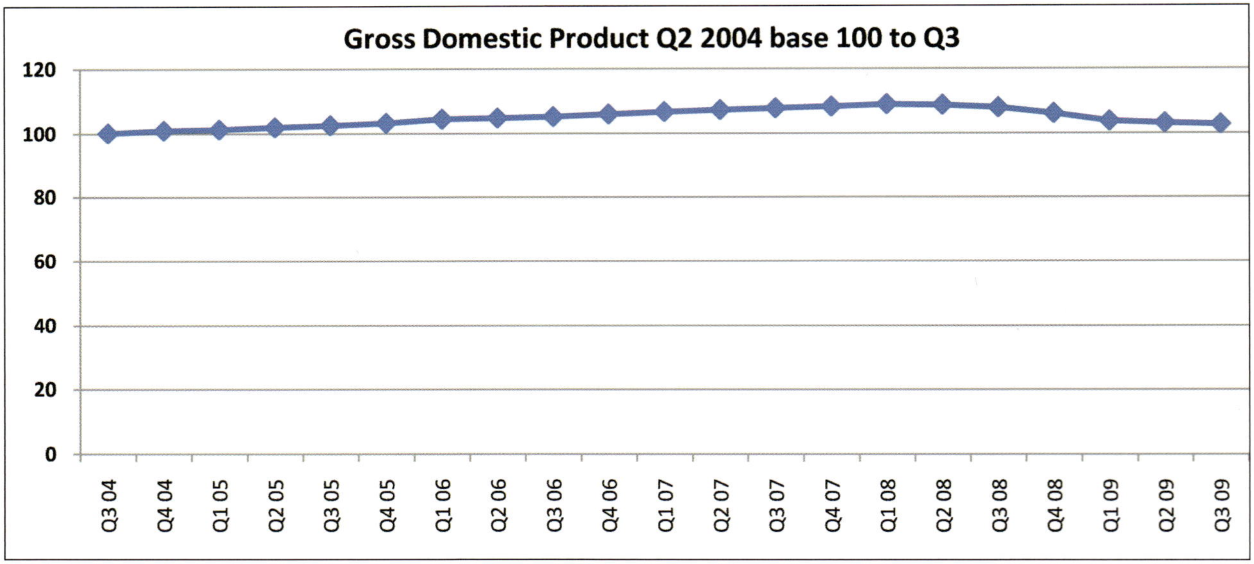

Just think, how many other operations are this steady and so prone to extreme worry by such a slight downward blip? This shows a very steady growth followed by a loss of that growth quite rapidly, had the economists, politicians and journalists not created such a firestorm of concern based on a very 'zoomed in' view of the economy, would the knee-jerk reaction from all affected have been so great?

There is a saying that comes to mind; 'all theories are useful, none are correct.'

As stated earlier – don't allow the scale of a graph to overwhelm the imagination. Our inherited doom and gloom and perhaps twenty years of national debt rests on theories of a few, and over-speculation of a few others.

The exact set of motivational aspects to start a Transformation for an organisation will be quite varied; the most likely one for the next decade will be financially driven. The recession caused many companies to considerably reduce employment levels (or for the longer term thinkers, reduce pay or working hours), which now is being reflected in the public sector. Overall unemployment may rise to 2.8 million people!

That will combine with a host of other issues such as: Working in partnership, recovery from a poor external audit, aspiring to greatly improve services, addressing new legislation, or initiating a 'beyond excellence' programme.

There will be many internal combinations; however, what is almost certain in every case is that there will be less money in real terms next year than this. So interventions will in the future have an imperative to address service improvement and cost savings to meet the aspirations of clients.

Consider also the comments from IDeA on their website for Performance Management, they state: 'The single most important factor in delivering LAA {Local Area Agreements} outcomes is partnership working.'

While that was possibly true prior to the recession, it is less likely now; there is also considerable operational drift since the end of Compulsory Competitive Tendering[2] (CCT) and the onset of Best Value[3] (BV). The loss of that commercial edge is very evident in the public sector and as a result there is considerable relaxation in Information Technology, Financial and HR attention to operational needs such that costs all increase as a result. Other legislation such as increasing human rights, equalities, equal pay, child care, maternity care and working time agreement all add to costs and reduce effective working time. Key question: ***Are there great business managers within your organisation?***

There is also a seed change in the public attitude – people are more likely to claim for accidents, the 'no win no fee' solicitors fuel extra insurance claims, not only from the public but also from employees[4]. Yet again the overlay from risk management comes in, many HR advisors shying away from winnable cases as the reputation of the council may be at risk[5]. So sickness levels crank up and accidents are reported that are at best, dubious, without CCT to sharpen operations managers' motivation, less is challenged and the situation gets worse.

The impacts of legislation changes tend to gain momentum over the years. We are now actually addressing issues that started to arise ten years ago, very much like Deming stated, 'you don't see the crisis until it's too late'. If additional measures and improvements were started ten years ago, draconian changes in employment levels wouldn't be needed now.

Traditionally decisions are taken in relative isolation from one another: with strategic development plans addressing needed legislation. Over the last ten years or so we have faced Best Value, Local Area Agreements[6], Local Strategic Partnership, Comprehensive Performance Assessments[7], now Comprehensive Area Assessments and One Place. These have brought with them a raft of Performance Indicators, Key Performance Indicators and now National Indicators.

Jargon and abbreviations increase by the day, clearly the abbreviations for the above list are: BV, LAA, LSP, CPA, CAA, PI's, KPI's and NI's. In addition there have been Gershon efficiency targets[8], a duty to involve and a duty to consult, with masses of new legislation for the environment, protection of people and reductions in highway accidents.

In parallel local government has been further fragmented with Housing being forced out in most places, fire, police, area planning, area regeneration development, business link, Primary Care Trusts (PCT's) and quasi regional government all being taken from local government.

Unitary councils have been established from single cities and boroughs, pairs of districts, up to whole counties, while other whole counties have been split in two. Some cities act as a unitary in the middle of a ring doughnut which is the residual county. All the time the Government talk about efficiency and effectiveness, but create an inexplicable jumble of options.

Various initiatives are established with three year funding, which race into existence, duplicate a number of other agencies, become useful and then are disbanded. The Government also hold up a series of 'best practice' concepts extolled upon the unsuspecting. Shared back office, customer call centres and improved unified IT systems being three examples where there has been huge expenditure and probably far more damage than improvement.

In all the above, the public sector has been continually pushed further and further away from excellent performance delivery with the customer being first in mind towards meeting the needs and objectives of the Audit Commission. Positive CPA evaluations have improved quicker for county and metropolitan authorities and slower for smaller districts[9].

This is then used as vindication that big is beautiful! At the same time the public are saying that districts are improving and the bigger councils are getting worse. Oh dear me, have the Audit Commission got it wrong? Of course not, what would the customers know about this?

Treating the Government as the prime customer through the Audit Commission (AC) has become so much of an issue that performance management and strategic management teams have massively grown in influence over the last ten years, often creating reams of documents to serve the AC which either add no value to services, or actually lead to essential service related information being culled. Yet when the AC officers meet the public and hear that the public cannot understand any of the highly detailed strategic plans created for the AC, they (the AC) shrug their shoulders, and say 'it's up to the council to give customers what they need as well as the AC'.

Then the next problem for customers is; who to go for what? The massive fragmentation of the public sector now means that there are around eight chief executives, HR departments, finance departments and IT sections in each borough where there used to be one. These then all use different IT systems that are difficult to inter-connect. When a customer needs an urgent solution to a problem, who should they go to? Well, in many cases the authorities aren't sure themselves and it's fairly certain the people in the call centres can't help.

These are the types of areas of concern that will need different forms of modelling, often referred to as soft systems designs. {Sometimes these issues are referred to as wicked messy issues} If you recall earlier, I referred to the IDeA statement that partnership working is so important; had the public sector not been divided up into so many, largely un-elected bodies, would partnering be so important?

Returning to motivation, it's quite likely that the initial motivators may be a pair of concepts such as 'Cost reductions and addressing the LAA' and that as the various threads of work move forward, a number of underlying (invisible) issues will come to the surface which are in many ways more important.

Within a Visualising Transformation process, there will be far more issues brought to light than imaginable via traditional silo-based operational reviews. It can assist a complete rethink of structure, systems and priorities, however, it can work to those at any pace the organisation needs, as all the operational reviews will add value and create additional capacity, so as progress is made, the ability to do more will improve.

The two diagrams below depict a single review process with the major stages of CPAD alongside a series of reviews running in parallel. There are more detailed visualisations of this later in the book. The strong message for now is that no single review or collection of reviews, will occur in isolation from the corporate body, and they will always reflect the ethos and ambitions of the host.

SINGLE PROCESS REVIEW

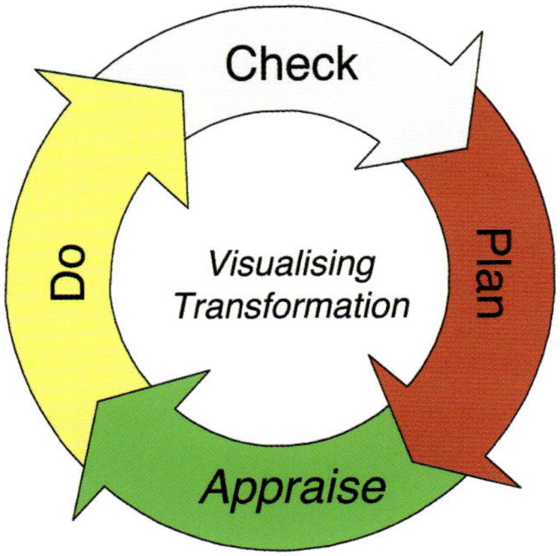

SERIES OF PROCESS REVIEWS IN PARALLEL

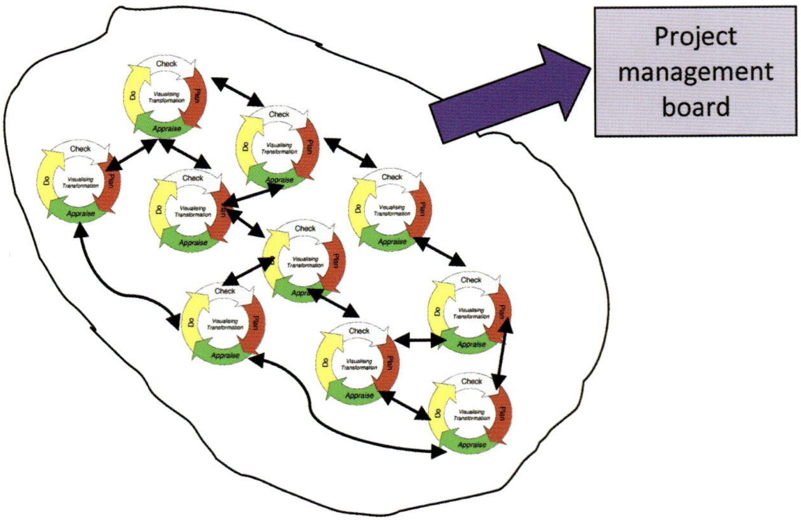

The effect of having many end-to-end projects running in parallel is far easier to enable than more traditional processes may infer. The front end training and project sponsor alignments aids mutual benefits naturally. There is more detail regarding multiple review leadership within chapter six.

The right hand diagram above shows how several reviews in a department could co-exist, which in turn can be applied to several departments at the same time, and indeed to an authority plus its partners via the LSP or indeed from previous procurement, out-sourcing or in-sourcing arrangements.

In order for maximum benefits to be derived a review needs to be end to end. For instance in something like housing benefits you shouldn't just look at an increment of the work, but look at the whole process from the point of customer need to resolution of payment. For parking fines; the process of sending out Penalty Charge Notices (PCN's) to payment is OK, but looking at the causes of appeal and resolving issues that lead to successful appeals with a view to stopping the causes will aid overall income and then in turn increase the initial purchases of parking tickets. (See the full example of this in chapter twelve)

Soft systems approaches will enable boundary conditions[10] to be drawn and considered with cogent reasoning. Drawing boundaries too tightly can sub-optimise[11] outcomes, while project drift into many related areas can delay implementation or lead to far too many restraining influences. Decisions as to what to include or not need to be reasoned with implications fully understood. (See boundary designs in chapter eleven)

Initiating projects, reviews and transformation can be quite emotive, what to include, what not to include, being difficult choices. To some extent there will be two positive outcomes from Visualising Transformation that most projects will not afford, at the outset the Check process will seek how many improvements and new concepts would like to be addressed if at all possible, ensuring clarity between must do and like to do issues. During the review in both Check and Plan, if it is clear from systems modelling that other services or teams should be included in the review, this would be raised with the sponsor straight away.

Later details will show how the various projects and boards can be coordinated, with benefits maximised such that governance risks and accounts are aligned and improved.

The after-effect of a transformation is that you have an organisation which can naturally adapt and react to future change. Continuous improvement is self fulfilling in that training, leadership and future proofing become second nature. If at the point of inception there is future legislation of unknown detail, the workshops and designs can scope the alterations with high level general designs as part of the initial core design with a futures plan clearly identifying what may be next. A later wash using CPAD will enable the details to be worked into original broader plans.

Host organisations utilise a massive array of procurement options, some procurement officers have significant concerns about buying the right consultants. While procuring change is difficult to specify or quantify, outcomes and payment processes can be as adaptive as the methodology. Where procurement officers have been involved in the change process they have invariably said that it will help them immeasurably with software or equipment procurement to follow as they fully understand what is needed and why.

Payment options for change professionals are also quite an interesting area to consider. At one authority one of the largest consultants in the UK were employed on a day rate. The host authority wanted to improve in essence but were ultra cautious in moving from Check to Plan, so they had a lots of costs associated with the governance of work, hence the delays added to the volume of consultant days to pay for, the only winner was the consultant.

Two things should occur as Transformation takes hold, the needs for an external firm should reduce as self-motivated well-trained teams become the norm, and the delays and costs from internal governance will also reduce as the council becomes more change comfortable.

Methods of procurement can be as a set fee, set input hours at agreed rates, percentage of savings achieved together with combinations of those. I favour a low day rate for core work with a profit share for savings achieved.

The style of risk and reward wanted by a host and acceptable to a consultant would give a strong indication of how confident the consultant is in their own abilities to add value.

Endnotes

1 *The Puritan Gift* by Hopper and Hopper shows many aspects of why America became a world force in business with narrative as to why recent decades show that world dominance has slid.

2 CCT had many negatives for councils in that it could be divisive and lead to awarding work on price alone, one of Deming's deadly sins. However, it gave considerable strength to management to maintain low sickness levels and high productivity levels.

3 BV supposedly addresses the whole council, but has greatly diminished the financial arguments for operational managers enabling greater strength to the corporate centre and the unions, thus operational management is far harder now than a decade ago.

4 In one assignment I was horrified to discover that the largest payments for injuries and accidents were from our own employees. The director, who was very competent, had no idea these claims and payments were being made. My analysis of insurance payments which took less than 45 minutes using Excel saved the council around £60,000 a year.

5 Risk and risk management have grown in strength over the last decade, with Audit using this as a review base for many audits. Considering risk in partial isolation from operational needs can create unseen burdens on operations and service delivery, each layer creating an ever more bureaucratic process as time goes on. Add in a claims culture, then the risk redoubles, so red tape increases. For highways trips and falls the accent placed on denying responsibility can take three times longer than curing the causes.

6 An LAA is effectively the designed plan for partners within an area to achieve a set of agreed visions. The LSP are the partners who will work together to the joined up plan. (Had local authorities not been divided up so often, would all these elaborate mechanisms be needed?)

7 CPA's and CAA's are the Government inspired ways of monitoring plans and actions for the individual and collective elements of a partnership to deliver services to the public. These are extremely central (upward) facing in nature, focusing far too much on the auditors rather than the public.

8 Gershon is the short text for a review which has caused authorities to reduce year on year expenditure by around 2.5% per annum. This has led to an over use of the term efficiencies which more often than not means stopping doing work that used to be done, rather than doing that work more effectively.

9 This was shown in a report commissioned by the Government carried out by Cardiff University in 2007.

10 Boundary conditions are important in order to define what is in and not in the project being reviewed. Boundaries can also be drawn round groups of issues to help simplify modelling until detail is needed.

11 The term sub-optimise is used to explain that a far better solution in terms of effectiveness or value could have been achieved which may be inhibited by a constraint exerted by the host or other body.

"The secret of getting ahead is getting started. The secret of getting started is breaking down your complex overwhelming tasks into small manageable tasks, and then starting on the first one"

MARK TWAIN

Following the scene setting , broad ideas plus some of the terms used, I shall at last start to address exactly why Visualising Transformation will add both value, which other systems are almost certain to miss and why by trade-marking Visualising Transformation, there will be protection against consultants who pretend to be experts.

Visualising Transformation is totally based on continuous improvement as initiated by Deming, Checkland et al. It is thorough, inclusive and self perpetuating. As with any reputable Systems Thinking intervention, there will be extensive knowledge transfer from consultants to the people involved in the work and those affected by it, enabling self achieved continuous improvement after the initial step changes.

However, the weakness with Systems Thinking and most associated systems approaches to change is that they are not regulated or licensed. The strength of PRINCE2 in particular is that it has rigour and regulation. If someone demands a PRINCE2 practioner, they can confirm that fact with a certificate.

There are many extremely good Systems Thinking practioners and consulting firms, but even some consulting firms that run associated training courses clearly do not understand sufficient breadth of knowledge and basic 'tools' to do the intervention any justice.

I've spoken with several dissatisfied host representatives who are very frustrated by far too many workshops and discussions, but no outcomes, achieved when working with their current consultants. The reasons for this could be that a consultant may be trying to design a divergent issue with a convergent solution, or simply the consultant is not good enough for the role.

I've also spoken with procurement experts who know what they want to some extent, but can't use their skills to achieve a contract with the best firm for the job. Without rigour and control under current procurement law, weeding the less capable firms out of the bidding process is very difficult indeed.

So Visualising Transformation will be offered as a solution, to be comparable with Six Sigma and PRINCE2 as a known product, rather than a vague description which means many things to many people. See also chapter eleven where many known styles of Continuous Improvement methodology are described with a web link to further reading offered.

There is a master link to the Support Services Direct website where links to a wide array of other experts, methods, case studies and diagrams will be retained and regularly updated. The web-link has a page by page capability, so ideas from this page can be followed via as few key strokes as possible.

Visualising Transformation has rigour and flexibility; it enables joined-up thinking based on greatly improved information within a structure that may also evolve, creating a far more effective and efficient organisation with improved ethos in terms of what matters to customers.

The information will be: ***Clear, Accurate and Stunning.***

As was discussed at the end of chapter one, via the Ackoff pyramid, defining data through to wisdom; wisdom is derived via initial hard work and several layers of rework which will be covered in the next chapter. Most organisations are 'data rich – information poor'. Invariably data cannot be trusted on arrival, so managers currently will need to probe and test the data to arrive at better data. Chapter one shows the possible current process to move from data to information within the current paradigm.

Visualising Transformation will lead to a bypass of all that work once embedded; information will be generated as a by-product of simply doing the work. It will arrive automatically if needed or on demand within any designated parameters. The automation of information will create capacity for the people doing the work, for their supervisors and for every strand of management and support service. That one very positive act, done right, will enable capacity to add value at every level of the organisation.

So in Ackoff's terms, information started from data, that data was cleaned, removing duplications, transposed decimal points, correcting incorrect names, or varieties of the same name, filling in gaps and going through the six basic questions of why, where, how, who, when and what. This would perhaps also employ the five whys to the process to add richness of information.

The starting point for the organisation with regard to volumes and detail of data, together with the ethos of approach, to being able to use information for decision making will be pertinent, as this affects the future desire for how much information will be routinely used, irrespective of the volume of information in use. It will be better information as a result of this approach.

The current usage of graphs and diagrams can also be very relevant. Within the Check process described in chapter five, a huge array of data will be processed into basic and improving information. Some information may create no interest or reaction; if it's not critical to progress it may be shelved for later. If it is critical, the core intervention team will use it and refer to it, with a view to creating inquisitive hosts as to what else may be there.

I can relate to many instances where bringing data together from within the hosts' systems and then presenting it in a joined-up informative manner can improve decision-making and save costs.

Example A: A London borough was failing to deliver enough recyclate returns, yet another contract was going to be entered into in order to avoid a £200 per tonne government fine. I calculated the cost of the proposed scheme to discover that the likely cost would have actually been in excess of £200 per tonne.

At the same time I used existing monitoring data from two sources for existing recycling schemes and compared it to the financial information relating to the same services. These services were running at less than 30% effectiveness compared to others in the same or neighbouring boroughs, it would have been perfectly easy to get a three-fold increase in the yield from those contracts if they were properly supervised and managed.

The council achieved far higher returns from their existing schemes than they could have achieved from the additional scheme. This was as a direct outcome of better information, without spending a penny of the £800,000 for the proposed new scheme.

Example B: A housing association was going to replace its core IT system as it was no longer going to be supported by the software providers in the medium term future, nor was it seen as capable of meeting operational needs. I worked with an IT consultant and the users of the system to repair some issues and add some easy reports. As a direct result of the improved information the operational delivery also improved from just over 90% on time to 100% on time. (This was for the first time ever.)

I also spent some time with the providers of the IT system and met with their user group, as a result they decided to standardise systems from client to client, add our recent reports as standard options and support the system for the future.

The housing association gained operationally and decided not to replace their IT systems saving them over £250,000 of capital cost for a new system, prior to considering all the additional operational costs associated with the major change and integration of systems.

In both these examples the host organisations were going to spend considerable sums purely because they didn't have the right information and skill sets, to get the right information, to manage well. Later examples will continue to build on this theme. So information needs to be accurate and have clarity to enable knowledge transfer and insight for better understanding. Information needs to be 'fit for purpose' in that it meets the needs of everyone within the organisation and taking the thinking wider, also for the customers of the services.

From an NI14[1] point of view, having information which is immediately accessible enables all to see where work is, gets the work done quicker with less likelihood of doing the wrong job and as it will be right first time quickly, there will be no need to chase work which is overdue. All these benefits come from simply having the right information instantly to hand, no changes of process have even been considered so far.

Consider also the concepts addressed earlier, where having corporate information systems that met the 'centre's need' was to the detriment of the service delivery. What is proposed within this first element is to ensure that the services have the right information and that as a by-product the centre gain live information which is always correct.

So the argument for clear and accurate information (evolved from dirty data) may be starting to make some sense, the last aspect I raised was for that information to be ***Stunning***. I have chosen this word with care, 'stunning' information enables faster, more accurate decisions to be made.

A recent project to improve the carbon management of an authority had not moved forward much for many months. The project manager was in despair as he could see the benefits, but the decision makers could not.

Every time he tried to enable a decision to be made he added more detail to the reports and still it wasn't approved. I got him to simplify the message, if we spend £50,000 the government will add £50,000 and we will save £70,000 per annum – and by the way it's very CO2 beneficial. This was approved, it could have been bigger and bolder, but it was unreservedly agreed and enabled phases two and three to follow straight after, reinvesting the initial savings straight back into those latter phases.

To build a strategy you need information, ownership and direction of travel. Too often this is done from an initial scoping meeting where direction is given and the next stage of the process many months later is to review the completed strategy which could be dozens of pages long. By that time a polished end format has been created – that will then take a lot of reading, it may be passed with only a few cosmetic changes made. Many hosts will like this, tell people what you want, they do it, then you accept it warts and all. Others may be happier to discuss raw thoughts and genuinely invest in strategy.

Using a 'Lean' technique for strategic development is well worth considering. One technique centres on having a single sheet of A3 with some relevant information, as in the following example.

The start of a process to develop the waste strategy for a council was to agree the core areas to consider, these were Cost, Customer and Environment. So the scoping meeting started with this triangle with a gradual increase in information as more research was carried out.

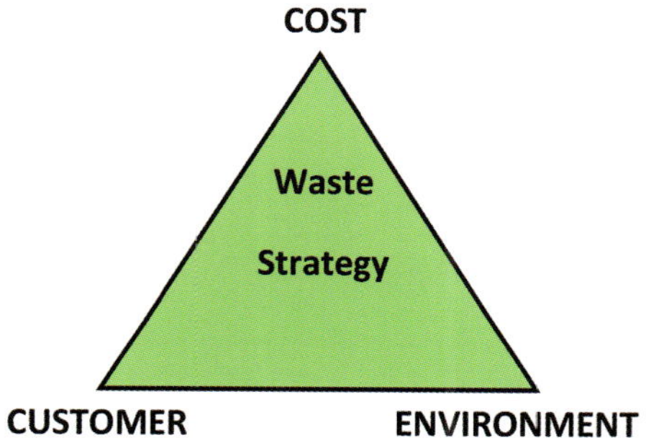

The first meeting looked at this concept, setting some core aspirations, such as; to not cost more than £300,000 extra to achieve outcomes, to increase recycling from under 40% to over 60% and to meet the wishes of the majority of customers.

To be able to devise the optimum strategy for these we needed to know:

- The capacity of the waste stream to divert materials
- The capacity of the current resources to change ways of working
- The costs of options to collect and process waste
- The desires, needs, wants and tolerances of the customers
- The value of materials in different formats
- The locations and capabilities of processing plants, now and in the near future.

Thus we devised a series of A3 information sheets addressing: How materials can be separated, what the composition and possibilities are for the current waste stream, what the trend has been so far in diverting waste and what the public opinion is regarding collection options.

As a direct result we started to gain more and more knowledge from information. Meetings were being held at many levels across the whole council guided by a steering group of cabinet members with senior officers, but all sharing an ever-increasing array of data.

The public were consulted via a three-stage plan, seeking broad concepts in various locations across the council, followed by an online and posted questionnaire and then towards the end of the process via further meetings around the council area.

RUN CHART SHOWING SUMMARY MATERIAL TRENDS

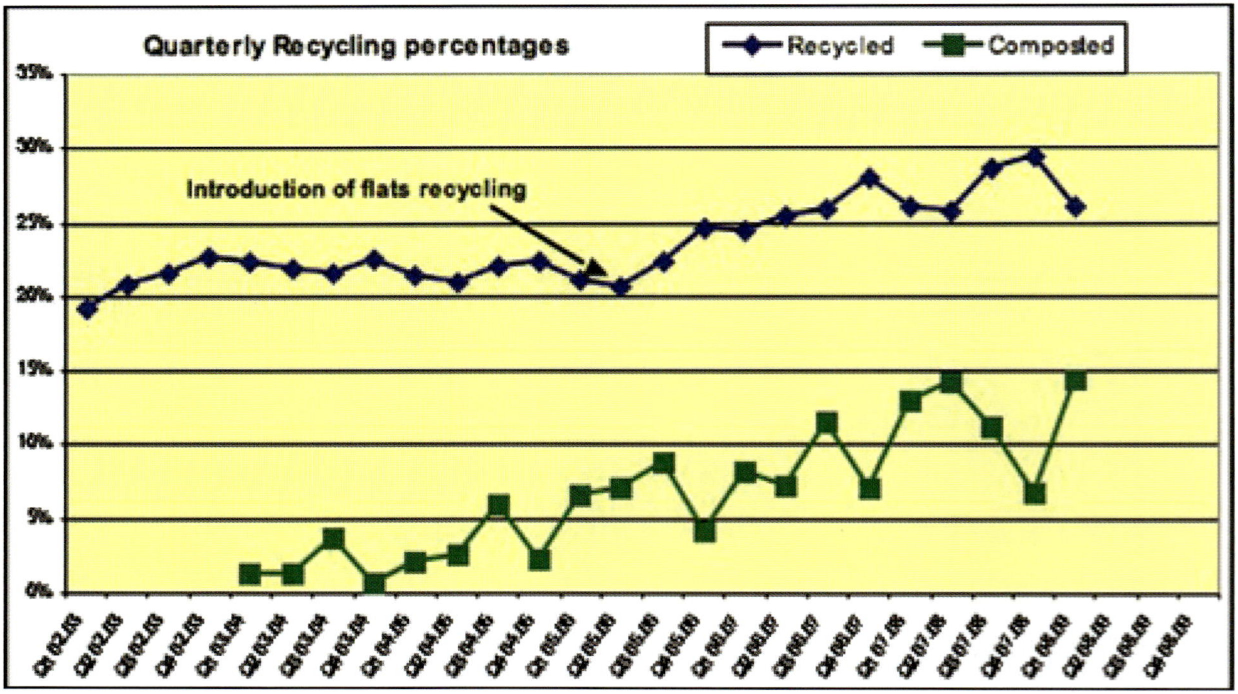

The above chart shows a number of interesting insights, first as a result of creating the charts I was able to ask what actions had been taken in early 2005 to transform a system in decline to one that step improved. It transpired that an additional member of staff was employed to introduce recycling to flats and work on the overall publicity of recycling. (This graph was on A3, big and bold.)

The composted material shows a continuous growth of material with a logical low point for January to March each year. A later graph from another council shows the relationship between rainfall and temperature for compost tonnes per month, which was a brilliant use of data to forecast outcomes.

MODEL FOR WASTE STRATEGY EVALUATION OF PROPOSALS (EACH ELEMENT HAS 1/3RD OF WEIGHTING, FURTHER DETAILED)

Scheme forecast to net current cost	8%
Greatest waste diversion per £ net spend	7%
Least volatility and risk to deliver	10%
Least capital impact	4%
Best revenue forecast	4%

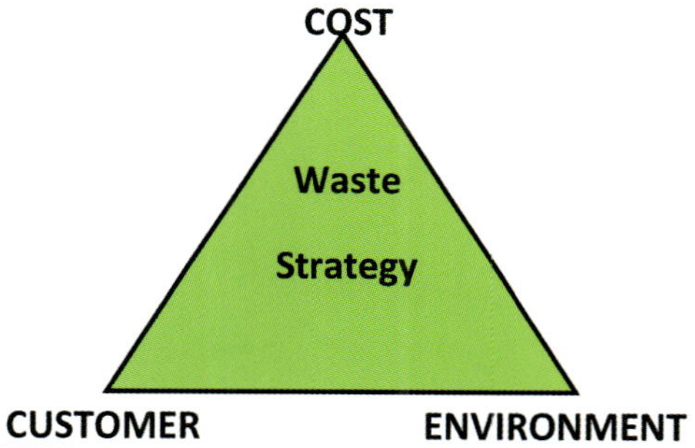

Greatest volume of doorstep recycling	10%
Simple system / maximum recycling	6%
Best mix bins and baskets	5%
Best option for flats	4%
Scheme with best user methods	4%
Easiest scheme to phase start-up	4%

Targets: BVPI's, NI's, internal, LAA	7%
Total waste recycling	10%
Best processing of recyclates	6%
Least Carbon Impact (haulage +)	6%
Best re-use of materials	4%

The simple triangle shown earlier became more important, leading the way for other analysis to become more relevant. The available options for recycling diversion were built up to 150 options that could be used in various combinations, with Cost, Customer and Environment aspects shown as a simple 1 to 10 marking, with red applied to 1 to 4, amber for 5 to 7 and green for 8 plus (more detail is available at www.supportservicesdirect.co.uk/visualisingtransformation).

Thus a quick inspect of RAG ratings (red amber green) allowed many options to be discarded without serious discussions. The 150 options were reduced to 25 options which again fitted on a single side of A3.

Further details of all three elements were added to the A3 page so as to detail information behind the bullet point aspects in the three coloured rectangles. As the process moved forward, we gravitated to outcomes which were very similar in Customer and Environment terms, but had quite different financial implications, so we evolved our assessment process to take this on board.

ABSTRACT FROM WASTE DATA HELD WITHIN AN A3 SHEET

Potential household waste collection
(Current recycling plus additional from residual waste, based on current door to door collections, plus 80% of potential residual, x 80% of properties)

Composition	Annual Tonnes	Per cent	Average property weekly
Total Weight	49,000 T	100%	15.4Kg
Paper & card	12,200 T	24.9%	3.83 Kg
Cans & plastics	2,500 T	5.1%	0.79 Kg
Garden waste	4,700 T	9.6%	1.48 Kg
Food waste	7,100 T	14.5%	2.23 Kg
Mixed Glass	3,704 T	7.6%	1.2 Kg
Residual waste	18,796 T	38.0%	5.9 Kg

Potential municipal waste (2009 / 10)
(This adds commercial waste and street cleansing onto household waste)

Composition	Tonnes per Annum	House-hold %
Total weight	55,800 T	108.1%
Residual domestic	18,796 T	36.4%
Dry recycling	18,404 T	35.7%
Compost / food	13,900 T	26.9%
Street Cleansing	500 T	1.0%
Commercial - waste - recycling	2,800 T 1,400 T	5.4% 2.7%

This was taken from an array of waste and recycling data held in several formats and locations, which was compared to studies of waste composition and success rates for new schemes elsewhere. I noticed that different people liked to consider information in different ways; some worked on the weight of a bin or box for each collection, while others were more comfortable with straightforward percentages. Thus tables carried mixtures of information such that choice was easy while still avoiding too much complexity.

FORECAST FROM LINKING ALL ASPECT OF REDESIGN AND APPRAISE TOGETHER

Original 'Budget plan' Waste Strategy

Budget Flow		**2008/09**	**2009 / 10**	**2010 / 11**	**2011 / 12**	**2012 / 13**	**2013 / 14**
Base Budget	Expenditure	£3,345,678	£3,455,970	£3,542,369	£3,630,928	£3,721,702	£3,814,744
	Income	-1,654,321	-1,695,679	-1,738,071	-1,781,523	-1,826,061	-1,871,712
Original net budget		£1,691,357	£1,760,291	£1,804,298	£1,849,406	£1,895,641	£1,943,032
Changes from base budget:							
Removal of growth refuse round		-£135,678	-£152,178	-£272,678	-£272,678	-£272,678	-£272,678
Removal of growth recycling round			-£52,020	-£52,020	-£52,020	-£52,020	-£52,020
Increase in commercial waste surplus		-£75,432	-£119,121	-£187,565	-£275,432	-£275,000	-£275,000
Increase in recyclates income		-£372,781	-£410,578	-£465,778	-£465,778	-£465,778	-£465,778
Improvement in garden waste position		-£149,945	-£230,000	-£287,000	-£317,500	-£331,000	-£349,000
Improved vehicle utilisation			-£7,667	-£16,100	-£23,000	-£23,000	-£23,000
Increase plastics and values			-£8,851	-£17,702	-£46,502	-£46,502	-£46,502
Improve values of recyclates			-£15,686	-£31,529	-£47,058	-£47,058	-£47,058
Increases in recycling to flats + marketing			-£10,104	-£28,291	-£40,416	-£40,416	-£40,416
Tracking, back office and comm waste system			£20,000	£113,383	-£201,972	-£201,972	-£201,972
Recycling Plan via phasing					-£229,526	-£459,052	-£459,052
Systems Thinking intervention and training		£156,789					
Increase in haulage and collection costs		£72,020	£73,436	£77,842	£82,512	£87,463	£92,711
Unknown and contingency costs		£75,319	£55,000	£56,375	£57,784	£59,229	£60,710
Additional costs			£153,832		£100,000	£100,000	
		Revised Forecasts					
Forecast net budget		**£1,261,649**	**£1,056,354**	**£693,235**	**£117,820**	**-£72,143**	**-£136,024**

This was derived from an array of background projections and accounts that had been positively vetted. All details are from individual project plans, showing how one aspect impacts on the other. The use of red to emphasise improvement of figures was high impact. The creation of this is seen in chapter eight.

In each set of information there was a clear capability to drill down into the data so as to understand how projections were cast and what assumptions were made. Even the methods of modelling the data were subject to open discussion, such that total ownership of information was created. This project carried a huge amount of data along. The final aspect of 'stunning' is shown in the next graph.

This was directly linked to a bar chart, the black bars represent the previous budget and the red bars depict the revised budget. This was an intended subliminal link, red is cheaper and more effective!

RED / BLACK BAR CHART SHOWING LONG TERM BENEFITS OF THE SCHEME

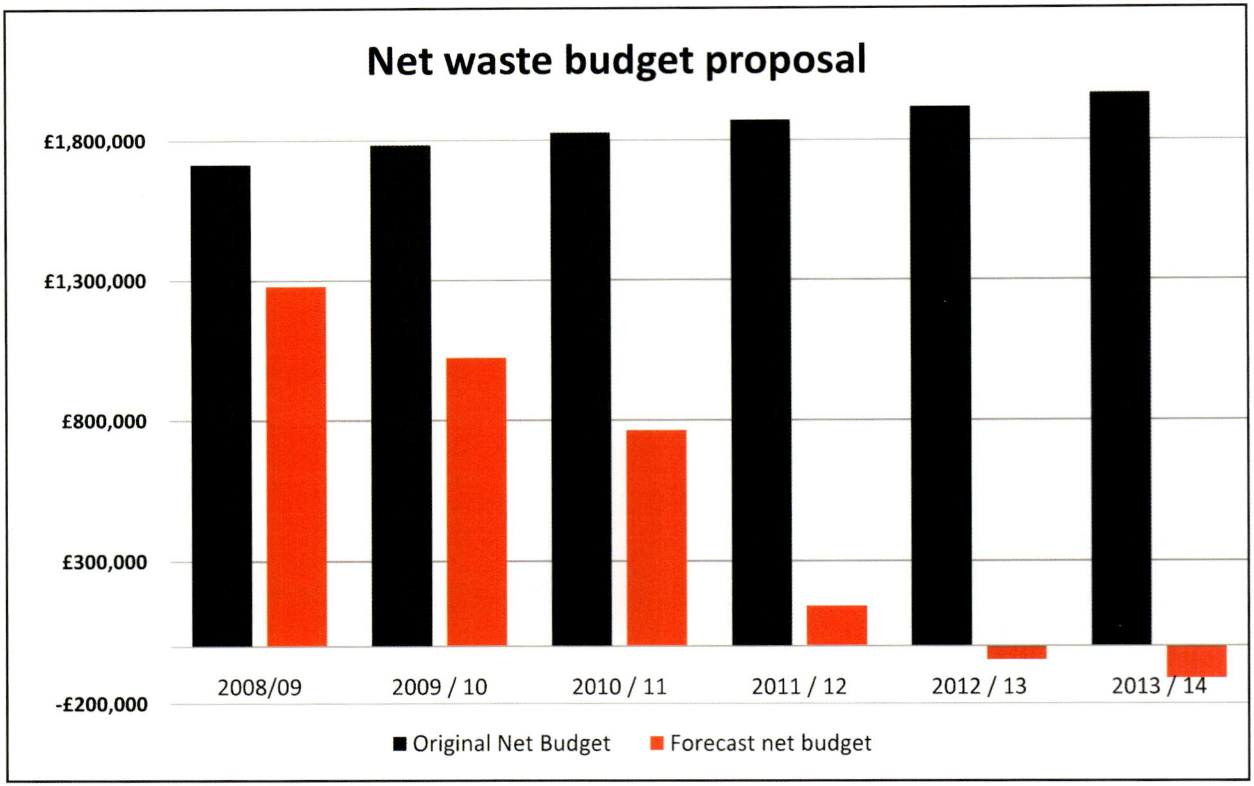

This shows the net cost of waste collection and treatment, prior to central overheads should reduce over time from £1.7M to less than zero. At the time of writing this book, the scheme was still fully on course to achieve this, and to move to 65%+ recycling diversion.

The latter chapters will return to this process, the contents so far have been included to differentiate data from information and to show how differing forms of 'stunning' may appear.

In the same way that there should be an understanding of the relationship between information and data, there should be an understanding of structures within an organisation in order for an intervention to succeed. This is not a simple mapping of who reports to whom in a standard employment diagram, but more how do real decisions get made or indeed how do unusual pieces of work get carried out?

The structures of how the council relates to customers, who are the customers and for the services under consideration; what their influence is for service delivery all need to be understood. Some councils give far more attention to paying customers than to normal service recipients, which perhaps is an insult to those who don't directly pay.

The customers are many-fold; the council tax payers, people who pay for work, the children of the payers, people passing through the area, people buying goods in the shops, your partners in the LAA, the contractors who are working for you, the Government and their various quangos and aligned organisations who have direct and indirect impact as a result of co-existence. When starting on a new way of working, all these need considering with some boundary drawing carried out in order to consciously include and exclude differing groups.

The politics of every organisation are always interesting, sometimes decision makers are very full on and leave you in no doubt as to what is wanted, while other very influential decision makers can stay quite quiet in meetings and workshops, only to raise issue outside of those meetings.

Part of the early engagement message must be that the more straightforward people are with aspirations and constraints of an intervention, the greater the cost benefit will be at the end, and the lower the costs of the intervention.

If a multi-layer review is started, as shown diagrammatically on page 56, the early reviews may enable trust to build and control processes to be understood. The more reliance that is placed in PiDs and detailed project plans, with gateway signoffs involving lengthy reports at regular intervals, the less intervention work will be carried out and the longer the consultants will be working for you. That is, too much control is likely to both add to costs of a review, and restrict the eventual value for money outcomes.

Consultants who are totally happy to comply with these approaches without voicing a view about value for money are most likely more interested in running up chargeable working days than they are about achieving ultimate value for money. Within Visualising Transformation we are content that a current paradigm exists with controls and procedures that are seen as sacrosanct, however, if an organisation needs to slice 10% off its overall budget then an open mind to challenge would help.

A quotation comes to mind:

We can't solve problems by using the same kind of thinking we used when we created them! **Albert Einstein**

Thus, as part of a Visualising Transformation intervention we would expect the host to openly question the effectiveness of project planning and control systems, perhaps moving gently through normal process methods, through a 'light touch' approach and hopefully through to a natural aspect of control emerging solely through the design processes.

This doesn't force an anxious host away from control; it merely enables a self-inspection to see what works and what needs to be improved.

This evolution will not be as powerful where heavy formal or perhaps even worse, heavy informal restrictions are placed on all change management. It is therefore strongly recommended that after a few projects or threads of work are complete, that the Visualising Transformation process be applied to project management and the whole council's performance management regimes. i.e. only use the process and systems when there is clear evidence that it is safe and effective.

This also leads to the need to understand the ethos of the organisation; why does it exist, what is truly important: how should it look, and where are the challenges and aspirations? Local authorities have a great many common aspects of work across the whole country. Comparing county to county or unitary to unitary, 95% of what is done is the same; however, the way a council is 'wired' in their internal working and external relationships tend to be very different indeed.

The worst consultants will inspect and benchmark another council and assume that a highly effective design there will work perfectly with the new host. It's this flawed thinking that causes work on the ground to get less efficient and effective to begin with during a traditionally managed transformation or change, prior to getting better later. It was also the cause of a reported 80% of BPR (Business Process Reengineering) schemes failing. There was little attempt to know the host, just an assumption we can do this better.

When reviewing the current ethos during Check, also seek to get understanding what the new ethos may look like, even if that is addressing broad wish lists. The more that direction of travel is discussed early on, the more likely that outcome will be achieved.

What is likely to happen from training and then improving ways of working is that you will achieve greater operational and corporate flexibility, with happier staff who know how to deal with previously difficult decisions. The council will become much more of an 'all one team' organisation with genuine support to the front line staff with managers better able to resolve issues as well as less issues needing to be resolved. Again more involved adept staff creates capacity.

Support will also become more adaptive, with some front line staff more able to rally to issues when the central parts of the council also need support.

Endnote

1 National Indicator 14 is one of two hundred indicators placed upon local authorities of late, replacing a previous larger set of Best Value Performance Indicators (BVPI's). NI14 has a target to reduce unnecessary customer contact. There is a 68 page booklet to give guidance on a single calculation of the formula (x/y) x 100 = z where: x is the no. of customer contacts that are assessed as avoidable, y is the total no. of contacts within the relevant services, z is the percentage of customer contacts that are assessed as avoidable. The best example in the booklet is where the call centre is bypassed by bringing the experts into direct contact with the customers. 'Hilarious that it's everything the Government mandate against!'

"The twin forces of Governance and Risk Management makes change ten times harder than it should be"

DAVE GASTER

5. CHECK

A Visualising Transformation intervention starts from the very first conversation, in that Check is entirely about data gathering and validation, with a view to gaining data, information, knowledge and insight for all that is currently done within an end-to-end process, so as to understand what also could be done to add value or perhaps to future-proof the service.

If a host is starting the journey to a new paradigm the consultant must make allowances for the fear that can accompany that position. The greatest fears are often generated by the unknown. If the host's experiences of change management so far have been something like the following:

- Change contractor appointed
- Contractor takes brief and confirms actions
- Contractor starts working with staff, causing alarm and disquiet
- Contractor benchmarks apparent work elements against national database
- Report is generated stating too many systems, ineffective processes
- Agreed action is to introduce better IT then cut 20% of jobs
- Implementation starts, staff disquiet increases, software incompatible with some systems
- Most of systems in place, meeting many needs, but not all
- Staff cuts are made
- Staff left with systems that don't meet all needs, and insufficient detail to work
- Morale, performance and customer satisfaction all get worse.

I acknowledge that the majority of interventions are positive in terms of most outcomes and cost savings. In reality the majority of work being carried out in many organisations was never designed properly in the first place. Systems are bought, people are trained on those systems and operational issues are addressed by the staff ingenuity and work rounds.

I've always chuckled to myself when you need permission to properly design a new way of working in an holistic way, but don't need permission to allow workers to work their way round systems that are ineffective.

So the point is this; the majority of historic change management interventions whether they were internally led or externally, will have caused various parts of the organisation some pain as a direct result. Thus, at the start of a process which could possibly transform the whole organisation, there will be fear, distrust and doubt.

Negative energy within a process is an inhibitor, including stretch targets. If the consultant approach is bombastic: 'they must work this way, they're wrong in their command and control lifestyle', then instead of enabling some positive energy, even more fear and anxiety will be created.

This is why the very start of a Transformation needs very careful handling. Remember, this is not about cloning a solution that worked elsewhere – this is using an array of approaches to enable maximum benefit possible for that specific host.

Starting with Check for the first few days will be a variable feast. What is the nature of the assignment? Is it a relatively small piece of work to gain trust? Perhaps it's four relatively small areas of work to see if the approaches are sound for different work styles and cultures.

Culture is important. Rarely does a host have a single culture; there will be areas where there is good leadership and great use of IT, and other areas where the manager is in reality a poor administrator who may have been technically sound and the area has just started moving from handwritten memos using carbon paper for triplicate copies.

Culture can be quite different from department to department, within divisions and even from one side of an office to the other. Part of Check must be to analyse what the approaches are to technologies, information, displaying data, attitudes to customers and attitudes to change, teamwork, natural support or perhaps, political games between sections.

This part of Check will be used to inform the Transformation Team[1] but not to run back to the host sponsor[2] with small items of feedback. There must be a build up of trust between all parties, such that the Transformation Team are seen as allies to all parties, or at least, as many as is possible.

Part of the initial Check process will be a series of small group and one-to-one interviews, gaining knowledge of systems, processes and the data available at that time. This will inform who needs to be part of the Intervention Team[3] and who will need secondary training[4] where they will only be part involved. Start creating charts and graphs, post them on boards in the workplace and share them with the workers.

It is anticipated that initial interventions will need to fully comply with the host project control systems, thus part of the Check process will be to gain information to create a PiD and project plan, creating conformance to procedure and comfort that control exists.

While the PiD is drafted and developed the Intervention Team will need to attend and partake in the four-day training course. As elements now start to parallel run, it's important to maintain a forward calendar so that key people and decisions can be made. It's advisable to establish a routine meeting arrangement, such that the sponsor meets weekly and the change board has diarised dates perhaps on a fortnightly basis, with an acceptance that meetings can be postponed where insufficient agenda items exist.

Again, the design and attendance of these board meetings will be determined by the current culture of the host. They may be best established as informal dialogues with people of influence. Agendas could be loose with a PowerPoint style[5] of presentation and enquiry.

The key to begin with is to gain credibility and belief, the balance between being actively involved in adding value to change and writing monitoring reports and designing control meetings is a difficult one. 'Pure' Systems Thinkers will say that these add no value to the process and simply sub-optimise effectiveness. However, we live in a real world, and the leap of faith needed at times is likely to have been tainted by previous projects that have gone wrong.

I have strongly pushed back against these controls and procedures, sometimes very effectively, on other occasions too strongly. Remembering the earlier quote from Einstein that high level change will be needed, but also that 'Rome wasn't built in a day' time will help to absorb and reflect on a better way.

So in the first few interventions, there will need to be a careful balance between the original ethos of the organisation and the possible ethos that may emerge as time goes on and positive results accumulate.

By the time that all the people in the Intervention Team have been trained there should be clarity as to what is in the review, what must be considered and what types of additional outcomes would be welcome. It is also very important to understand what must not be changed or what constraints are imposed by the host. Some of the data gathered early on will be used for context in the training sessions.

The first meeting with the sponsor after training will be an interesting one to reflect on at the end of the meeting. Invariably the language of the meeting is transformed by the training, the nature of discussions will have moved forward, concepts are now understood and clarity of process become obvious.

As the training will include a Check Plan *Appraise* Do cycle, all participants will understand how Check will greatly assist in moving forward. I'll now return to the model of work input comparison between Visualising Transformation and traditional project management, analysing each step for context.

VISUALISING TRANSFORMATION COMPARED TO TRADITIONAL PROJECT MANAGEMENT

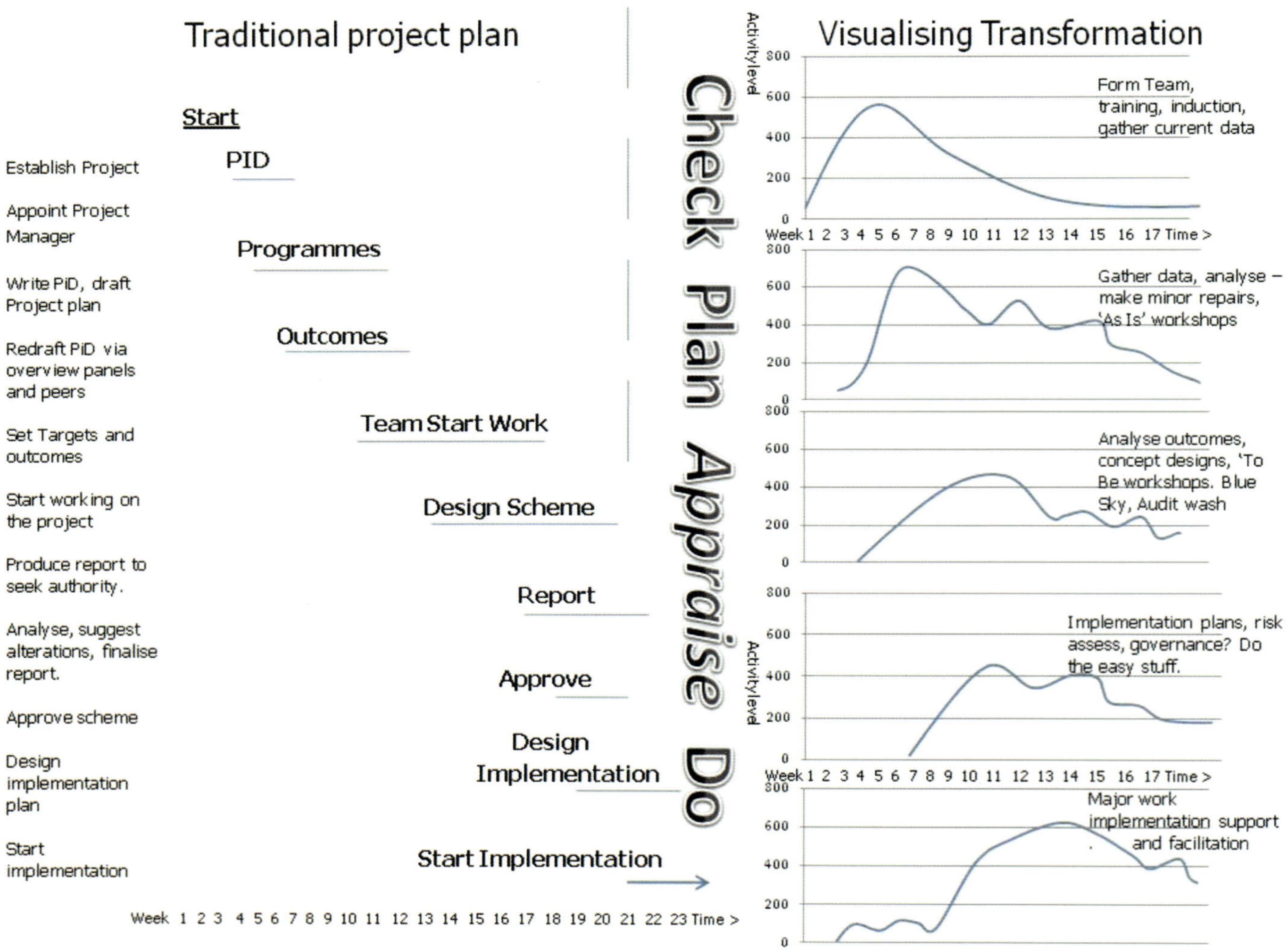

As the first few interventions will be more conventionally led, there will be a need to draft a PiD and project plan, with a fair amount of preparing of documents compared to positively working on the Check process. However, as Check moves forward and the Intervention Team now understand the nature of the intervention from their training, data gathering and knowledge development will accelerate.

CHECK

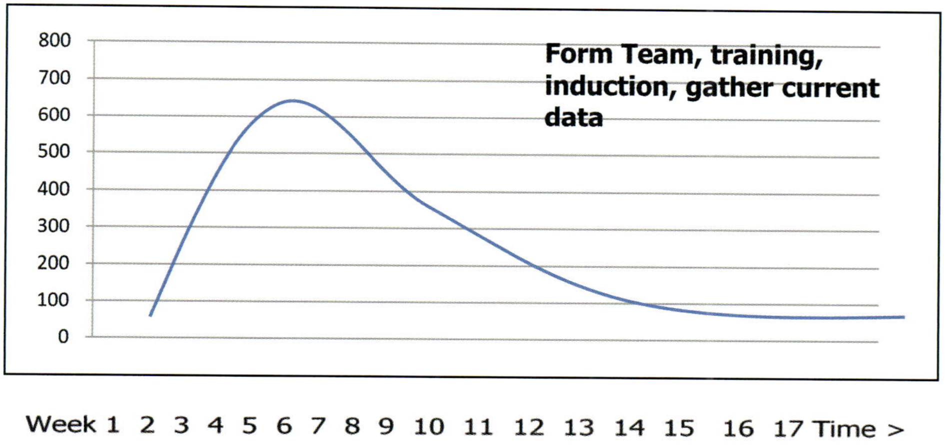

This shows that there may be a rapid build up of activity, with the training followed by quite intense data gathering, initial analysis and cleaning of information required. It is highly likely that the process of data gathering and cleaning will become far more effective after the four-day training than prior to that. This is mainly due to the new insight from the delegates and their understanding of the importance of sound information.

There will be positive support and a ready acceptance regarding the causes of incorrect data. This new insight will automatically lead to better ways of working not only in the areas where data gathering is occurring but also where support services are involved.

There will also be a sudden, very positive, attitude change between service sections. The call centre will perhaps see how they have sided with customers who have been making false claims, or where simple errors in communications cause the wrong work operations to be commissioned; the back office may see how their administration of a process is not so helpful for operations, who in turn may understand why completing processes to say 'job done' is important to the back office and call centre.

There will be defensiveness as well; handling irritations and conflict will be definite roles for both the Transformation Team and sponsor. Strangely the highest degree of resistance usually comes from highly skilled professionals or managers. Part of the reason for this is that they have the most to 'unlearn' whereas the majority of workers will see the common sense of the approach very easily.

The very nature of the approach to change and coordination at the board level is designed to understand and help develop this unlearning process. Starting small and moving forward incrementally has the benefit of the least line of resistance for the host, but could then suffer from excessive control or perceived lack of impact in initial stages[6].

Again, Check is vital here, as the approach would need to be quite different if say two cabinet members and the Chief Executive have been involved in this style of working before and can't wait for the rest of the organisation to catch up. In all circumstances there will be resistance and pockets where understanding is different. In time the significant degree of achievement will start to change mindsets.

In one authority where the stretch challenge had been set by the Leader to save £600,000 a year from the budget and the first offer in reply was, 'we can save £800,000 next year, but that will improve the year after', her reply was, 'I don't know how you are managing this, but we want more of it!'

At first it will not matter too much that the project management board have not been trained in this new way of working; however, in just the same way that the conversations with the project sponsor are transformed by the training, the transfer of insight from the Transformation Team to the project board may be inhibited by their lack of cultural shift.

Experience has shown that even getting the board to a half-day training course will be extremely difficult. This may be easier where the Leader or Chief Executive has inside knowledge of the new paradigm, or has enough intuitive awareness that it's worth the investment. Even after scheduling such a training event, it's quite likely that the next crisis at that level will be seen as more important than mere training, with the training slot being hijacked.

To some extent that's why this process seeks to provide 'stunning' information to the board. There will be no spin, no exaggeration, as much corporate ownership as possible but irrefutable evidence that the proposed course of action is well worth moving forward on.

In addition to the PiD and project plan, I would suggest that a risk log[7] and benefits realisation[8] sheet are created and maintained, probably keeping both in Excel, and using them to show evolution, such that additional sheets are attached to benefits, with issues and pipeline opportunities logged.

Following on from the initial training and data capture the two main elements of work will be the design and running of workshops and the analysis of data and information before and after those workshops take place.

CHECK DATA ANALYSIS AND STARTING 'AS IS' WORKSHOPS

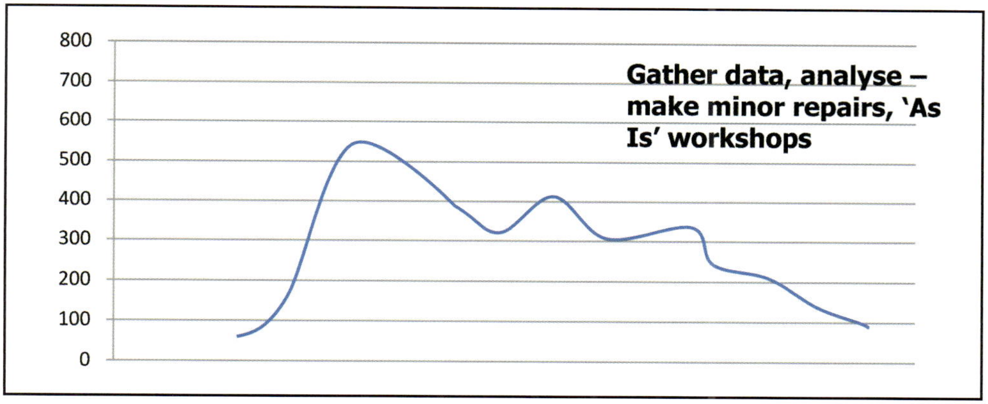

While I have discussed the differences between data and information via the Ackoff pyramid to show the relationships, I've not attempted to show some of the aspects that this will entail. This also feeds back to the composition of the team. The Transformation Team should include a balance of skills and backgrounds; there needs to be good trainers, communicators, with IT literacy and researchers, however one of the most essential skill sets at this stage is someone who can gather data and analyse it in dozens of ways, such that we understand what the data can tell us from a very wide set of view-points.

When my son Daniel, who has an ITC Degree, has worked with me, I used the terms ferret and gopher as parts of his Job Description. The ability to relentlessly wring the truths out of data is essential to enabling understanding. Think about the five whys again with this in mind. Why is there that saw tooth effect from week to week? Why are there more issues on Tuesdays than Fridays? How can the average time be thirteen days when some stuff takes three hours and others takes three months? Why are there more instances of failure at the end of month than earlier in the month?

We tend to use Excel as the main probing tool, along with Access and WinChart[9]. The process can be soul destroying as battle ensues from 15,000 records, a proportion of which will be incomplete or inaccurate, to become an agreed set of information sources. However, one major element is to find which work is within the scope of common cause and which is subject to special cause[10] and then find out why!

Some examples of data presentation, good and bad, are included within this chapter. However hard the journey is, examination and re-examination of data are imperative, not only for the Transformation Team but also to gain agreement from all involved that the information is sound and reliable. On one occasion we had to work on one set of data for about a fortnight simply to convince the head of IT that our analysis was relevant and meaningful. Not having her acknowledgement would have potentially cast doubt on our findings and the outcome of the intervention.

PART SORTED CONTROL CHART FOR HIGHWAYS TRIPS AND FALLS CLAIMS

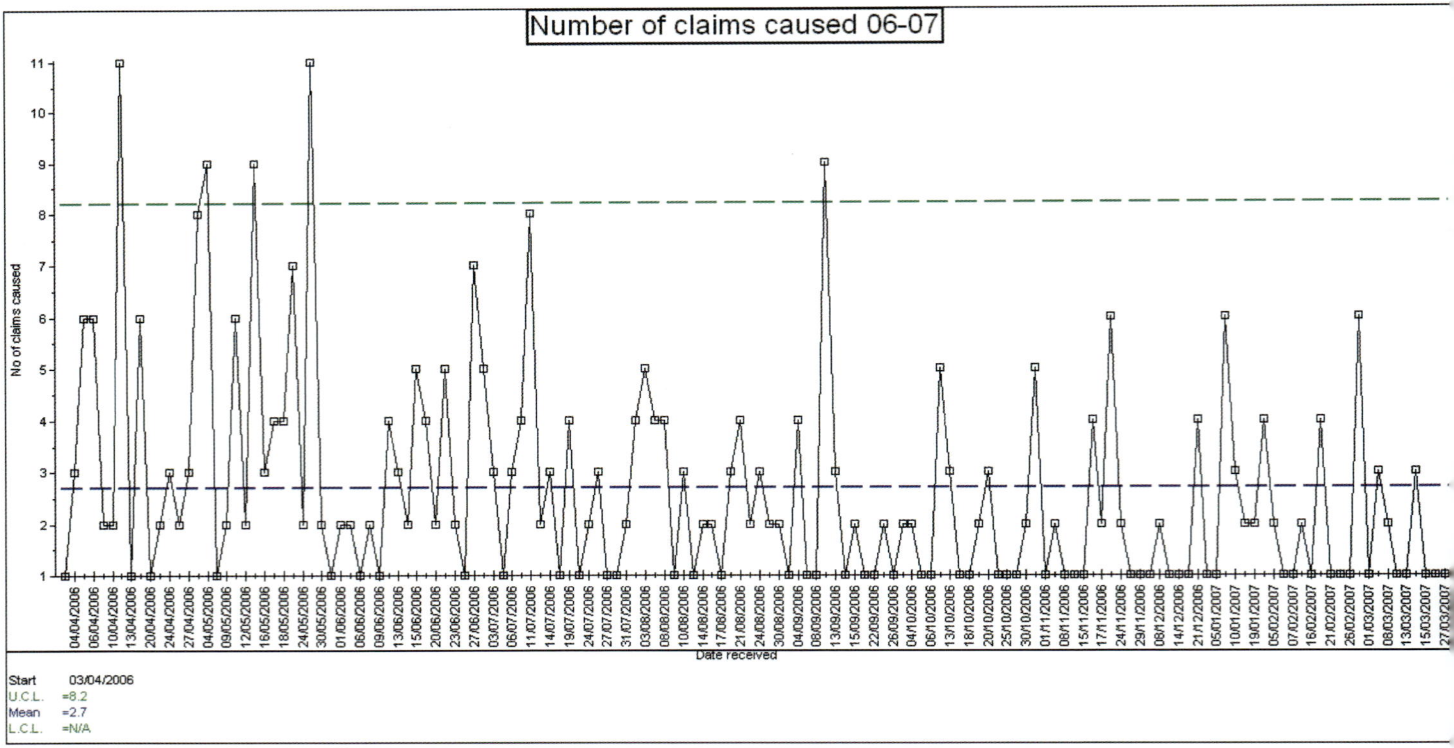

This shows an analysis of the number of claims registered during one year. It is an interesting mix of part filtered information, in that some data is a week apart while others are on consecutive days. Placing this in a control chart is only part correct at this time, in that the interval of time period should have been standardised first. What it does reflect is the impact of not entering data in real time; batching some work for several days causes backlogs in the system prior to even starting to do work to resolve issues.

This also shows how special cause will identify issues; most peaks are for several days while most troughs are for a single days or no data entered. Clearly when producing such graphs and control sheets, there needs to be conscious thought in data entry, with a cleaning and standardising process prior to production.

CONTROL CHART FOR HIGHWAYS TRIPS AND FALLS, DAYS TO RESOLVE A CLAIM

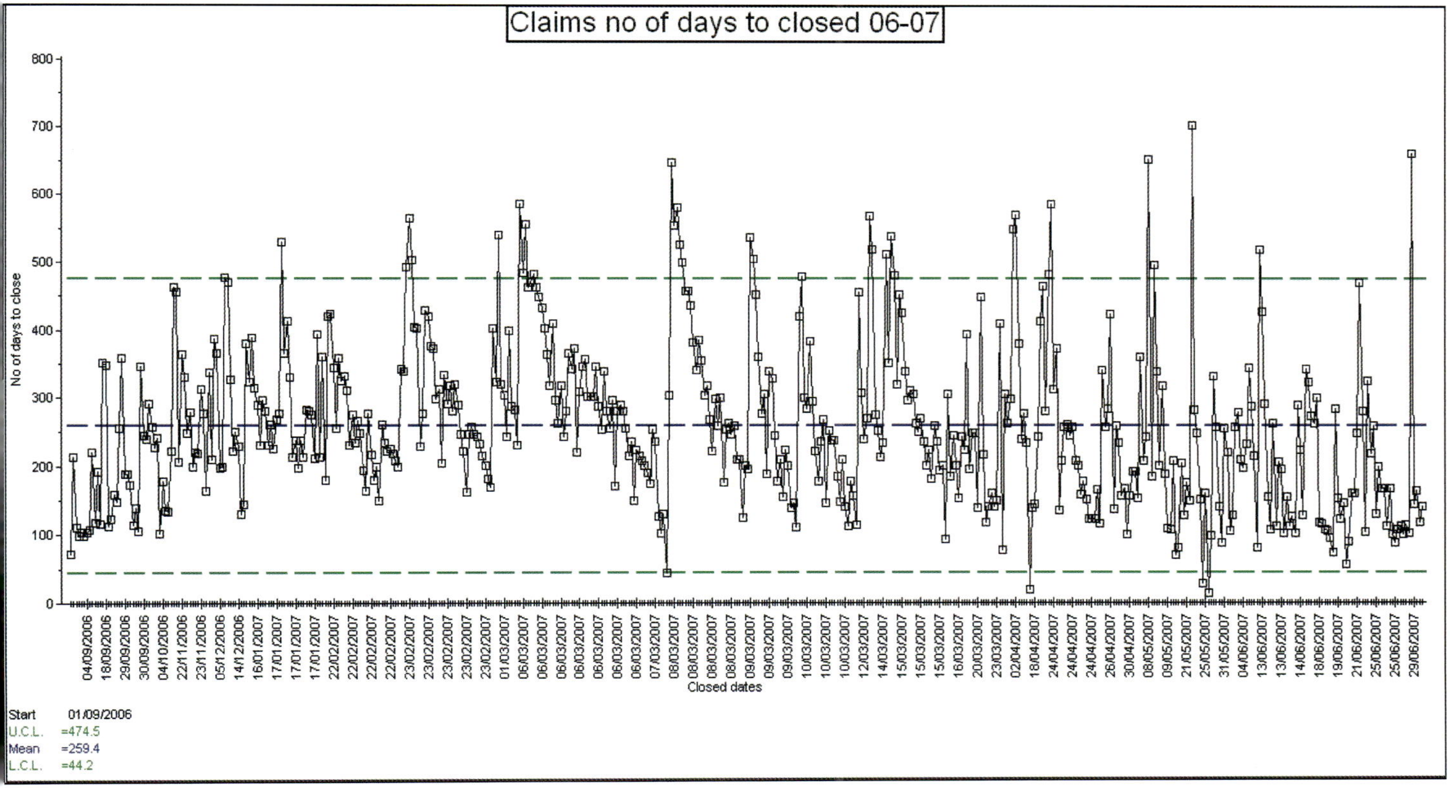

The second control chart is far more informative, with a number of apparent trends and huge variation of time-spans to resolve claims. The mean time to resolve (average) is 259 days, more than eight months as an average to settle a claim for a damaged wheel in a pothole? Outrageous? Perhaps so, but most councils will have equally poor service delivery areas. But also look at the boundaries of common cause resolutions, from 44 days up to 474 days. So at this time a claim could routinely take 15 months to resolve.

Just think about the systems required to work that badly: A core database to record progress, stage points in the system to record 'who needs to do what next' to that piece of work, admin staff to keep files and chase progress. The worse the performance of a system the more work is needed to keep it moving. That then leads to statements that this is highly complex and needs complex systems to run it on. Key learning point: ***Poor systems need far more work to be carried out to keep them going.***

The apparent trends are also very interesting:

- From September to December 2006 work takes an average of around 200 days but gets worse
- Some degree of stability through January and February
- Then a big rush in March with more work closed that month than the other eight months
- Lastly a generally quicker resolution with more aged jobs being addressed.

This is indicative of a service where targets are being met; various priorities lead to holding up work and batches being pushed through together. Where that happens, previous incomplete work is identified and re-work will frequently be needed. (This is the service where the average front end of the process to carry out a site visit and create an accepted final report improved from 90 days to 2.65 days.)

The sketch on page 85 shows the most frequent failure modes for highway claims. The production of this for a workshop led to a number of interesting discussions, which in turn, enabled some seeds to richer enlightenment in that the majority of claims faced by the council, had started from a re-instatement of a hole or trench by the utility companies.

In most cases the failure was many years after the work was carried out. The council had reduced inspections of that work as they believed it was not cost effective. The cost of the claims system was over £1,000,000 per annum. During a walk in one night I found sufficient information to fine statutory undertakers £6,000 for defective lighting, signage, repairs and final works to recent trenches.

FOOTWAY CROSS SECTION: EXAMPLES OF FAILURE MODES

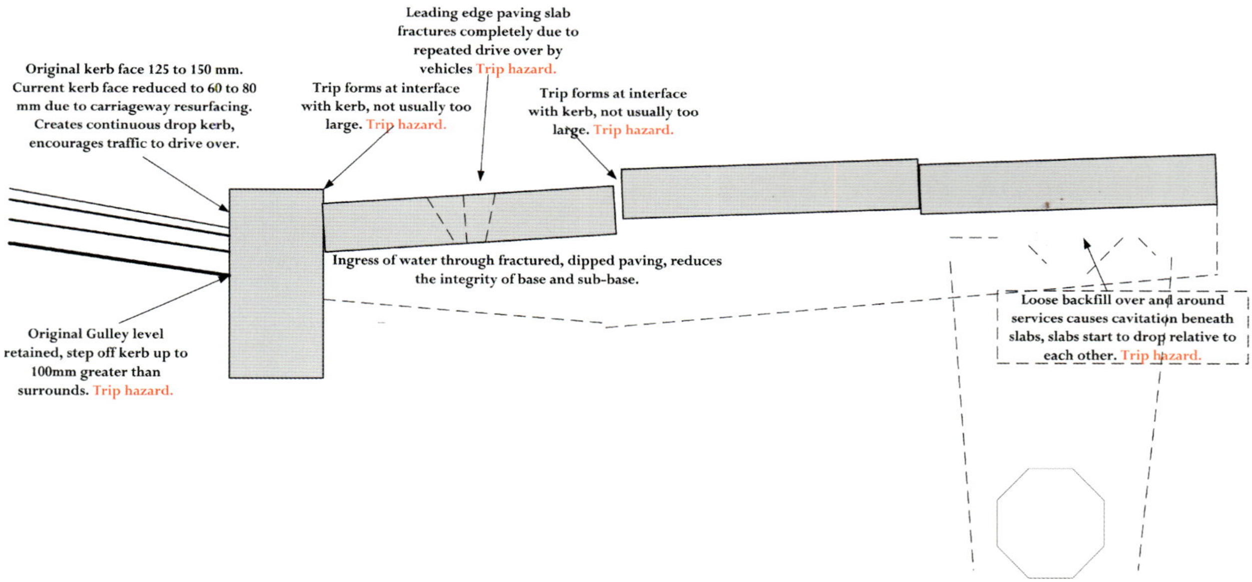

Repudiation is where the council successfully defends a case, or the claimant no longer pursues the case. The six thinner lines in the graph on the next page are for the six areas of the council, while the dotted line shows benchmark information from other councils. The thicker black line is the average for the whole council.

It was interesting that two areas were always below average and both were getting worse prior to the intervention. There were a number of pet theories as to why one area was better than the other. They had five electronic data systems of control between them, with at least three versions of the same data for each different area, plus the claims loss adjusters' system.

GRAPH SHOWING CLAIMS REPUDIATION RATES OVER TIME

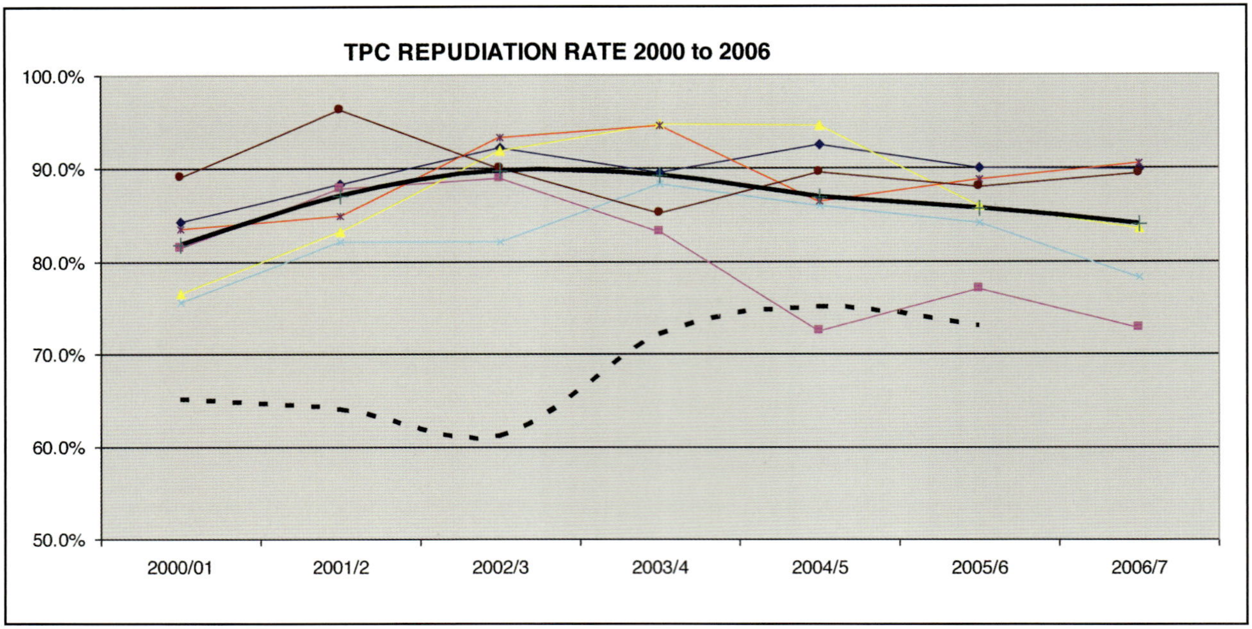

The council had devolved highways management to six areas, each with an area manager; each was allowed to operate uniquely compared to each other or to the county. They had a common contractor across the whole county who maintained their highways and street furniture, with each area using differing repair methods and materials. There were no linkages between the areas to evaluate value for money or to compare the effectiveness of approach.

Some areas claimed to post-inspect statutory undertakers work to the legal maximum; it was in one of those areas that I found the £6,000 worth of opportunity in a single night.

From a benchmarking point of view, the council was better than average, so they had no problems. They were spending over £1m p.a. due to failure and were getting worse. They improved services, reduced cost and became safer!

TYPICAL SOURCE OF RAW DATA

Occurrence No.	Category Of Claimant	Cause	Highways Ref No.	Status		Date clm recvd	Close Date
TG 2304	Householder	OTH PROPERTY DAMAGE DUE TO H'WAY	N/05TPC0118	Final		15/06/2005	27/03/2006
TG 2305	Motorist	TRIP/VEH ACCIDENT - POTHOLE	05TPC0109	Final		06/06/2005	22/09/2005
TG 2306	Other Private Company	VIBRATION DAMAGE TO PROPERTY	05TPC0005	Final		07/04/2005	10/11/2005
TG 2307	Motorist	TRIP/VEH ACCIDENT - POTHOLE	N/05TPC0028	Final		19/04/2005	20/12/2005
TG 2308				Final		30/06/2005	18/01/2006
TG 2309	Pedestrian	TRIP - FLAG	05TPC0150	Final		12/07/2005	28/03/2006
TG 2310	Utility Company	HAND EXCAVATION	N/05TPC0170	Final		19/07/2005	31/07/2006
TG 2311	Pedestrian	TRIP - UNEVEN SURFACE	05TPC0093	Final		24/05/2005	26/01/2006
TG 2312	Cyclist	TRIP/VEH ACCIDENT - POTHOLE	N/05TPC0114	Final		09/06/2005	10/05/2006
TG 2313	Pedestrian	SURFACE DRESSING/BITUMEN/TAR	N/05TPC0027	Final		18/04/2005	16/03/2006
TG 2314	Motorist	TRIP/VEH ACCIDENT - POTHOLE	N/04TPC0054	Final		05/05/2005	03/03/2006
TG 2315	Motorist	INJURY/DAMAGE CAUSED BY SIGN	N/05TPC0239	Final		09/09/2005	30/01/2006
TG 2316	Motorist	TRIP/VEH ACCIDENT - IRONWORK	N/05TPC0025	Final		15/04/2005	18/04/2006
TG 2317				Final		26/04/2005	26/01/2006
TG 2318	Motorist	TRIP/VEH ACCIDENT - POTHOLE	05TPC0156	Final		13/07/2005	21/12/2005
TG 2319	Householder	OTH PROPERTY DAMAGE DUE TO H'WAY	N/05TPC0034	Final		22/04/2005	26/07/2005
TG 2320	Motorist	TRIP/VEH ACCIDENT - POTHOLE	N/05TPC0017	Final		14/04/2005	03/03/2006
TG 2321				Final		26/05/2005	22/09/2005
TG 2322				Open		26/10/2005	
TG 2323	Cyclist	TRIP/VEH ACCIDENT - POTHOLE	05TPC0157	Final		14/07/2005	26/01/2006
TG 2324	Motorist	TRIP/VEH ACCIDENT - POTHOLE	N/04TPC0047	Final		28/04/2005	22/09/2005
TG 2325	Pedestrian			Final		14/07/2005	26/01/2006
TG 2326	Pedestrian	TRIP - FLAG	N/05TPC0074	Final		17/04/2005	13/12/2005
TG 2327				Final		14/07/2005	08/05/2007
TG 2328	Pedestrian			Open		06/02/2006	
TG 2329	Motorist	ROAD TRAFF.ACC.	N/05TPC0032	Final		21/05/2005	22/05/2006
TG 2330	Motorist	SLIPPERY SURFACE - MUD	N/05TPC0065	Final		09/05/2005	10/01/2006
TG 2331	Pedestrian	TRIP/VEH ACCIDENT - IRONWORK	05TPC0086	Final		24/05/2005	12/04/2006
TG 2332	Motorist	TRIP/VEH ACCIDENT - POTHOLE	05TPC0154	Final		12/07/2005	24/11/2005
TG 2333	Motorist	TRIP/VEH ACCIDENT - POTHOLE	N05TPC0045	Final		27/04/2005	26/01/2006

The data on page 87 had been abstracted from a very large file which had all accidents for some seven years, there were very few lines in the database that were absolutely trustworthy, I particularly liked the line where a person had tripped over a loose paving slab breaking an arm which was resolved by buying two new wheels and tyres. Note cases started and no data entered.

CAUSE AND EFFECT CHART. ELECTRONIC REPRODUCTION OF HAND-DRAWN ONE IN CHAPTER ONE

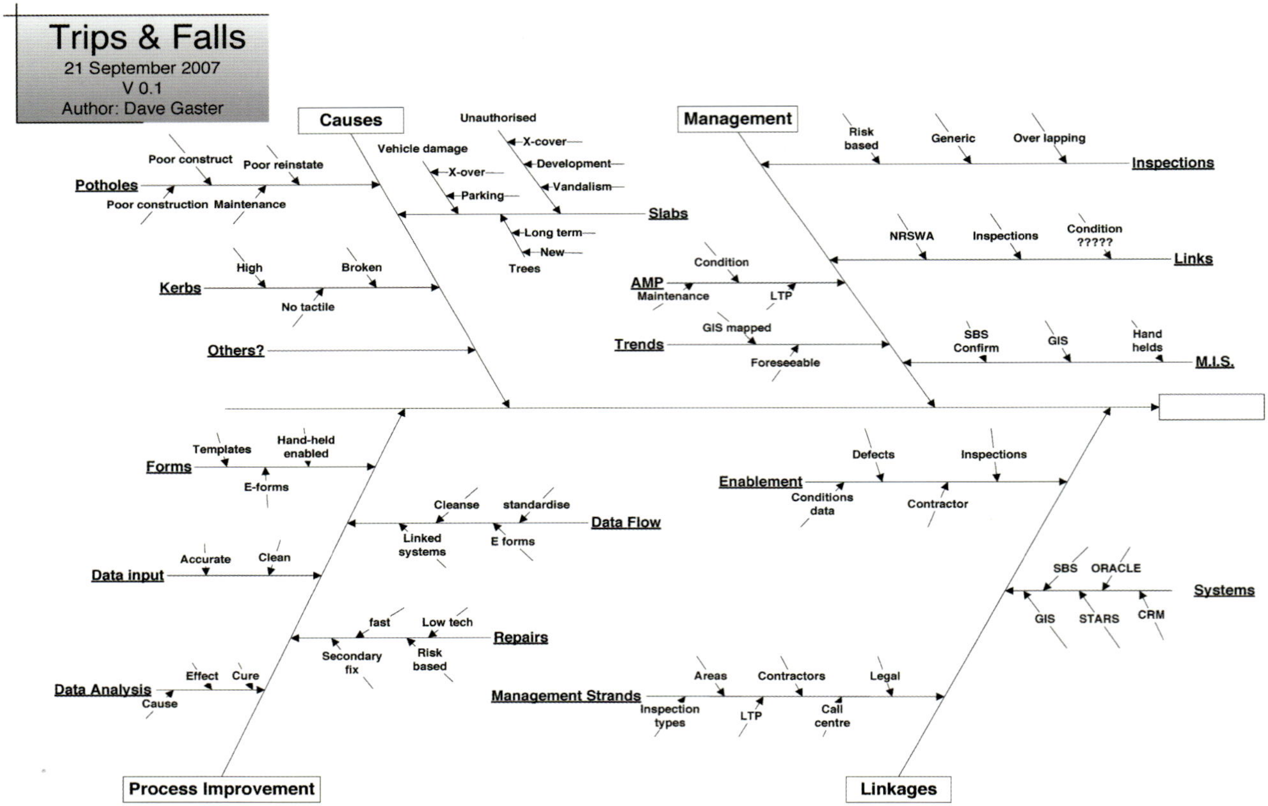

This was one element of analysis trying to use current IT systems to map ideas. While I still prefer pen and paper for cause and effect and mind maps, there is a greater likelihood of professional acceptance for a typed version. The basic premise stands here; there are lots of information on one sheet to discuss and sort where issues are. This was used in conjunction with several other strands of analysis to improve response and eliminate causes.

RUN CHART FOR MISSED WASTE COLLECTIONS

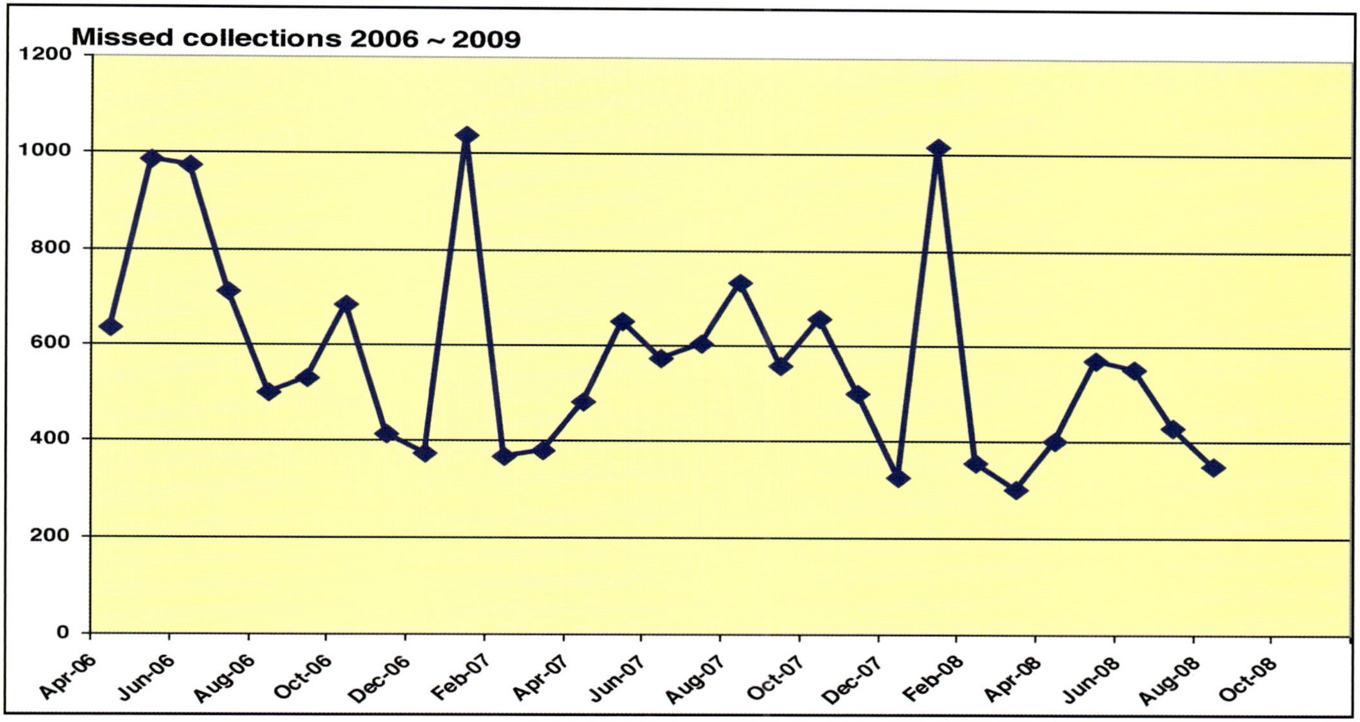

This chart was created from a number of sources which needed considerable data tidying. You will see that there are two strong special causes quite clear to all now, which is the post-Christmas collections that impact on each January and an apparent trend towards improvement through the whole time.

There is also a tendency for summer collection services to be worse than winter. Much of that is explained when garden waste collections are excluded from the figures; less demand in winter so less failure. I will return to this area for quick wins and segmented control charts.

All this digging for data and seeking the best ways to visualise it must take place to enable and support the workshops which will be the main engines for service improvement. Even gaining access to data can be problematic, with senior officers sometimes stating that we can't have 'their' information, because they created it for themselves. (Not to serve the customers better!)

The launch of the first 'As Is' workshop is very important, you need to set a very positive, can do, all seeking a better outcome approach. There needs to be room for challenge, but within a positive scoping. As there will be quite a diverse cross section of people, it's often useful to get everyone to introduce themselves. It's also important to enable freedom of speech, sometimes the people who know the most about a system are the ones who initially keep the quietest, so good chairing skills are needed.

Although it may be counter intuitive I would strongly recommend that there is union representation throughout the workshops so that there is no doubt that this is a system designed by the people who will be working in it. Raising issues while in design stages enables a far easier implementation later.

I prefer to design and manage workshops via PowerPoint probably having several slides too many so that you can run past them if need be, or refer to them when it seems most opportune. The starting point should be to remind people of their recent training, show some of the outcome slides, from their own redesigns of services.

PERFORMANCE IMPROVEMENT FROM A TRAINING SESSION

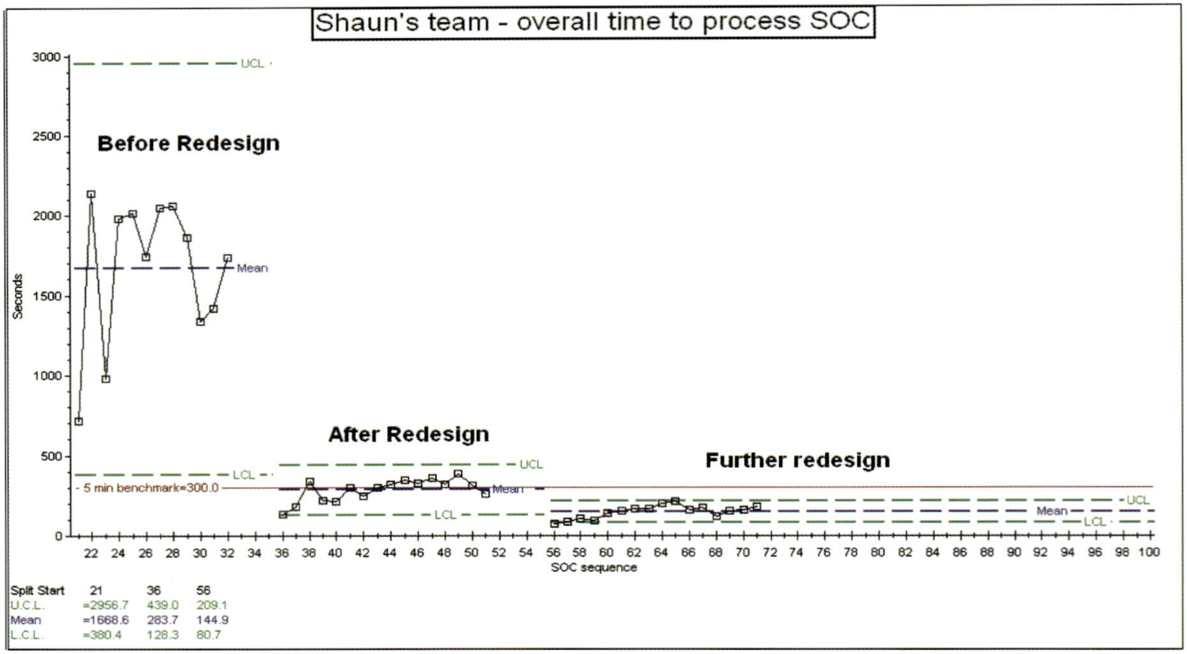

This is a real example of improvement from over 27 minutes to less than 2½ minutes. High impact, with a lasting memory.

Introduce the review with a pace that the majority will be comfortable with, apply newly learned techniques to the service review in focus. Have various breakout teams working together, then compare their findings. In this way everyone gets involved and stronger influences are heard but not dominant.

The workshops will address some cause and effect approaches to the services, using 'post-it notes' to write ideas and then allocate to various issues impacting on the service. This is like a brainstorm session, but with a control as to what to do with the knowledge.

The simple cause and effect chart below enables the groups to allocate their issues against these five standard headings, or indeed service specific ideas. These can raise a hundred or so aspects to consider from 20 minutes work. The important aspect is to follow up and ensure solutions to issues are addressed.

SIMPLE CORE CAUSE AND EFFECT CHART TO USE IN INITIAL WORKSHOPS

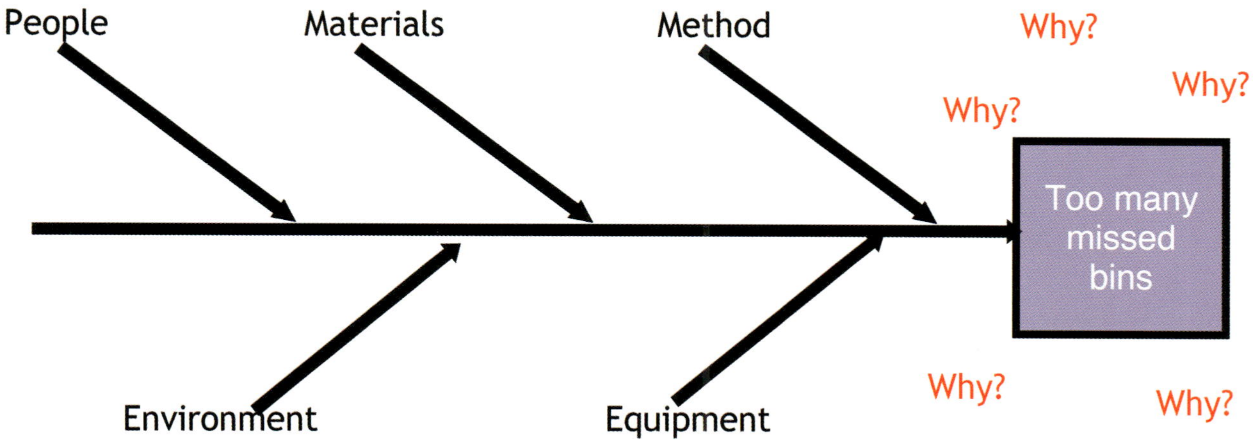

The cause and effect chart on the following page arose from the first workshop to improve waste collection, each team worked together, attaching post-its to individual flip chart pages. Afterwards the teams toured the room looking at each others ideas, prior to a quick round the table on lessons learned.

At the end of the day, these sheets were collected, all the post-its being taped on to the pages to retain their locations and summarised onto one sheet. While this 'boxy' approach works well within Excel, sub-dividing issues as earlier cause and effect diagrams helps to focus effort more cleanly.

SIMPLE CAUSE AND EFFECT CHART FROM INITIAL WORKSHOP

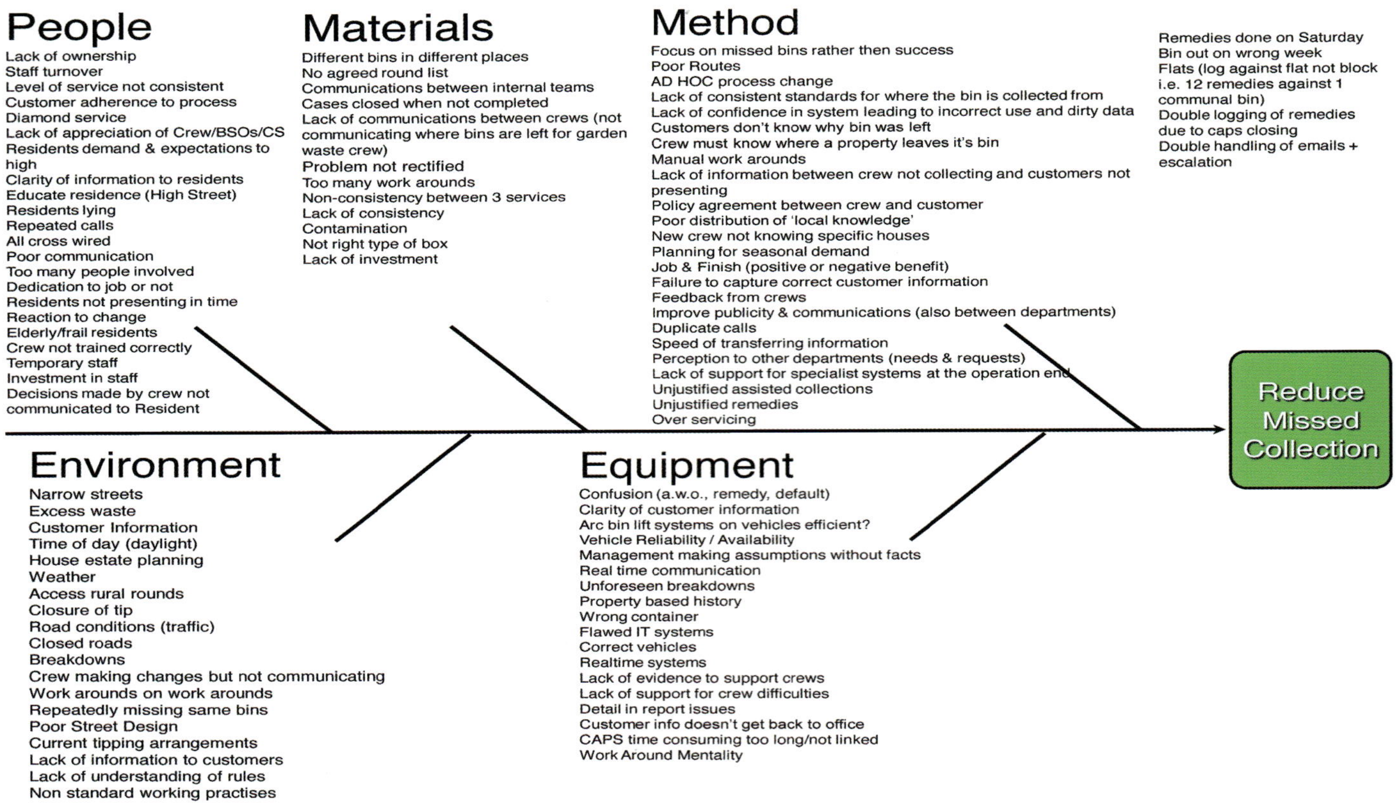

This C&E chart as above, was printed on an A0 sheet of paper, displayed at the following workshops to remind delegates of all their initial ideas and concerns. In every workshop, the session leader needs to be well prepared and knowledgeable, in order to maintain a positive direction. It is very important to pre-consider distracter questions, it's also good to have ways of maintaining direction, have two flip-charts ready to queue issues and opportunities. If a tangential issue is being raised, have one of the Transformation Team members record it, and transfer that to the issues log[11] later.

The first workshop works best as an all-day event with plenty of time for discussion and thought development. After the warm up as above it's worth then addressing how the major pieces of work actually flow through the organisation.

Traditionally workshop-based flow charting is carried out at a high level lumpy level initially, followed by increased detail. Again this can be done via post-its on brown paper sheeting. Even early in the process I would recommend flow lanes so that handovers[12] through the process can be clearly seen.

INITIAL FLOWCHARTING WORKSTREAMS

At all times the delegates should be filling out the majority of the flow charts. There will be some natural leaders and some people who need a little support.

I would expect the Transformation Team to have worked out the basic workflows prior to the first workshop, always open to learn nuances as detail expands.

There will be invariable disputes regarding all the processes involved often due to the fact that several people do the work in different ways. That's part of the reason why foreknowledge helps.

By the end of the first day there should be some clarity as to how work is carried out, using only rectangles and diamonds to represent an operation or decision. The start and finish of the process should be shown with an oval. If the system is very complex, an area can be shown as a cluster of elements, (post-its stacked on top of one another) then details for that area can be added later.

These two pictures are quite typical as outputs from a solid day in the workshops. At the end of the day, the flowcharts should be preserved by taking pictures of them and using sticky tape to hold the post-its in place. Sometimes pictures can be used to help identify to others the positive energy created in the workshops. In a full Transformation scenario, positive communications will be an important aspect.

TYPICAL SET OF FLOW CHARTS AT THE END OF A WORKSHOP

These large plans should be entered onto Visio using different levels of details in some services areas. All the sub-routines can be tested by discussing with sections of the service; then the whole service can ultimately agree the current process. The original sheets should be retained until sign-off is achieved.

Between workshops the teams will need to gain detail in the workflows, keep improving their joint understandings of information, share information and seek ways to help each other work smarter.

Towards the end of the Check process there will need to be some additional work on *Appraise*, in that we have gained knowledge of where we are, we need to know where we could we get to. That's why either the sponsor or a team member will need to have professional/business insight to the services.

There are options to this, the lead consultant or one of the permanent members of the Transformation Team could be a professional for that type of work. If no internal option is possible, consider co-opting someone from a neighbouring authority, a professional body or via a consultant. This is vital to being able to add value and future proof the work.

It's also at this point that the whole team should be discussing what success would look like. It's possible that when the PiD was drafted that some aspirations are included with some financial outcomes as well. Traditionally these are relatively lower case compared to what starts to get discussed at the *Appraise* stage. The Benefits Analysis will have been increased in size as opportunities and quick wins occurred, and as the double impact of causing less mistakes and working smarter start to arise. It is advised to keep financial and customer benefits separately detailed.

However, in the early days of these interventions experience is also an issue, if the revised aspiration moves from say £100,000 savings to £300,000, the danger is that the host effectively banks the saving without the full follow-through to enable that to happen. This will both reduce the effectiveness of the review and perhaps reduce the capacity realisation which is possible. Discussions with the sponsor and then the board will need to be aware of these risks with a careful evolution of message on the way.

While the concerted effort will be to resolve revenue issues, invariably capital savings can be achieved in parallel. At the same council where £600,000 revenue savings were delivered in the first year, nearly £400,000 was taken out of the capital replacement programme with immediate effect.

Addressing the council strategies in parallel to the operational review will add even more value to outcomes. Clearly, part of Check will focus on where the service is in relation to the strategy, if however there is a challenge back to strategy, creating greater harmony between plans and reality, and then opportunities to improve in many more ways increase exponentially.

The strategic 'review' and analysis will benefit more from a soft systems approach, using mind maps, cause and effect charts and affinity diagrams.[13] The more complex an issue is, the more worthwhile it is to visualise the issues in simple formats. In a BV review for an inner London council, we had a huge array of data, trial information and interview-based feedback from customers. Thus, prior to knowing how to create and use affinity diagrams I modelled the information by hand in three different ways. (Six years later, I still have these evolving diagrams.)

Eventually I returned to my initial learning from Deming (after attending a Deming Forum), and showed the system as below. Even in the largest systems there can be flow with many contributors.

'AFFINITY DIAGRAM' THE STREETSCENE DEPICTED AS A SYSTEM. (SOMETIMES KNOWN AS A RICH PICTURE)

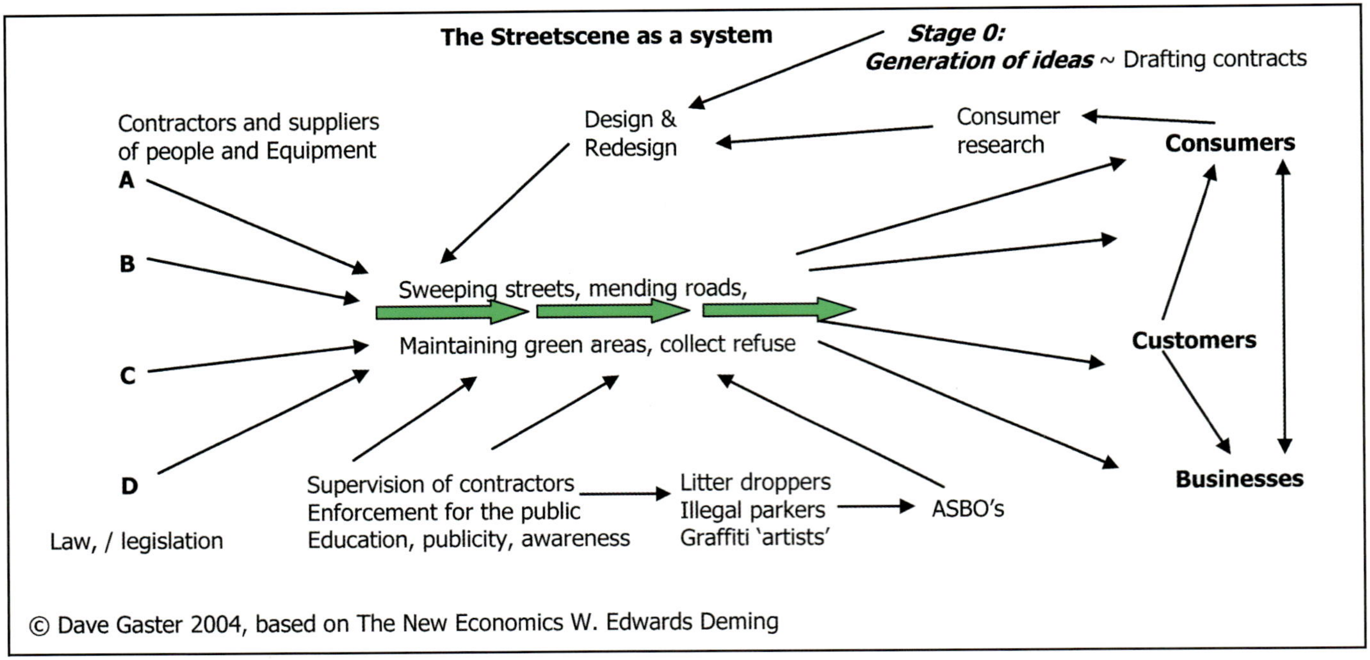

The diagram above purely shows a huge set of services as a system. This is a partial bridge between 'hard and soft' systems, with some boundary conditions added. It is not pure in any usual defined description for affinity or rich picture concepts.

The intention early on in that review was to procure a joined up contractor-based service, perhaps by increasing spend by up to £3.5M per annum. The outcome from the review was to retain existing systems with far greater joining up of resources on a win-win basis voluntarily, with no increase in budgets.

Most interventions over the last eight years have used GIS extensively, to design new rounds, to understand demographics, to visualise highway maintenance needs, to enable integrated monitoring of issues for resource deployment and to understand the cause and effect of budget cuts in one service and its impacts on another.

The final stage of 'As Is' would be to have a last major workshop with the sponsor present, to agree all the common understandings and jointly agree the prime contents of a presentation to the project board. The flowcharts within Visio will now detail how work links together and flows through the organisation, what issues arise and how they are currently dealt with, together with the volumes of work, issues and special requirements of the system.

Improvement work to flowcharts now will be to use a simple graphic technique of differentiating value work (from a customer point of view), from value enabling or non-value work. An example of this is shown in the Plan section of this book. This simply differentiates those processes that add value as one colour, while value-enabling and non-value are other colours. Thus, without the need for training or micro-management all senior staff and the board will be able to immediately see the effectiveness of designs.

The project management board should be able to share the energy and insights found, hopefully with a couple of host workers taking part in the presentation of what we've learned, the quick wins and what we believe we can do next, prior to moving to Plan.

This will also be the first real taster for the board to demonstrate how many opportunities exist within benefits analysis and pipeline projects, together with how *Appraise* may add considerable value beyond that of a conventional change process.

Chapter three introduced the concept of one intervention running, followed by the implications for several threads of work being carried out simultaneously; the sketch below was used to identify the high level linkages and relationship to the project management board.

This shows that several reviews are being carried out concurrently, there will need to be coordination and commonality for these to work well.

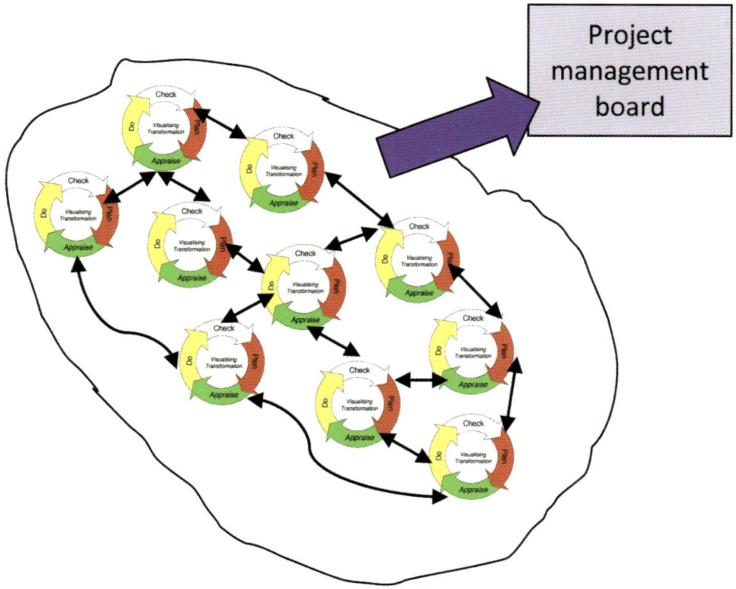

Some of the risks to consider are that there will be call on the same staff for several reviews, such as IT programmers and business support officers.

If the first end-to-end review shows that there are many opportunities within creditor payments and procurement, then that learning would inform that a 'procure to pay' (P2P) review would be useful across the whole host.

Thus when further reviews are initiated the Transformation Team would highlight options for each subsequent thread for P2P to apply.

The project management board would be reviewing the work of all threads, sponsors would need to coordinate actions at an operational level ensuring not only that these threads are properly supported, but also that service delivery is not impaired by the additional workload.

For this reason more than any other, it's recommended to enable capacity to be generated from quick wins and initial implementations, rather than harvest the capacity[14] as soon as is possible. In that way capacity is increased, with a growing number of people who have been trained to work more effectively.

Thus the host will be able to accelerate the benefits from many parallel threads, deliver more services for less overall budget while increasing income streams. A fuller discussion on governance and risk management will be dealt with in chapter seven.

This chapter has hopefully shaped some thinking which will enable an open mind to project management being via the threads and coordination between them, creating a virtual self managing team, rather than a heavily controlled process from the outside. By drawing the boundary conditions, the Transformation Teams with the sponsors can run many work threads taking reports to the project management board showing quick wins, outcomes and identifying barriers to progress. This helps (in time) to move the board from a regulatory inhibiting force, to a celebratory enabling force.

Endnotes

1 The Transformation Team will be the core consultants (mainly full time in a large intervention, probably mainly external people initially, gradually gravitating to internal as corporate maturity increases) who will help educate and develop all the host workers to Transform to better more effective ways of working. This team will need to share and reflect what they learn on at least a weekly basis. They will also maintain a common use of words and approaches to change across several threads of work, so that there is no ambiguity with the host.

2 The sponsor will be the person who is responsible for guiding and assisting the Transformation Team and affected areas of the reviews. The sponsor must have the same level of training as all people who are deeply involved in the whole Check, Plan, *Appraise*, Do process. The sponsor will act as a go-between to the change committee, Directors and Team Leaders affected by the intervention. They must be able to use authority to enable the intervention to be effective. Ideally the sponsor will thoroughly understand the service under review, or the review will be directly involved with a professional person who does understand the business.

3 The Intervention Team will be a mixture of people from across the service being reviewed, such that all major elements have direct knowledgeable people represented. There will be front line workers, administration, supervisors and managers involved. The project sponsor will be part of major events; the Transformation Team will be always involved. At times specific support experts will need to be co-opted, such as IT, audit or HR. There should be some solid customer presence in workshops, if this cannot be done directly, perhaps some staff who are customers could assume that role?

4 Visualising Transformation is a step forward from Lean Systems Thinking (LST). LST works best where all the people in the Intervention Team attend a three-day training course to open the eyes and mind to far better options at work. This includes a multi-stage business simulation where a failing process is worked on by self directed teams to become far more efficient. Under Visualising Transformation this is a four-day course where the value added from *Appraise* is built in. People who will be affected by, or occasionally involved in, the Transformation should attend an awareness course which will last one day.

5 PowerPoint can be used to bring in previous information, guide discussions and keep progress moving. Have more slides prepared than are intended to be used, bring in slides when a conversation moves that way, if they help. This is neither rigid nor rigorous, purely a way to complement a flow of creative thinking and sharing.

6 The risk log, benefits realised and issues log will all inform and reassure the project band that everything that they would want to see as project control is built into the system, hopefully enabling gradual freedoms.

7 The Risk Log can be a simple issue, impact and probability matrix enabling a RAG rating for the issues, as issues are dealt with the traffic light rating should decrease. Sometimes issues are due to lack of access or support from the host which will cause risks to get worse.

8 The Benefits Realisation log can show the broad aspirations at the outset, with a logging of quick wins and step changes en route. Pipeline opportunities should be logged here, to add to aspirations and to later direct how the *Appraise* wash can deliver other opportunities. In general this control sheet can then be used to compare initial targets at the PiD stage to final outcomes.

9 WinChart is a highly sophisticated piece of software to help analyse data creating control charts without needing to know the statistical processes to create those limits. A simpler and cheaper system called BaseLine is being examined for future use.

10 Common cause and special cause variation are best found via creating a run chart and then making that into a control chart. The control chart will have an upper and lower limit, within which the majority of work will operate as common cause. Statistically any work that is outside these limits is likely to be due to special cause. Special causes for extra complaints for refuse collection could be Christmas, a strike or the staff being heavily affected by the flu for instance.

11 The issues log will be kept with the risk register so that the sponsor, audit and all team members are aware that it was raised and will need to be part of the final design.

12 Handovers are where one section deals with a piece of work in part, then sends it to another section to carry out the next process.

13 An example of an affinity diagram for obesity is included later in the book, simply because it is so graphic and beautiful. The idea again is to understand the core concepts on a single sheet of paper. This approach deals with what are sometimes known as 'wicked messy problems'.

14 I use the term of harvesting capacity to align to normal projects where redesigns are carried out, restructures are undertaken and several posts are designed out. By retaining those people and either using them in future transformations or to invest in the business area to create additional income far greater value can be achieved than those costs saved from employment alone.

"Have no fear of perfection – you'll never reach it"

SALVADOR DALI

The Plan stage of Visualising Transformation is probably where the most intense work occurs and often where there is the most fun and learning. The initial thrust of this chapter will be based on the Plan stage for a single end-to-end thread of work. Towards the end of this chapter there will be extensive emphasis placed on *Appraise* which is further dealt with in chapters seven and ten.

The Intervention Team should now be very positive, with high energy from their training, learning and some quick wins within Check. It is very important to retain as much positive energy as possible through the rest of the review.

There is also the consideration of one thread moving through Plan while other threads will be a mixture of further ahead or behind this thread, the opportunities to share ideas and processes between the active threads will be dealt with straight away. At this point I'll sow a seed for consideration to return to later.

PLAN WORKLOAD

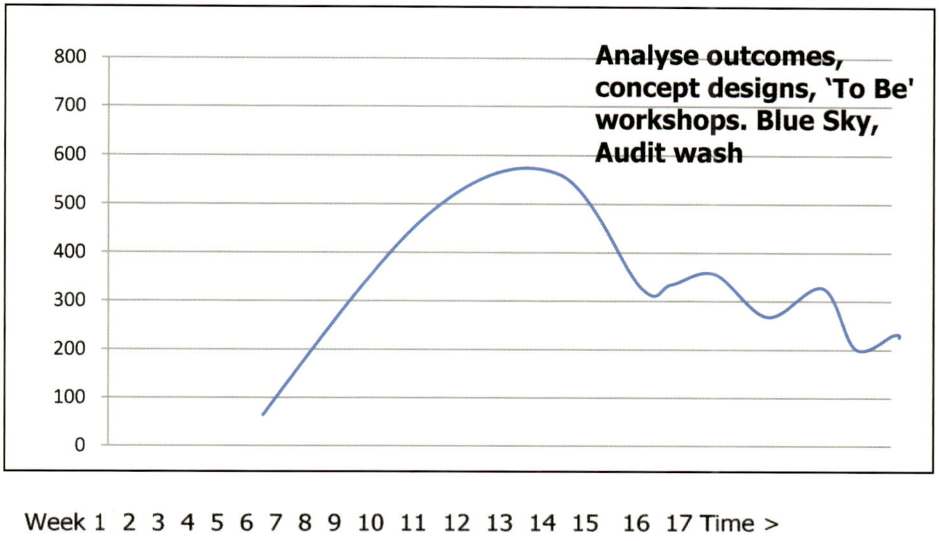

Various elements of Check Plan *Appraise* Do (CPAD) can happen at the same time, as new data is collected and cleaned it may enable new insight, leading to a potential enquiry to the host as part of check. The CPAD cycle will always be in progress for minor elements of work while the major work moves forward.

One single thread will always, on its own, be easier to lead than an array of pieces of work. So the core focus is naturally on one service and its progress through plan to produce a set of designs and forecast outcomes to then be implemented. The difficulty with the first change within a new way of working will be the newness of approach. It's quite possible that none of the host staff will have done this before; so many aspects will be a little mechanistic, not natural.

If however, there are fifteen threads under development in a mature organisation at the same time, there will be a far easier flow of resources as both practice and comfort will quickly be established with natural leadership and seamless deployment of staff. Leading change is no different to leading any resource-based operation, the more routine it becomes the less 'management' it will need. So part of the process for change leadership is to make change fundamentally routine. That is, change itself should, in time, be treated the same as normal operations.

The E2E review can and should be both addressing the operational and strategic aspects of the service at the same time. This will enable a step improvement in customer service and increased breadth of capability concurrently. Dealing with both operations and strategy at the same time can create four times the amount of potential that either could achieve alone[1].

As with Check, Plan will start with a workshop with all involved. It will again need to be well planned, with masses of relevant information, charts, graphs, flows and graphics available, the majority of which will have been shared and agreed previously. The routines will be established in that there will be smaller break out group sessions, with constant recording of issues and opportunities.

People who had not been involved in Check, but are now seen as vital to Plan will have hopefully been coached on the approaches to work, following a one-day induction crash course.

Within the larger group there will need to be a refresh of what was discovered in Check, some positive discussions regarding quick wins and new insights, concluding with broad agreements of information and the current flow charts representing how the work works at present.

If some minor redesigns are needed after this team discussion, then that adds to the knowledge.

A simple analogy for service redesign can be used; we call this the garage design or 'Blue Sky Thinking', the concept is that you are a small business running out of your garage, and you wish to win this new contract to do the work with the least constrictions and set-up costs as possible.

However, where very effective communications or operational systems are available those can be deployed. So you start with the perfect design, simple, unrestrained by current situations and the very best model possible. After the perfect design is agreed, known constraints are added to create the first core deigns to discuss.

We find that it's helpful to provide some rules and guidance to this design process.

- ▷ Design against value demand
- ▷ Customer defines quality
- ▷ Only do the value work
- ▷ Minimise number of hand-offs
- ▷ Put information in the hands of front line staff
- ▷ Decisions about the work should be made by people who do the work
- ▷ Do the work perfectly (leave it clean)
- ▷ Challenge "dirt" and "failure demand"
- ▷ Pull ICT to further improve flow only once the work is clean.

Value demand is work that actually adds value to the customer. The flow chart on the following page shows that a large percentage of work even after the first phase of redesign started was not value adding.

The 'customer defines quality' aspect can be difficult if direct access to customers is not allowed as part of the review. Where possible we harvest information from the call centre, by listening to failure demand and the occasional compliments. You can also use questionnaires, via on line, posted or left with the customer at the end of a task. We also frequently use other employees who are not involved in the review, who are a customer of that type of work.

Where possible, seek to reduce or eliminate all aspects of work that do not benefit the customers. This is likely to create quite a lot of discussion to identify and separate non-value work from value enabling. It's amazing how defensive this can get, but it also is quite sobering.

The issue with hand-offs is that: the more people that are individually involved in a piece of work the longer it is likely to take, the greater the probability that it will have errors, that more systems will be used to record information, and there will be more duplications of elements of work causing the service to be costlier.

Current management thinking encourages hand-offs as one section carries out specialist work in batches to enable a low cost per transaction. The analysis would be carried out based on Activity Based Costing, (ABC) such as for processing debtor payments[2].

I was talking with a colleague recently who is looking only at debtors. That authority is considering not chasing parking fines more than once as it costs more per activity than the income achieved. (They are only looking at 'that' activity.) The ratio of fines challenged, to paid, is low. The number of fines issued per day is low, and there is likely to be a relatively low percentage of parking tickets bought per day, as friends get away with ticket sharing to deal with occasional enforcement. There is a reverse cause and effect from not designing a service as end-to-end. Key learning point: ***A sub-element may save perhaps £10,000 a year but could cost £500,000 in lost income.***

Good information and the ability for decision-making need to be with the people doing the work. The union reps always support workers being armed with all the information needed to do the work; this will greatly improve the speed of implementation later. Seek a quick win early on to create useful energy.

Local government tends to appoint well qualified, ambitious, decisive people, who are capable and competent to do their work without constant management, and then via induction tell them all the rules and regulations about control, authority, cross checking. Effectively the handcuffs of 'management by distrust[3]'necessitates far more effort to get work done and as a result is, by design, less efficient than it should be.

The average recycling collection operative will make more decisions in a day than any director or chief executive will in an average week. Is the box close enough to the road? Is the toy on top of this for collection or just left there? Are the materials all correct for collection? Which houses have assisted collections? Is this from one property or six flats? Is this person getting rid of business material illegally?

I've often heard about waste collectors working to rule; if they had the same decision constraints and needs for detailed information that 3rd tier officers normally endure, you'd never get waste collected. So the concepts of empowerment are well established where auditors have been out of their depth to review operating procedures.

Doing the work perfectly may appear to be common sense, although I've often discovered that common sense isn't that common. The most likely area where less than perfect is common is where work volume quotas need to be achieved, parking fines are batch completed in the last few days of the month, the number of calls per operative in the call centre has to be achieved, so people are passed on rather than dealt with, or calls are concluded prior to the resolution of issues.

Where an 'aged debtor' skim is used to look at the oldest work left as incomplete, 80% will be pieces of work that need re-work, perhaps because insufficient information was to hand originally, or the work is far more complex and it's easier to do five other pieces of work than that one.

Challenging failure demand[4] and 'dirt' in the system is healthy for the organisation in that difficult problems are identified and dealt with. In time the role of supervisors and first line managers will increasingly be to help with the redesign of the service so that more and more issues are resolved by design rather than guesswork. The role of more senior managers will become far more enabling, removing the barriers to getting good work done, instigating far more partnership working between sections, divisions and departments.

The whole concept of Visualising Transformation is based on creating a culture of genuine continuous improvement. The ethos, skills transfer and ability to make hundreds of improvements resolving issues will naturally enable capacity to increase for the long-term future, and to engender the ability to deal with problems from emerging legislation, population growth and socio economic pressures of an aging community.

Lastly from the list of bullet points is to 'pull ICT to further improve flow only once the work is clean'. The tendency is to have an information or work flow issue, procure an IT-based solution and then try to do the work with the new system. While the new system may resolve many of the old problems, it's likely to create new problems and not be able to address some of the continuous improvement requirements.

Thus, a staged implementation is often best, where new sub-systems are designed to meet most needs, which can be followed by a later design or purchase of a better system. If the new IT systems are work-flow designed[5] as well, then there is greater likelihood of compatibility and development options.

An additional item to that list should be: Do the work as soon as it arrives, do not queue or batch work.

The flow chart below shows the progress from post-its on a brown paper sheet through to the first interpretation of a new design. This has value steps shown in light blue, value-enabling in pink and non-value in red. So even after the first phase of design, there was far too much non-value work.

FLOW CHART AFTER FIRST PLAN WORKSHOP

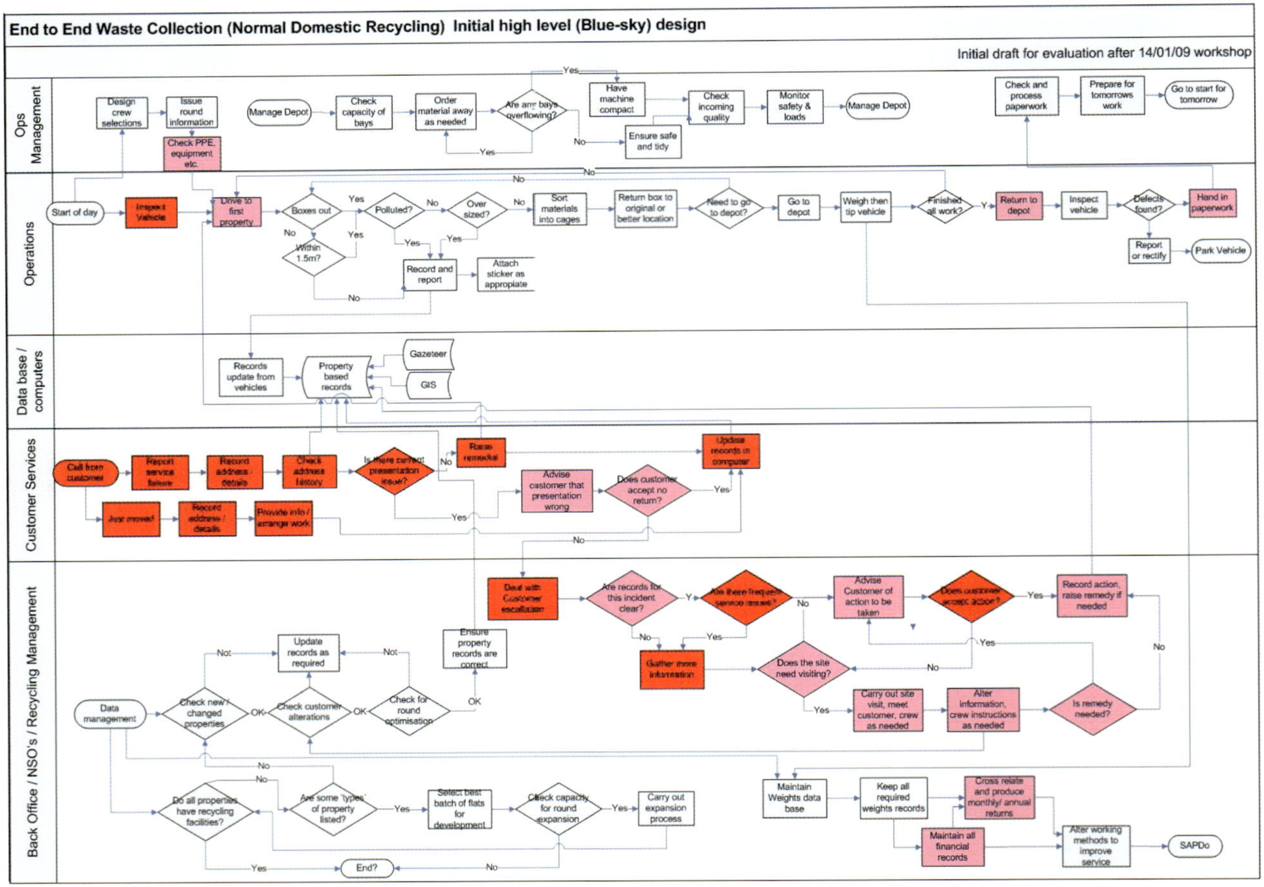

The swim lanes have been simplified and a tight definition placed on the work being designed. A given constraint was that all customer contact would be via the call centre (in customer services). This was award winning and prestigious. It's interesting how much red and pink sits in that area! This detailed chart is available at www.supportservicesdirect.co.uk/visualisingtransformation.

Considering again the concept of visualising stimulating, high impact graphics, we exported the work demand volumes into a simple pie chart to discuss existing and possible designs with the sponsor and project board. The reality of the call centre retention was not lost on the board.

PIE CHART SHOWING THE BALANCE OF VALUE AND NON VALUE WORK

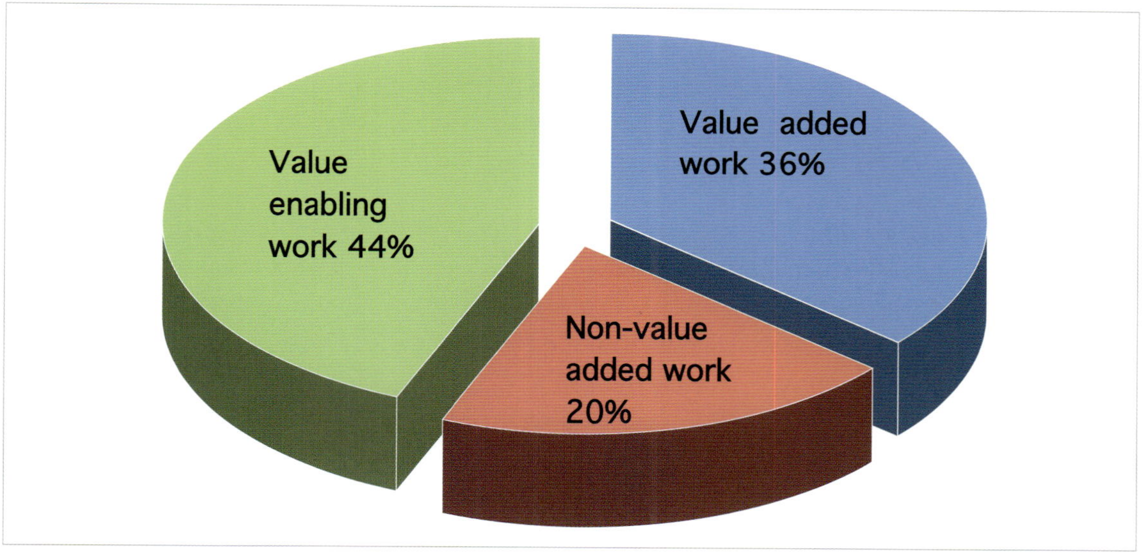

So even in redesign only 36% of elements were true value work, with a further 44% being value-enabling. This doesn't instantly show that a further 20% could be sliced from the overall resources, as the individual elements are not all the same volumes of work.

Remember that the translation of quite complex operational details into high level information which will enable people, such as the board members, to make very good decisions needs the proposition to be blindingly obvious to them. There is not an absolute need for them to be able to read and understand the flow chart; although it will help, the colour codes give instant insight. Red and pink need to be minimised!

As stated, this is one of many designs and considerations. Within the E2E review we will need to manage a great deal of data sorting issues. There will be main-stream process common cause variation, and some areas which are separate to the core designs, or maybe should be treated as special cause.

Not all workflows were obvious to all the people involved, thus while gathering information about the E2E process we had back office staff visiting the call centre and going out with recycling crews. After a while there had been many visits by many people to each other's work areas; while this may seem wasteful, it very much helped create increased knowledge rather than retaining pet theories. The approach to IT systems and its importance radically changed, the questions and technical approaches in the call centre became far more realistic, with an immediate drop in twin miss issues[6].

We were still facing a situation where the whole Intervention Team had not seen how the work works, we therefore designed a 'waste collection game' to re-enact the collection of materials down half a street which was familiar to the crew and half that was unknown.

The briefing for the game said that it was a cold wet day; you are wearing heavy gloves, and cannot hold a pad of paper and pencil. People were supplied with reasonable information under the current way of thinking to do a good job. Once collections started, several people suddenly realised that this was far more complex than it looked, and that simple solutions couldn't be achieved straight- way.

Within the Toyota Production System (TPS), there is a term of 'going to the gemba[7]', which basically means that the easiest way to see how the work works, is to watch it in real time. Site visits and work simulations significantly help to eradicate some pet theories, create knowledge and enable an all one team approach to crystallise quicker. There are two wonderful books from the mid 1990's by Peter Scholtes[8] called *The Team Handbook* and *The Leaders Handbook*. I would thoroughly recommend reading or browsing through them, they retain their excellent validity today.

There are many aspects from the initial training which have not yet been discussed, partly to not overload the previous chapters. There are many concepts and analysing tools available, the majority of which I will try to include, similarly the four-day course, which initially will be only via PRISM consultancy and SSD, has a wealth of high quality diagrams and examples.

The Joiner triangle provides a very useful foundation for considering the process of service delivery and managing change. The three corners of focus for the triangle are: Quality, All one team and a Scientific approach. Nigel Clements of PRISM has helped to develop these considerations adding in: Voice of the process, Voice of the customer and Voice of the people (See right).

Much of the four-day course focuses on this anchor diagram, drilling down to the details of variation, understanding cause and effect, making decisions based on information which matters to the customer. It also ensures that everyone being part of the same team is fully understood.

THE EVOLVED JOINER TRIANGLE

This is part of the reason why I refer to this process as holistic, in that it seeks to achieve the best outcomes in every way possible, note the elements in voice of the people, having a belief in people, treating them with dignity, trust and respect. This is not a simple process-driven methodology; it is rounded and very much all inclusive and the final stages of Plan and *Appraise* will show how added value from many aspects will be driven into the designs.

I had previously mentioned that future proofing the designs would be needed; one aspect of today's society is that it expects current elements of 'providing a little bit more' to be a standard offering shortly after. As a personal example – I rarely use trains to get around the country as I live so far from a station; however, having had sockets to charge my laptop on some trains, I really miss that now when the next train hasn't got power.

MEETING THE NEEDS OF THE CUSTOMER BASED ON DR. KANO

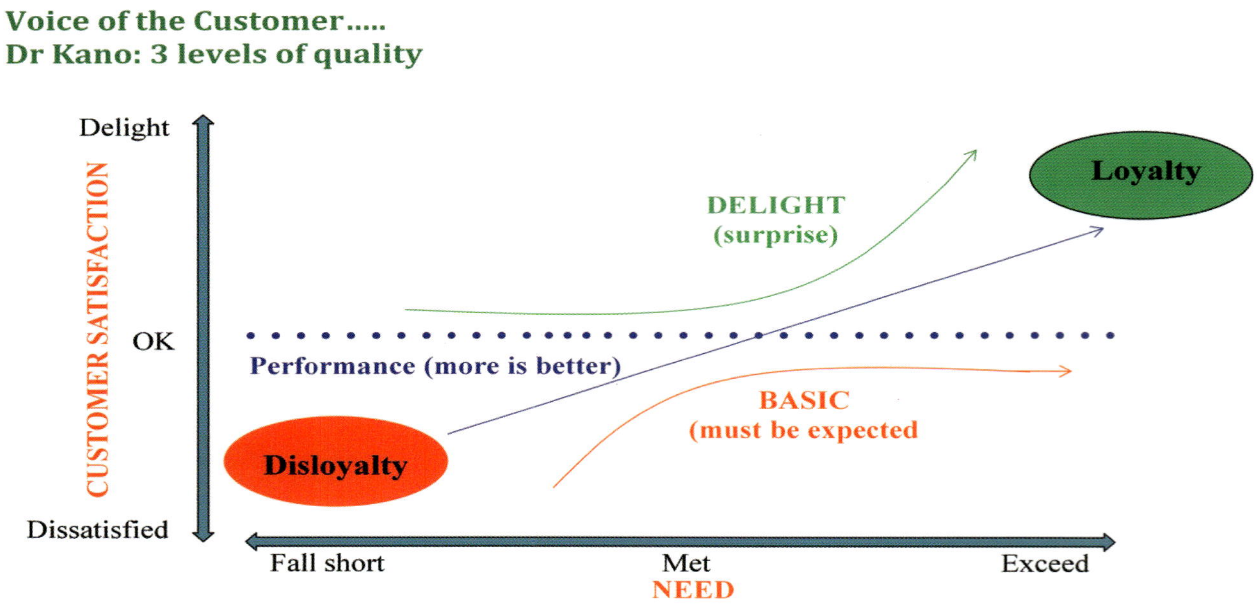

It's quite customary for the public sector to not consider what will lead to customer delight, when the simple act of doing the basics can be so difficult. When you review the operation and strategy in tandem, getting everyone in the room to start thinking about what surprise and delight could be will help to create a queue of concepts for further developments, many will be possible at no extra cost.

"Why should we delight our customers? We only need to do our jobs, which gets harder to do all the time, with less money and ever more difficult targets. Anyway, we provide a good service so they can take it or lump it!" Well, while these comments are rarely voiced, but there are often these types of thoughts and murmurings in the background.

So, why should we delight customers? Under the National Indicator for avoidable contact (NI14), delighting customers is a real risk, as those delighted customers will phone in to say 'what a good job that was', or, 'I'd hardly put the phone down and the pothole was filled!'

Delighting customers causes avoidable contact. {NI14 is technically supposed to address continuous improvement via shared front offices & call centres & setting targets, there's so much wrong with it, the only good idea is to dump it!}

Delight can be caused by many types of actions, for blue badges – issuing a badge within a few minutes of the person arriving and then offering services X and Y which may also help the customer. There is the opportunity to create a single file for customer credentials rather than parallel ones for blue badges, bus passes, and benefits. Rectifying errors quickly, without fuss and in such a way as the fault will not recur often makes people happier than never causing an error.

There is a wonderful podcast called 'Shift happens'; the one by Sony is my favoured version. This shows quite stunningly how fast technology and society is changing. When considering delight, being three steps behind the leaders is not good enough.

Another recent experience: *I've been dealing with one of the most prestigious firms in the world who sell a niche product from the 'swishest' shops in the best cities in the world (for my wife). They have a problem with their system design, it causes errors. If it causes them to overcharge you, that is fine by them. However, if it causes them to undercharge you, not only can they not rectify the issue, but it takes months of work to get them to comply with international contract law. They took £600 for a £1,000 product, contract agreed! Then it was unilaterally broken!*

They have a contact centre, called 'customer care' whose main aim is to get between sensible people and customers. They don't understand issues, but will not escalate them. Eventually I forced the contact centre manager to get involved, who having got legal agreement, he advises all will be resolved within a week, at the originally agreed price. Well perhaps two weeks. Well perhaps several more weeks. So one of the most expensive firms in the world are in fact all gloss and PR but hopeless at real customer service.

This took ten weeks to resolve via constant research and badgering. Even after all this, they tried to negotiate a price rather than do what their own legal department and customer care had said.

Finally by talking with the MD in the country the purchase took place in, they accepted deplorable service, and agreed to sell the commodity at the original agreed price and then told me that they would take the difference of price from the sales-person's pay. I explained that the error was due to the system design and managers were responsible. They then sent the item to the wrong address!

Each review needs to be end-to-end, as viewed by the customer, however within the whole work, segmenting the designs further increases the opportunities to add value. As an example – for highways you can consider: road users from commuters, school run, delivery driver and bus driver perspectives; then pedestrians, cyclists, joggers. Even after all that there will uses at various times of the day, conflicts of access to safety to parking. The greater the drill down the more likely that best fit holistic solutions will be found.

Therefore you should never design a service or product from one user point of view, if it's inescapable for many people to need to use it or be affected by that service. I've often seen the designs for refuse collection to be great for virtually 90% of the households; those that are detached, semi-detached or terraced houses with reasonable front gardens, it may even suit some flats. However, its odds on that the design doesn't work for high density housing such as back to back terrace with no front gardens, flats over shops nor for other non-conforming dwellings.

Then the recycling services have even poorer designs, as communal recycling is always destroyed by a single rogue family who just don't care. So refuse and recyclates get left and messy, then stuff is slung alongside and suddenly nothing works at all and it gets full of rats...

That's why the service designs need to address the mainstream services and most of the secondary ones. If there are ten thousand homes with a poor design for collection, how could the collection service ever be better than mediocre?

If we go back to some earlier points, how can we apply the five whys to the data to start to get to information? Are we looking at the information at the right level in the rights way? Can we diagnose some issues within the performances that are happening now to enable a quick win?

Returning to the integrated waste management review, the service there was OK, but not stunning. They had one problem for every 1,000 collections on average. A failure rate of 1 in 1,000 sounds quite good, for instance, how many cabinet reports are right first time? Or how would one error per 1,000 invoices feel?

But refuse and recycling collections are different in many ways; one way is that there are generally over 100,000 collections a week. So a failure rate of 1 in 1,000 gives you over 100 customer issues a week. If you have 100 missed bins per week, that's a lot of admin, supervision and operational capacity taken up which in turn reduces capacity to do core work.

If you have a rectification crew who simply put things right, there will never be any motivation for things to be perfect in the first place. If the original team rectify the work, it will often take ¼ hour to rectify one collection. A crew can collect from two properties every 40 seconds in a good road, so 15 minutes error correcting is a loss of capacity of 45 properties. One hundred misses a week denies you around 4,500 properties capacity (or a small round).

Don't forget that on top of your operational lost capacity, you have your call centre, back office and supervision to factor in prior to escalations because work isn't rectified quick enough, so a 1 in 1,000 failure rate could add 10% to the collection costs, thus a near perfect collection service will be far cheaper than a poor one.

The control chart on page 114 shows that the whole waste collection service generally has a mean failure rate of 116 errors a week from mid January to September. We were aware of Christmas being a special cause for additional design.

The transformation intervention was to start in late October, so it had been decided to use the team to initially address 'the Christmas blip' so that it could be used as a mini exercise for a quick win soon after. This would also have the benefit of releasing review resources in January.

Note how the use of notes actually written into a graph brings the information to the fore. We employ this technique in order to raise a graph from a mere data placement to information or insight.

CONTROL CHART WASTE COLLECTION MISSES

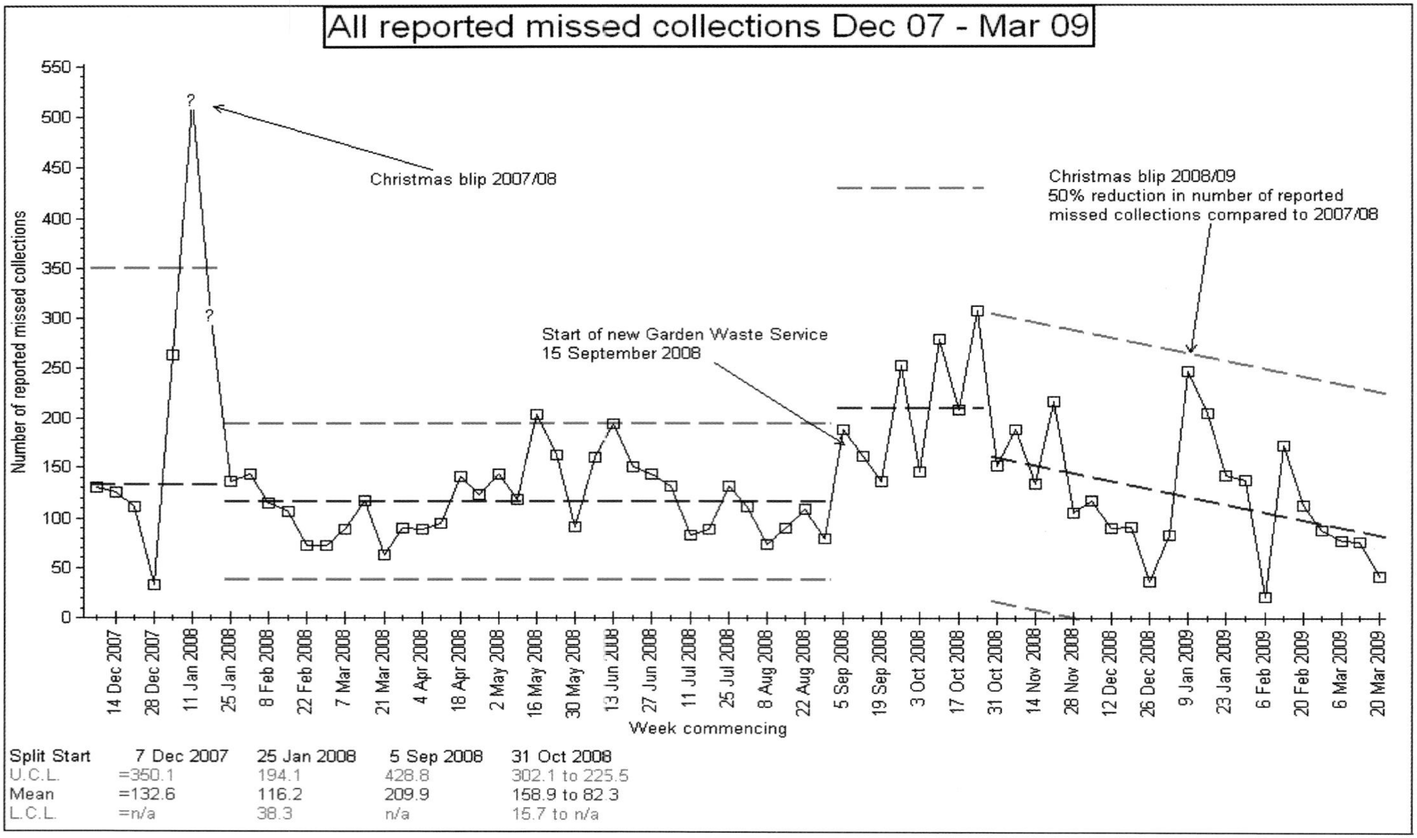

Note how well a special cause is immediately identified by the control chart from September 2008, when the garden waste scheme commenced. That had been designed under a traditional project management methodology, with far too much emphasis on IT and financial services, with little operational input being listened to, leading to very significant operational problems. I will also return to the 'saw-tooth' (that is alternating good, then bad performances) causes from mid-September until the end of October. That is not natural; there will be a special cause.

CONTROL CHART FOR GARDEN WASTE

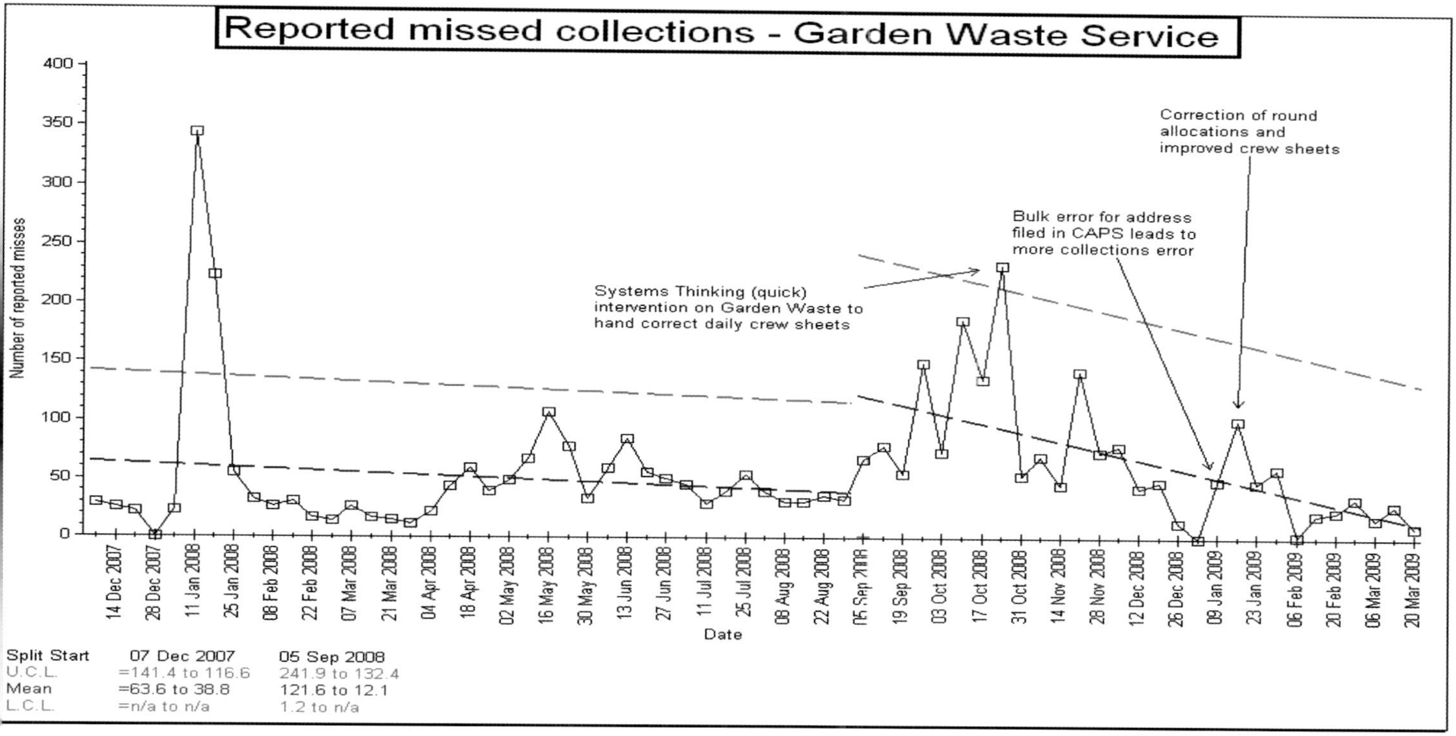

This displays slightly different characteristics in that the service had a mean of around 50 misses prior to September, followed by a significant melt down with that distinct 'saw-tooth' affect between week one and week two of collections. (The service was fortnightly.)

We started an immediate rapid intervention for this part of the waste service the day the intervention team was appointed. We discovered that the computer system was creating incorrect crew sheets, (that is the daily instruction as to where to collect from) with omissions and duplications, so the first aspect of a quick win was to create a computer generated crew sheet and then manually altered it to be correct every evening (in advance of correcting the original problems).

We used the 'five whys' concept to drill down to why the problem had occurred in the first place and from that, how to design a long-term resolution of the issues. The saw tooth effect was traced to a round with wrong data entries for three days of one week.

CONTROL CHART FOR ONE GARDEN WASTE ROUND ONLY

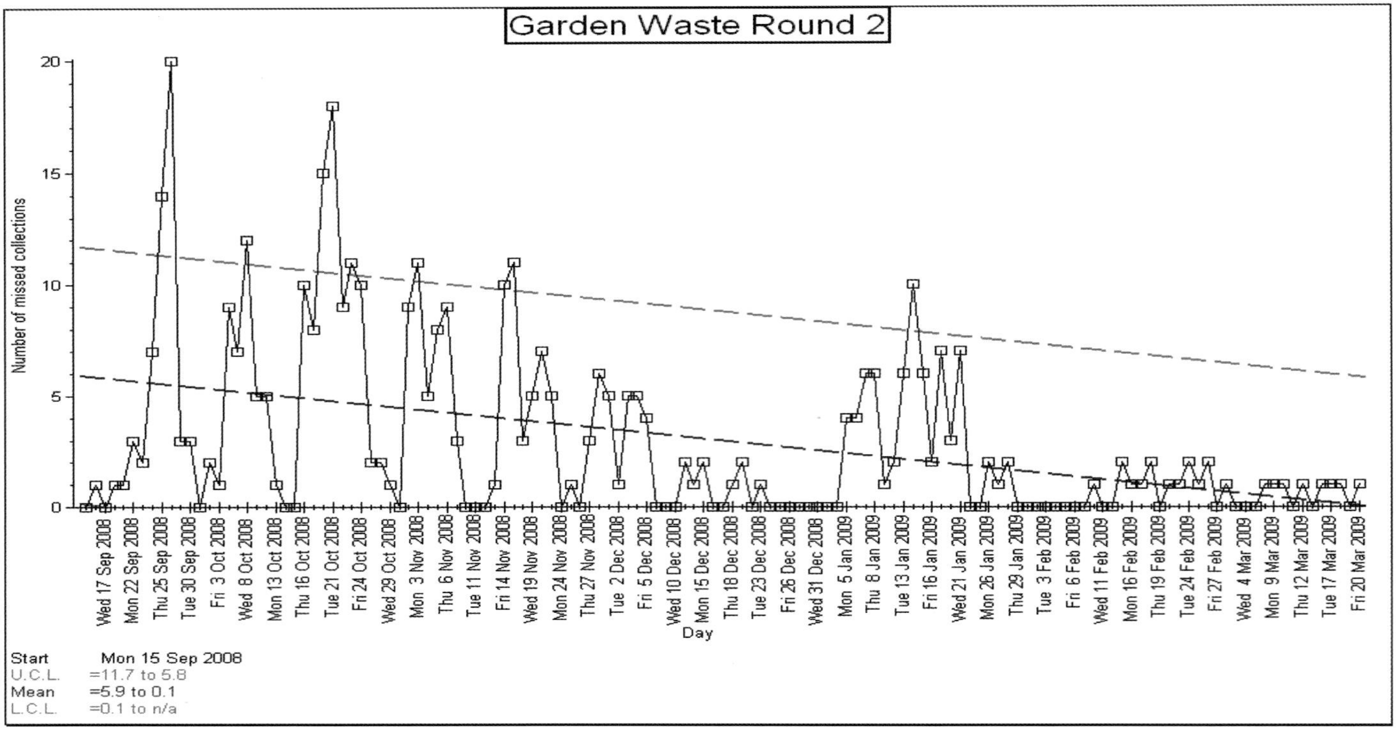

When the information is broken down into operational days, we get an even clearer understanding of the problems. Remember that points above the upper control limit are likely to be due to a special cause.

The likelihood of perfect collection days being alongside days with 15 to 20 errors for a round without a reason is most unlikely without a special cause. As time goes on and actions were taken, 'perfect days' become more common and the maximum errors per day reduce to only two.

It is 'well known' that change causes failure! However, this was entirely due to incomplete design and a lack of operational attention from the PRINCE2 project manager. Where systems thinking approaches have been applied to round changes, there are rarely any discernable losses for the customer service.

The service meltdown that occurred in September caused around eight man days from admin, back office, call centre and IT extra rework ***every day***. This was entirely avoidable and virtually stopped within two days by a quick intervention by people who knew how a system works and how to get information from data.

The quick win process was also applied to Christmas, resulting in a 60% reduction in issues compared to the previous two years. That is 600 less dissatisfied customers, and around 2,400 less processes for the call centre and back office to process. Key learning point: ***Improving the quality of the service by design will always increase the capacity to do value work.***

The garden waste intervention was not part of the original transformation plan, but it was an extremely useful demonstration of how a service in complete meltdown can be rescued very quickly. It also created a belief in the upcoming review that this was something quite different. These quick wins are always great points of reference for training and development of people who may need proof in the pudding before they may be willing to totally commit to a real engagement.

So even in the biggest reviews it is well worth keeping an eye open for simple improvements without meddling. The detour is often paid back many times with increased positive energy from delegates. This may also enable increased capacity so that the review creates less capacity strain than thought.

As the Plan processes are moving forward, maintain positive contact with the sponsor, all work teams and support personnel. Make sure that simple observations are validated and are as true as can be achieved. The main service design starts from the first workshop; however, all the supplementary service designs need consideration. As the waste examples have shown above, the three strands of waste (residual, dry recyclates and garden waste) have different characteristics of containment, collection and offloading, leading to different access and storage issues.

The designs need to be generically similar, enabling single core methodologies while enabling the correct options for the various non-core elements. The end of the next chapter will catalogue possible designs and outcomes, as an indicator for how 'Do' can be designed. These options need to be understood, catalogued and shared so all parties have knowledge of the whole service design with insight of how their elements impact on all the other areas. This gives both inclusion and helps safeguard against meddling[9].

As the sub-sections of work are being designed, constraints are challenged and worked to; it's worth starting to deal with aspirations and a first phase of *Appraise*. What improvements to the current way of working have you been trying to achieve recently without progress, or is going far too slowly?

One of my favourite discussions in the built world/street scene has been: "We've been trying for years to connect our operations database to PDA's (mobile computers) so that we can see what needs to be done when we are on site and be able to send completions back to the main database once the work's done."

I then ask the computer expert who is in the room; "Can that be done at present?" The answer is often something like this, "No, we are waiting for the update version of system xxx, but we can't do that update until system yyy is updated."

> "So, you can't start mobile working before then?"
>
> "No"
>
> "If you took the information from system xxx and transferred it into Access using a flat file conversion with comma delineations, would a simple PDA be able to take that?"
>
> "Yes, that could be done."
>
> "How soon could you do that with a simple PDA?"
>
> "We could do it by next Monday!"

At this point the operations manager squawks quite loudly as he's wanted this for seven years!

The fact is that by asking better questions and having a little knowledge and not stopping at a simple 'No' that quite amazing things can happen. When the GIS link in the database is then considered against the basic GPRS in the PDA, it's often possible to show all related work which is 'live' within a mile of where the supervisor is standing. Quite a jump forward in productivity can then occur with virtually no additional cost. Key learning point: ***Always try to consider indirect linkages if direct ones are not yet available.***

The 'flat file conversion' paragraph enables linkage, I've no idea how to do it, but it has worked in housing maintenance, highways, street scene, parking enforcement, parking payments, waste collection, finance transactions and ASB. The ASB issue was that Councillors wanted to know where enforcement had been taking place, the IT department went through the usual routine of pointing out that the GIS module had not been purchased for the ASB system, I tried the flat file paragraph, this time between the ASB system and the existing GIS and that was OK – we had the print for it the next week.

That does make me wonder how many councils buy software and systems needlessly because the IT professionals do not, and will not, think laterally. I've probably saved the public sector £3/4M through that one paragraph alone. This is a simple extension of the five whys concept, why can't that connect? Why don't you link it through a common system to both?

The work discussed so far has largely been operational in nature, the mix with strategy is important, the use of mind maps, cause and effect charts together with the flow diagram on page 96 all show ways of visualising strategic issues at the same time as operational ones. The next diagram is based on an affinity diagram[10].

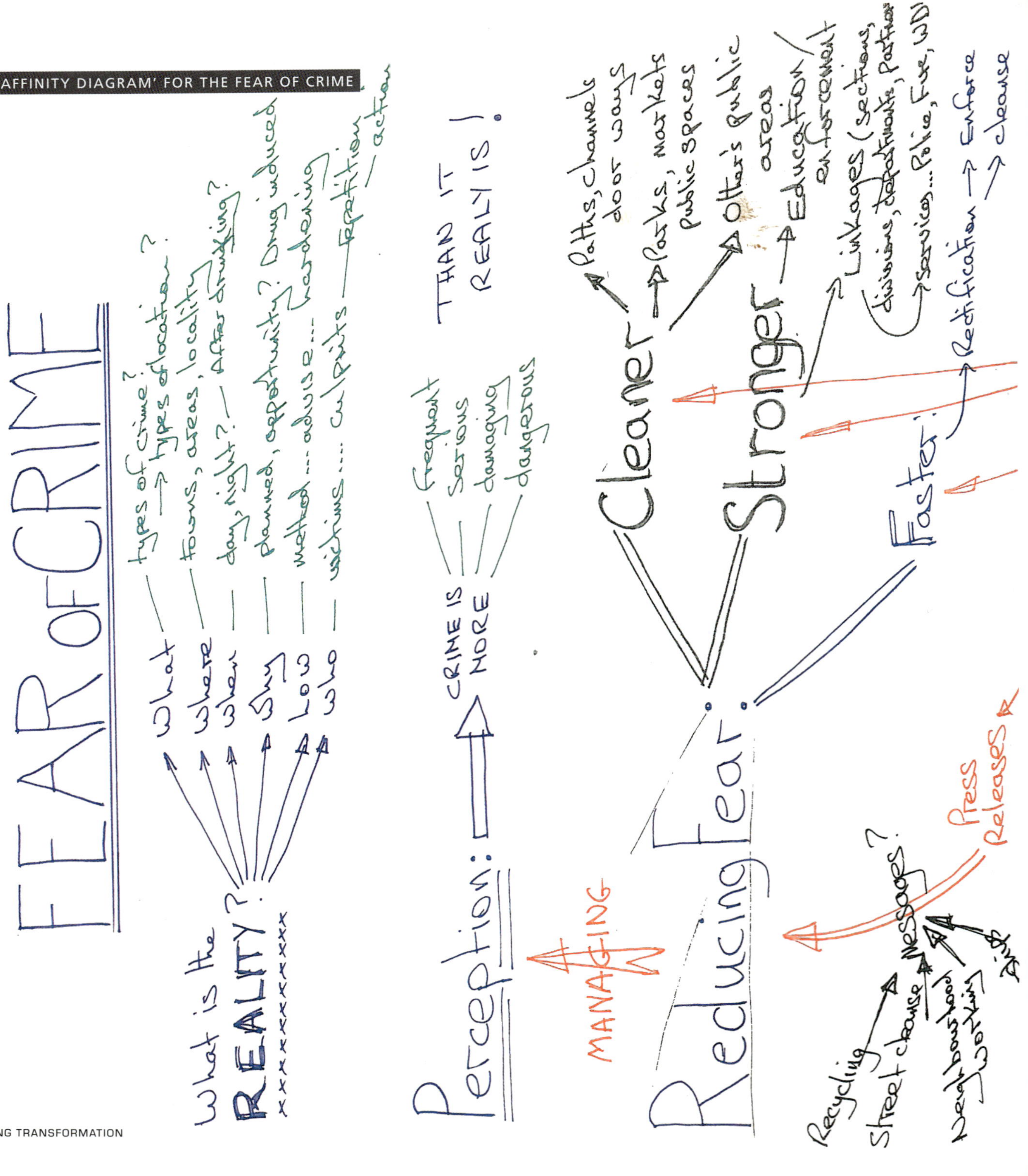
FEAR OF CRIME
What is the REALITY?
What — types of crime? → types of location?
Where — towns, areas, locality
When — day, night? — After drinking?
Why — planned, opportunity? Drug induced
How — method ... advise ... wandering
Who — victims ... culprits — repetition — action
Perception: ⟹ CRIME IS MORE frequent serious damaging dangerous THAN IT REALLY IS!
MANAGING
Reducing Fear:
Cleaner → Paths, channels door ways → Parks, markets public spaces → others public areas
Stronger → Education → Education / enforcement → Linkages (sections, divisions, departments, partners → Services ... Police, Fire, WD)
Faster: → Rectification → Enforce → cleanse
Press Releases
Messages?
Recycling
Street cleanse
Neighbourhood working

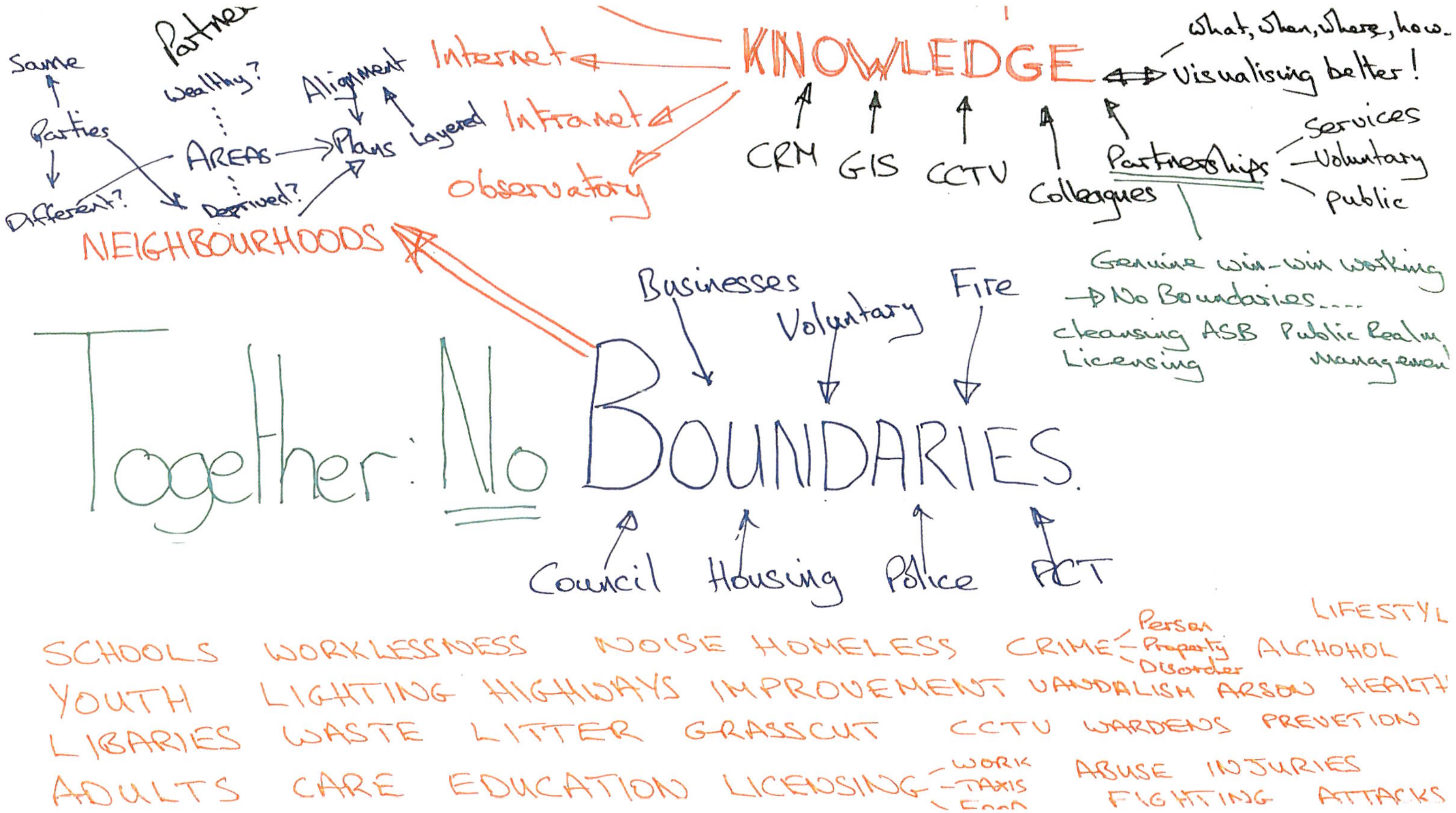
KNOWLEDGE
What, when, where, how.
Visualising better!
CRM
GIS
CCTV
Colleagues
Partnerships
Services
Voluntary
Public
Genuine win-win working
No Boundaries....
cleansing ASB Public Realm
Licensing management
Internet
Intranet
Observatory
Partner
Same
Parties
Different?
Wealthy?
AREAS
Deprived?
Alignment
Plans
Layered
NEIGHBOURHOODS
Together: No BOUNDARIES.
Businesses
Voluntary
Fire
Council
Housing
Police
PCT
SCHOOLS
WORKLESSNESS
NOISE
HOMELESS
CRIME
Person
Property
Disorder
LIFESTYL
ALCHOHOL
YOUTH
LIGHTING
HIGHWAYS
IMPROVEMENT
VANDALISM
ARSON
HEALTH
LIBARIES
WASTE
LITTER
GRASSCUT
CCTV
WARDENS
PREVETION
ADULTS
CARE
EDUCATION
LICENSING
WORK
TAXIS
ABUSE
INJURIES
FIGHTING
ATTACKS

The key issue was to reduce ***the fear of crime***. Crime levels were very low for this district and were actually improving. The council, police, housing associations, fire brigade, PCT and voluntary sector were all involved in working together and had very good written strategies via the LAA and LSP. However, the fear of crime was just as bad in this district as it was in an adjacent city where crime really was a problem.

Here LSPs are into a completely different management need. The operational methods that worked perfectly well, were failing to translate into an improvement for the public perception. Perception management now needs to address several parts of the 200 NIs that the government has produced for local authorities. The approaches to manage perception must be different; simply using publicity runs the risk of credibility and concerns about marketing spin.

The 'affinity diagram' starts with questioning reality, using the six questions of where, what, why, how, who and when crime is committed at present. That is: we must fully understand the issues. These issues vary from town to town, from a city centre to the outlying countryside. Something what doesn't even register as an issue in a city centre would be a calamity within a small hamlet. This hand-drawn diagram was scanned and shared among all the parties involved, it was adopted without any form of adverse comment.

Then we move on to the current issue, Which is, the *perception* of crime is that: it is more serious, frequent, damaging and dangerous than *reality*. The organisations thus need to understand why there are such differences in the current perception from reality; and from *understanding* that *perception*, then try to *influence* the perception. NOTE this is no longer a piece of work to improve crime reduction, although that was occurring in parallel, this is solely about perception management.

So we are now looking at ***reducing fear***, to do that the last thing we needed to do was publish more statistics about crime being low. There was also a perception that places are safe by day but not by night. Between the public and us was the press. Newspapers achieve profit by selling papers. They need sensationalism and bad news stories to succeed, so no matter how we presented any good news, the public would only hear one message, that this is crime on the streets, and you should be afraid.

So we needed to analyse what we could do. We already had thematic joined up working within the council for Cleaner, Safer and Stronger localities. The police had a series of PACT meetings, where police representatives would meet with community representatives to discuss local issues. (Due to initiation issues and a lack of operational linkages, these were frequently not attended by other bodies, so promises would be made by the police, not passed on to other agencies and thus would not be acted on.) The major housing association had meetings with its tenants, again often without other 'partners' present, with an outcome of dealing with their issues, but not the more difficult inter-agency ones.

The reality was that the services who should deal with the fear of crime were totally fragmented with resources all working in parallel, often duplicating efforts, but not working in harmony.

We therefore had at least two major problems; operationally we needed to coordinate, align and jointly work on the thornier issues, and all the parties needed to independently understand the types of issues which needed mainline resolution and then publicity.

There were also moves to establish an information observatory. Effectively a database linked to GIS in a well managed way will enable this such as for Nottingham with Nomad plus[11]. There was an array of organisations with their separate budgets, systems, sub-systems and websites all needing to be coordinated and aligned. GIS tends to be treated fairly 'lower case' in each body, and data sharing was not strong. So we could have had a dozen versions of the truth, none of which was correct.

We needed as much as was possible to create common 'knowledge' from our information and from the areas we could agree on, then work out what positive messages we could promote. We had the highest cleanliness results ever, virtually no graffiti or fly-posting and improving green spaces. The recycling results were improving quickly and partly due to the recession total waste was also reducing. So we started with a strong campaign for 'Cleaner Greener' raising the awareness of better environments for people to look at.

Separate to this we brought all the teams together who were dealing with side waste and fly-tipping and worked through to a new strategy for reducing issues and improving response times. (Inside three months we reduced customer complaints for the whole of waste services by sixty per cent.) We also established strategies for improved enforcement, for business involvement and many other linked concepts, such as greater working with the probation service and improved tasking with response teams, using GIS linked data to visualise local issues quicker.

Across the agencies we created a far stronger link from our CCTV centre to harvest far more of the 700 opportunities a month, liaison for the PACT meetings, enabling us to align to the 44 PACT areas with a form of 1 to 1 marking, such that we were able to react to issues raised, reliably, within a fortnight. The 'affinity diagram' enabled us to discuss our boundary conditions openly. This in turn helped us to create links from the police to council and vice versa, internal and external messages became more 'on theme' and seamless working started to become a reality.

Returning to the major waste intervention it was decided to split that into four main pieces of work:

1. The overall waste strategy for the council
2. Waste collections services
3. Vehicle optimisation
4. Information systems

The first three threads were led by external consultants while the fourth was led by the council. The thread leaders met and shared their work progress at least once a week, some delegates would be involved in only one thread, while others were involved in several.

The strategic development had started before the operational reviews, and had indicated that an operational improvement of £250,000 a year was possible prior to starting the transformation process.

Over the following few weeks, the aspirations of the interventions increased as knowledge was gained. A subsequent benefits realisation record showed the opportunities had grown to £600,000, plus £250,000 for part 2 and £200,000 for part 3.

The benefits realisation was recorded on a simple Excel spreadsheet, version control was maintained, and pages were added to record opportunities and new concepts, such that there were 'pipeline[12]' options and delivered outcomes from quick wins as work proceeded.

BENEFITS ANALYSIS ABSTRACT

	Description	Efficiency		Qualitative		Owner	Start Date	End Date	Status
		Cashable	Non-Cashable	BVPIs/LPI	Other				
1	End to end review of missed collections. Dealing with all aspects of the workstream from initial customer contact through Customer Services, Back Office, Operations to resolution and information recording.	£600,000 a year. Linked to item 2.	Reduced missed collections, leading to: Increased customer satisfaction, reduced work load in Call Centre and Back Office, reduced resource needs operationally.	Reduced cost per household, reduced misses per 100,000 collections. Target sub 40 per week by Christmas, long term sub 10 per week.	Improving customer satisfaction	Gurmit Sandhu Nic Lindsey Danny	Aug-08	Ongoing	Started properly in November 2008, dealing with Garden waste and Christmas Blip as special causes. Two 3 day courses designed and run, follow up sessions started. Data collection and reports started.
2	Integration of data systems, including: Fuel Issue, Aggesso, Trace, Blue ??, Avery, Waste weights, CAPS, Commercial Waste and GIS.	£250,000 a year. Linked to item 1.	Elimination of parallel running of systems with a view to creating single entry of data with multiple use. Creating routine output reports, including dashboard awareness.	Increase in recyclates diversion. Improved income from recyclates and commercial waste.	Free time to better market Recyclates sales, penetration of recycling into flatted areas, Commercial waste management.	Alex Dave Gaster Geoff	Nov-08	Mar-09	Initial issues started to be mapped, Trace / finance linkage pilot work started.
3	Data representation of rounds via GIS. Preparedness to use GIS round modelling by February 2009.	Potentially £200,000 per annum, if not re-invested into increasing recyclate volumes.	Round designs can be robust, enabling future development integration. Absolute clarity for new rounds down to individual properties enables no service disruption on day 1.	Increased recycling diversion within net budget. Reduced misses per 100,000 collections during transition.	Likely improvement in service delivery, later net financial.	Dave Gaster Maggy	Aug-08	Feb-09	GIS plans created of refuse rounds as a start to visualise data, assisting Garden Waste data cleanse. Rounds data on CAPS being improved, initial demos of tracking systems started.
Total		£1.05M per annum							

The 'prospect log' had seventeen options developed in under four months, most of which were integrated into the final designs.

A change log was also maintained to record alterations to the normal ways of working prior to the final reports being generated. The abstract shows how the change log was set up, with a record of when a change was decided against when the change was implemented. There were twenty three changes agreed, with sixteen implemented during the actual review period and several part-implemented.

Two of these changes areas were for 'The Christmas Blip' and for Garden Waste, as below.

CHANGE LOG ABSTRACT

	Description		Efficiency		Decision monitor	
		Action	Cashable	Non-Cashable	Decided	Acted on
1	Christmas Blip - Additional resources to deal with increased demand.	Hire three RCV's for a fortnight.	Plus £7,000.	Operatives and drivers not worked to exhaustion, less mistakes made.	11/11/2008	13/11/2008
2	Christmas Blip - Additional resources to deal with increased demand.	Additional drivers, altered usage of garden waste RCV to card collections, and use of spare cage vehicles for recycling collections.	Plus £7,000	Operatives and drivers not worked to exhaustion, less mistakes made.	11/11/2008	20/11/2008
3	Christmas Blip - Additional resources to deal with increased demand.	Less failure demand to customer services, back office, less returns to rectify work. Greater proportion of recyclates recovered.	More productive time available to staff. Less overtime, resources needed. More income from recyclates.	Far fewer customers experience dis-satisfaction.	11/11/2008	11/11/2008
4	Christmas Blip - Don't start collecting Christmas trees until its light enough to see these clearly.	All trees seen on first pass, greatly reduced needs to return to properties, less call via Customer services and back office.	More productive time available to staff. Less overtime, resources needed. Less cost of rectification.	Less likelihood of several vehicles working in one area at a time.	11/11/2008	11/11/2008
5	Christmas Blip - Improve communications for customers and employees alike.	Advertise special Christmas message on side of RCV's. (in budget).	Promotes recycling, reduces calls, reduces wrong day presentation.	Easier for customers to be aware of changes, less calls enquiring, reduces NI 14 position.	11/11/2008	14/11/2008
6	Christmas Blip - Improve communications for customers and employees alike.	Seek to increase message to as many households as possible re date change and operations. Thus less calls received.	Information on paper, web-site and calendars, thus less calls to discover info, less failure demand.	Easier for customers to be aware of changes, less calls enquiring, reduces NI 14 position.	11/11/2008	mid December
7	Christmas Blip - Improve communications for customers and employees alike.	Ensure total clarity of who and how work is to be done, brief crews, management, back office, customer services and IT.	All people know what and how work is done, FAQ's focus on special causes, less rework	Less stress in customer services and back office, easier to focus on real issues.	11/11/2008	mid December

	Description	Action	Efficiency		Decision monitor	
			Cashable	**Non-Cashable**	**Decided**	**Acted on**
8	Christmas Blip - Focus on flats for refuse, recycling and tree collections	Identify likely issues, design additional resources and FAQ's to meet demand.			11/11/2008	mid December
9	Garden Waste - Alter round structures for week 2 Thursday Friday.	Increase to 3 rounds as work is out of proportion.	Scheme is designed as three rounds, prevents failure escalation and customer fall out.	Shows caring employer, enables back office and IT to resolve causes.	4/11/2008	05/11/2008
10	Garden Waste - Manually inspect crew sheets daily before printing.	Manually update crew sheets against database records, highlight known problems, write on corrections.	Reduced failure demand, less need to return to customers, less calls into customer services and back office.	Reduced stress on all involved with the service.	4/11/2008	04/11/2008
11	Garden Waste - Instruct all drivers and collectors re corner properties.	Advise crew to always look around the corner for potential collection for corner and near corner properties.	Reduced back office generation of maps for every corner property. Reduced error rate associated with 'unusual locations'	Greater capacity to do value adding work.	4/11/2008	05/11/2008
18	Create dashboard reporting systems for service failure on all waste rounds	Management information will enable daily focus on the rounds that matter. Far greater ability to make a difference. Thus eliminate a quantum of failure related costs.	Less calls to customer services, less back office time, less fuel and ware and tare to RCV's. More capacity for rounds.	Better public perception of service.	27/01/2008	

I think it's helpful to see that there are several levels of design in any one item of work. The Christmas blip for instance, has eight work activities, which were led by several different people. If authority to spend money was required, that would have been part of the process.

The simple dashboard report, as shown on the next page, was designed in Excel to show how the outputs from the current IT systems in place, could easily be transferred into a daily report for all the waste supervisors and managers to use on a daily basis. While dashboards can cause an organisation to focus far too much on the negative, i.e. ambers and reds only, this did enable the council to provide simple automated basic daily performance reporting.

This is an example where a transition process can add value; the dashboard was created prior to a more fundamental change of IT systems. The colours are auto evaluated in Excel 2007, based on the averages from each service currently, as service improves, relative performance will still be displayed.

Waste Dashboard

Weighted position

Refuse		Recycling	
1	6.0	1	0.5
2	7.2	2	6.5
3	2.3	3	10.5
4	9.8	4	7.3
5	11.5	5	1.5
6	15.0	6	12.7
7	4.0	7	1.8
8	1.2		

Garden 1	
1	5.5
2	7.0
3	3.0
Garden 2	
1	28.7
2	14.8
3	10.2

Others	
Trade	0.3
Clinical	1.0
Bulky	0.2

Statistics

	Miss / 100K	Current O/D Rems
All	67.3	11
Refuse	37.9	5
Recycling	30.6	3
Garden	581.8	3

The dashboard report is a balance of missed collections from yesterday, over the last week, together with any overdue remedies that were in place. Within the two biggest services, it shows Refuse rounds 4, 5 and 6 have problems, and that Recycling rounds 3 and 6 also need attention.

Garden 1 and 2, show the same crews working alternate weeks, this again shows the problems we had for week 2, round 1. The miss per 100,000 collections show how deplorable the garden waste service was in comparison to the other rounds.

The chart on the next page is a simple report which brings together the properties per day, loads per day and average finish times for residual waste collection rounds only. I have used it to depict the imbalance between designed rounds at a high level. This may be slightly more balanced when miles per day and other issues are added.

The green highlights show where there are relatively low workloads in a day, and the yellow highlights show the larger workloads, in terms of the number of properties to collect from. Rounds 7 and 8 were rural rounds, dealing with narrow streets, farms and villages in general. Waste collections started at 6.30 each morning.

Round summaries

Round 1 Monday	Props	Round 1 Tuesday	Props	Round 1 Wednesday	Props	Round 1 Thursday	Props	Round 1 Friday	Props	Total
Total	1668	Total	1799	Total	1605	Total	2208	Total	1761	9041
Round 2 Monday	Props	Round 2 Tuesday	Props	Round 2 Wednesday	Props	Round 2 Thursday	Props	Round 2 Friday	Props	Total
Total	1723	Total	1656	Total	1703	Total	1858	Total	1651	8591
Round 3 Monday	Props	Round 3 Tuesday	Props	Round 3 Wednesday	Props	Round 3 Thursday	Props	Round 3 Friday	Props	Total
Total	2397	Total	2122	Total	1532	Total	1682	Total	1272	9005
Round 4 Monday	Props	Round 4 Tuesday	Props	Round 4 Wednesday	Props	Round 4 Thursday	Props	Round 4 Friday	Props	Total
Total	1882	Total	2259	Total	1831	Total	2283	Total	1800	10055
Round 5 Monday	Props	Round 5 Tuesday	Props	Round 5 Wednesday	Props	Round 5 Thursday	Props	Round 5 Friday	Props	Total
Total	1624	Total	1577	Total	1550	Total	1675	Total	1174	7600
Round 6 Monday	Props	Round 6 Tuesday	Props	Round 6 Wednesday	Props	Round 6 Thursday	Props	Round 6 Friday	Props	Total
Total	1597	Total	1493	Total	1679	Total	1667	Total	1450	7886
Round 7 Monday	Props	Round 7 Tuesday	Props	Round 7 Wednesday	Props	Round 7 Thursday	Props	Round 7 Friday	Props	Total
Total	790	Total	837	Total	1279	Total	779	Total	956	4641
Round 8 Monday	Props	Round 8 Tuesday	Props	Round 8 Wednesday	Props	Round 8 Thursday	Props	Round 8 Friday	Props	Total
Total	459	Total	354	Total	636	Total	930	Total	493	2872
Total Monday	12140	Total Tuesday	12097	Total Wednesday	11815	Total Thursday	13082	Total Friday	10557	59691

	Total	Average finish time	Average weight T per day	Average wt per prop
Round 1	9041	12:31	15.56	8.61
Round 2	8591	13:30	16.21	9.43
Round 3	9005	11:53	15.60	8.66
Round 4	10055	13:20	16.88	8.39
Round 5	7600	13:22	13.19	8.68
Round 6	7886	14:01	15.45	9.80
Round 7	4641	11:54	10.67	11.50
Round 8	2872	12:23	8.64	15.04

Key		
	Yellow	Max
	Green	Min
Note	Rounds Are	7 & 8 smaller

ABSTRACT FROM AN AREA ON GIS REFUSE ROUNDS

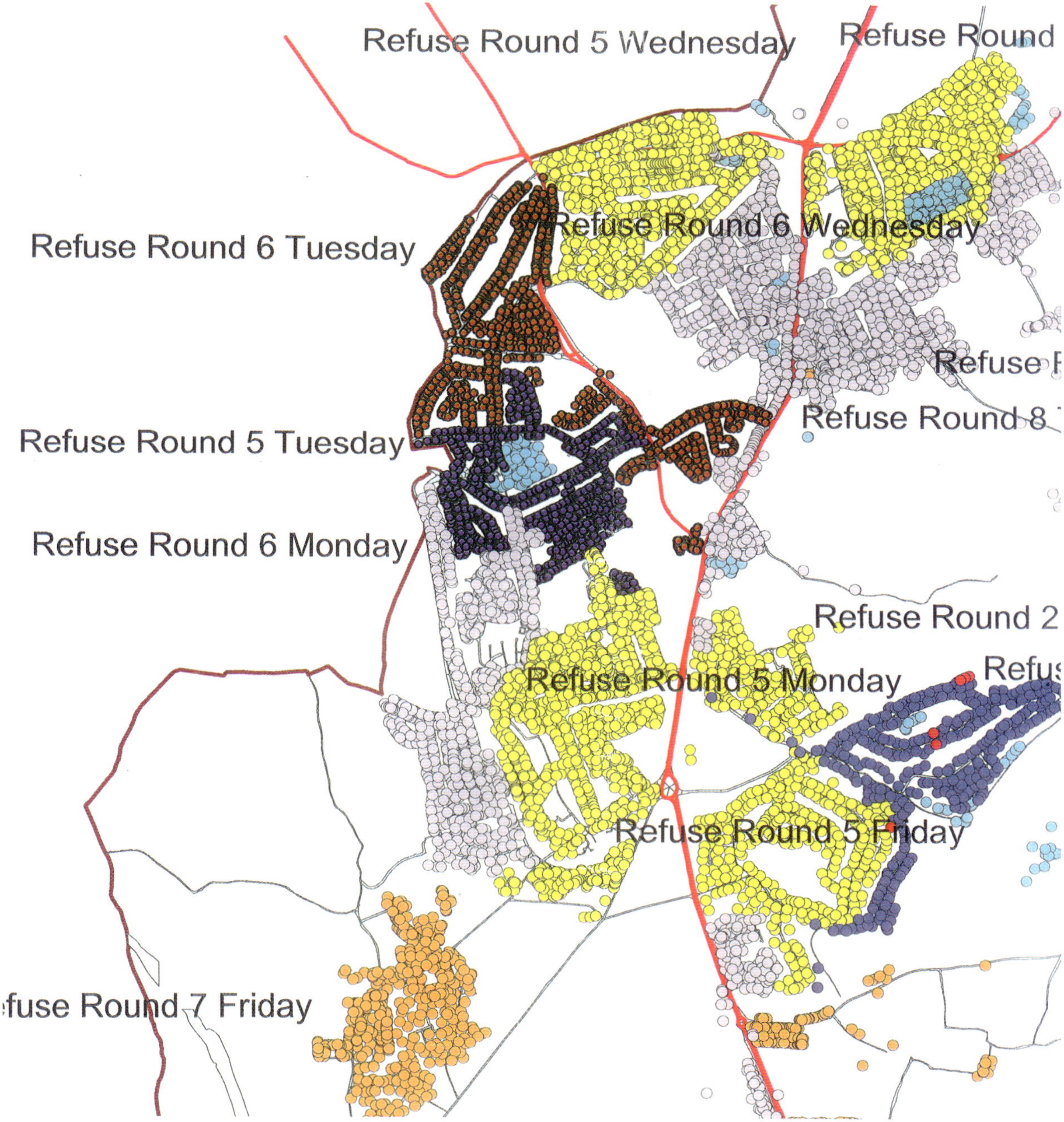

The capacity visioning report shows that the design of work to be allocated to each crew does not appear to be fair or reasonable. However, the above GIS abstract makes it quite clear that there was no form of rational design for refuse rounds whatsoever!

Each coloured dot on these plans represents a location for refuse collection. Each colour represents a day of the week for collection. Thus within a relatively small area of the council there were several crews collecting every day of the week. We also showed this in terms of the rounds making these collections; it was almost as random as the days of the week.

When I passed this back to the teams who had arranged the new garden waste collections mentioned earlier, they had simply said that garden waste would be collected on the same day of the week as refuse, never suspecting that there was a pile of spaghetti in that design, rather than what they had assumed to be one based on sound logic.

As a direct result of the review, these rounds have all been successfully restructured enabling the reduction of resources for both the refuse and recycling rounds, when the original intentions when first engaged, were to increase resources by a round for each.

Within our controls processes adopted from the council's way of working, I mentioned earlier that we kept a risk and issues log; these were again maintained with regular updates. While most risks reduced, the council failed to provide the staff needed for their thread, always being distracted by other pressures. They did not appreciate us updating the official risk log showing their area moving from green through amber into red, while all other issues gravitated to green.

After we applied as much pressure as could be exerted within the contractual tolerance, a fair amount of the council thread workflows were addressed by the contracted consultants in addition to our agreed work. These were completed to some extent at the end of the assignment, although not to the standard we would have been happy with.

The issues log was aimed at showing control by design; many of these were IT based, all of these were shared with audit. Part of the end of Plan is to ensure that the new designs meet the needs of the authority, without question, and in their entirety.

Using the issues log in this way, may seem a little over the top at first, but it both helps the flow of initial high level designs and then helps the detailing of sub-systems and support systems.

RISK REGISTER ABSTRACT

	Risk Type	Risks identified	Inherent Risk			Resp.	Control Measures	Residual Risk		
			Impact	L'hood	Total	Off.		Impact	L'hood	Total
1	Outcomes Risk	Availability of and dependency on key workers in core process. For example, sufficient involvement as outlined in Resources section in System Improvement Document, from customer services, back office support, crew, IT, Finance and Commulimations.	5	3	15	LM, DG	Highlight risk in System Improvement Document. Escalate to VFM Board if problem occurs	5	2	10
2	Resource risk	Lack of support and co-operation from Managers and Leaders from the Waste Collection System and other supporting systems, for example IT	5	2	10	LM, DG	Highlight risk in System Improvement Document. Work with VFM Board and request sufficient resources	5	4	20
3	Outcomes Risk	Lack of buy-in by key staff of the redesigned process	5	3	15	LM, DG	Highlight risk in System Improvement Document. Work with Managers and leaders of the system to increase buy-in	4	3	12
4	Outcomes Risk	Lack of time to sufficiently experiment with method as Experimentation is all about testing, learning and refining a better way of working	5	2	10	LM, DG	Highlight risk in System Improvement Document. Escalate to Lead Sponsor if problem occurs	5	4	20
5	Outcomes Risk	Risk to successful delivery of Waste Strategy	4	2	8	LM, DG	Highlight risk in System Improvement Document. Raise awareness if risks are not mitigated/managed	4	2	8
6	Outcomes Risk	Core Redesign Team is not empowered to make decisions on new ways of working whilst testing	5	3	15	LM, DG	Escalate if problem occurs	5	4	20
7	Outcomes Risk	Lack of operational leadership and support for Redesign	5	3	15	LM, DG	Discuss issue with operational leaders if appropriate. Discussed with George 16/1 and Jim 19/1.	4	2	8

Again this uses a RAG system to automatically draw attention to issues that may be occurring. The normal process is that any amber or red issues have control measures designed to reduce risk. The block to the right hand side can then be duplicated to show the position at one date, and then what the position is several weeks later. The details in this abstract have been changed for illustrative purposes only. In this case IT support is less than expected, and experimentation time curtailed.

ABSTRACT FROM ISSUES LOG

Issue No	Date raised	Raised by Validation Team VT	Issue Description	Issue type (Q,S,C	Priority (1,2,3)	(Resolution) Actions	Resolution needed by Redesign Team RT	Owner	Status (Open/Cl
			People Section						
1	18-Dec-08	VT	Lack of ownership	S		To be addressed in Redesign	RT	GS, DG, AC	O
3	17-Dec-08	VT	Level of service not consistent	S		To be addressed in Redesign	RT	GS, DG, AC	O
4	17-Dec-08	VT	Customer adherence to process	S		To be addressed in Redesign	RT	GS, DG, AC	O
30	17-Dec-08	VT	Non-consistency between 3 services	S		To be addressed in Redesign	RT	GS, DG, AC	O
6	17-Dec-08	VT	Lack of appreciation of Crew/BSOs/CS	S		To be addressed in Redesign	RT	GS, DG, AC	O
7	17-Dec-08	VT	Residents demand & expectations too high	S		To be addressed in Redesign	RT	GS, DG, AC	O
8	17-Dec-08	VT	Clarity of information to residents	S		To be addressed in Redesign	RT	GS, DG, AC	O
11	17-Dec-08	VT	Repeated calls	S		To be addressed in Redesign	RT	GS, DG, AC	O
13	17-Dec-08	VT	Poor communication - between teams and within teams	S		To be addressed in Redesign	RT	GS, DG, AC	O
			Materials Section						
24	18-Dec-08	VT	Different bins in different places	S		To be addressed in Redesign	RT	GS, DG, AC	O
24	17-Dec-08	VT	No agreed round list	S		To be addressed in Redesign	RT	GS, DG, AC	O
26	17-Dec-08	VT	Cases closed when not completed	S		To be addressed in Redesign	RT	GS, DG, AC	O
28	17-Dec-08	VT	Problems not rectified	S		To be addressed in Redesign	RT	GS, DG, AC	O
			Method Section						
36	18-Dec-08	VT	Focus on missed bins rather than success	S		To be addressed in Redesign	RT	GS, DG, AC	O
37	19-Dec-08	VT	Customer not fed back on resolution	S		To be addressed in Redesign	RT	GS, DG, AC	O
36	17-Dec-08	VT	Poor routes	S		To be addressed in Redesign	RT	GS, DG, AC	O
37	17-Dec-08	VT	Ad hoc process change	S		To be addressed in Redesign	RT	GS, DG, AC	O
38	17-Dec-08	VT	Lack of consistent standards for where the bin is collected from	S		To be addressed in Redesign	RT	GS, DG, AC	O
39	17-Dec-08	VT	Lack of confidence in system leading to incorrect use and dirty data	S		To be addressed in Redesign	RT	GS, DG, AC	O
40	17-Dec-08	VT	Customers don't know why bin was left	S		To be addressed in Redesign	RT	GS, DG, AC	O

The issues log ties back to the cause and effect chart, sub-divided by 'People, Materials, Method, Environment and Equipment'. As new risks are identified they were added to the bottom of each list. As designs are created, they were referred to this list for a 'conformance to need' check.

The next chapter picks up the end of the design phase by addressing *Appraise*. It is hoped that the documents in the last two chapters have helped demonstrate that between Check and Plan, that many of the council's existing procedures and documents can be adopted with an array of value adding methods and considerations creating far more value and self directed control than may be usually the case with a systems thinking based intervention.

Hopefully it will also show that a change of balance can be designed into the system, so in time there is less reliance placed on the PiD, project plan and governance, and more reliance placed on the regular involvement of the project sponsor with some key stage reports being presented to the board. That is there should not be monitoring and management of the process due to habit alone.

Endnotes

1 The four times impact is from personal experience and from feedback from similar end-to-end reviews. The hardest area to add value to is when winning an operational contract where virtually every aspect of work is tightly defined in the specification. To be able to add value, some freedoms are needed, the greater the freedom, the more the scope to add value. That is why Check includes for mapping out boundary conditions, and why later phases may identify where those conditions inhibit improvement.

2 Activity Based Costing can be a useful indicator for comparing methods, however, using ABC as a prime system of compare can lead to creating 13,000 elements for £9.00 a time rather than 10,000 for £10.00 each. Designing out demand often is cheaper than reducing the cost of each element. There are further references to this later.

3 Quality or Politics deals with management by distrust, where controls, procedures, governance and risk management look at every way the council could be corruptly managed and then apply all those aspects of distrust to people of the highest ethical standing, purely because a small minority of people do abuse the system.

4 Failure demand is any work that doesn't go right, missed bins, incorrect invoice payments, slow payments, leaking roofs, flooded houses, unpaid benefits.

5 If an IT system is designed and implemented in the same way as the initial service is designed, then it will meet operational and reporting needs in a totally seamless way.

6 Refuse and recycling were collected separately, thus unless a road was inaccessible the chances of a normal customer having both materials missed on one day were very similar to winning the national lottery, that is 1 in 14,000,000. These twin reports nearly stopped being passed through overnight.

7 Liker in *The Toyota Way* p224 says Toyota actually use the phrase "Genchi Genbutsu" meaning "going to the place to see the actual situation for understanding". He goes on to say "Gemba" is a term that has become more popular. It refers to the "actual place" and means about the same thing as "Genchi Genbutsu".

8 Peter Scholtes sadly died in 2009, he was a tremendous supporter for the work and ideas of Deming. He worked with Joiner Associates in the USA passing on many accolades to his whole team. He was also a great supporter of the Deming Forum in the UK.

9 Meddling (or tampering) is a term to explain the difference between managing with good intentions as opposed to designing with knowledge. Meddling can occur from managing by walking about. "what's that doing there, throw it in the skip", can lose a large item for a job that was specially produced but wouldn't fit in the van. Or altering a sub-set of a large database for one part of an organisation can corrupt another element downstream, which then needs to be addressed. Computer programmers can have full time work correcting their last mistake!

10 Affinity diagrams can be used to consider core issues and all aspects that impact on the core issues. The diagram for Fear of Crime is not correct in many ways, but was useful to enable multiple discussions with stakeholders across several weeks, which in turn informed action plans in several organisations.

11 Nomad plus has a wealth of integrated project delivery mechanisms, with GIS based analysis of needs and deliveries, these can be accessed via the SSD website from this page number reference.

12 Pipeline options would include ideas from workshops or from an *Appraise* process creating thoughts as to how the service may be improved to delight customers, expanded to new work areas, or create options to add value generally.

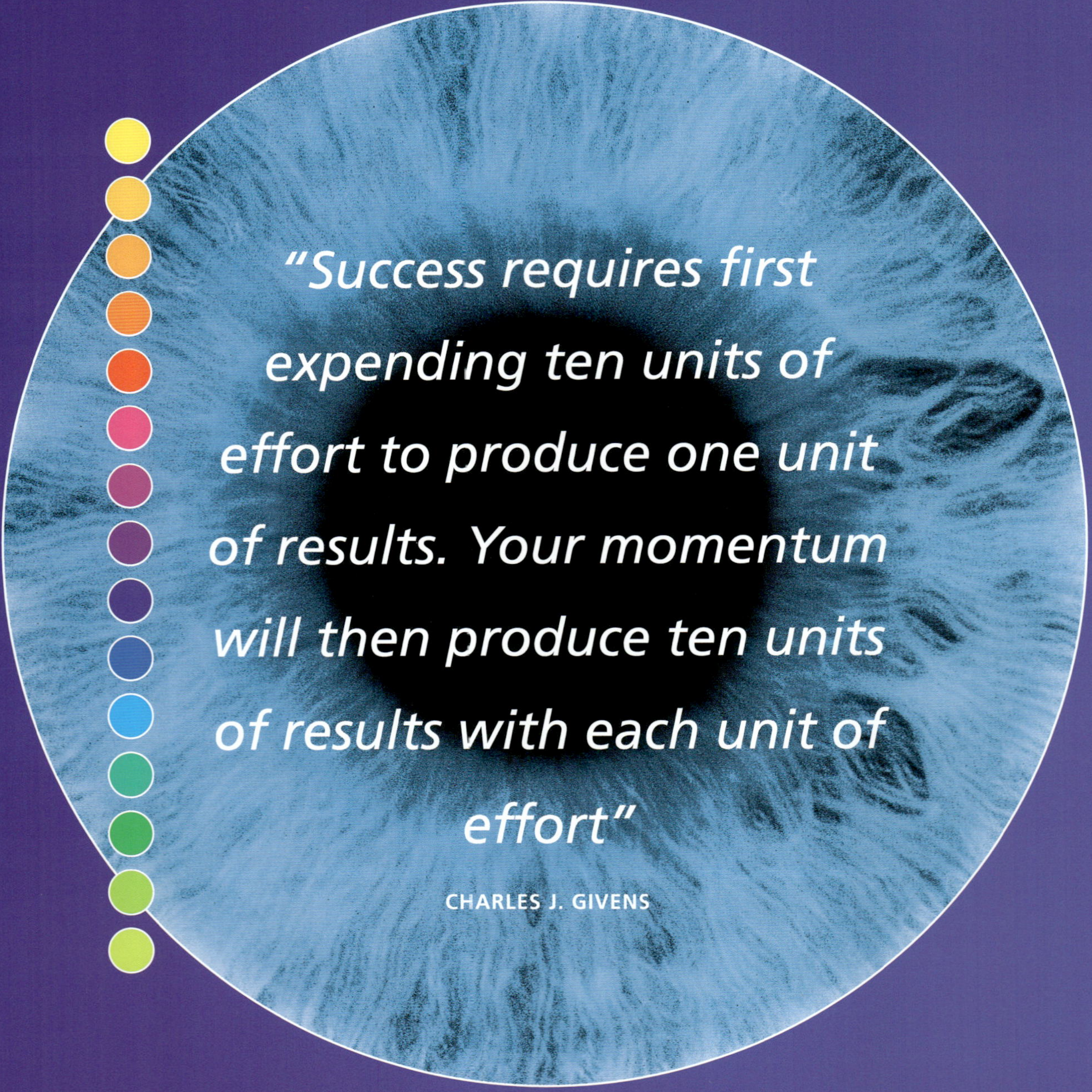

"Success requires first expending ten units of effort to produce one unit of results. Your momentum will then produce ten units of results with each unit of effort"

CHARLES J. GIVENS

Appraise has been added to the normal 'Check Plan Do' review cycle in order that wider dimensions can be added to a transformation review. In some ways the initial works of Deming would have included *Appraise* in that reviews took many years to work through. Deming is quoted as stating 'Continuous Improvement will take five years for an organisation to achieve[1]'.

During those five years the (Deming) chain reaction and normal operational evolution would have occurred with a great deal of customer interaction in between. Now the whole world works quite differently, such that, for example an E2E review will occur in months rather than years, which could run the risk of creating a new design without fundamental consideration for the business and legislation issues that could also be addressed. This is why there is an *Appraise* element, examining all pipeline options and the business positioning as a whole, creating innovation as a result.

APPRAISE WORK ACTIVITIES

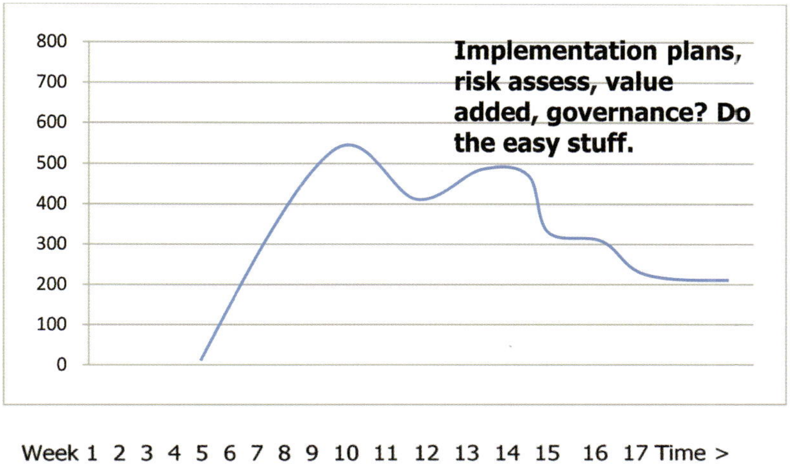

So *Appraise* is an additional wash over the entire Check Plan phases with a view to maximising the benefits which are possible.

Chapter ten addresses many examples of what *Appraise* can look like within an operational context. It is hoped that future books can address some industrial and Health Service aspects in the same way.

Within Plan, we saw how a waste collection service was to have additional residual and recycling rounds at a cost of over £200,000 per annum; in fact they have already implemented improved services with fewer rounds. In any consulting concern that would be taken as an exceptionally successful intervention. However, the design of these services from an adding value aspect had aspirations to achieve even beyond that.

The *Appraise* elements of the review highlighted that flats and high density housing were not recycling as much material as they could do. There was a strong potential demand from businesses to reduce the costs of trade waste, which was further pressured by the £8.00 per tonne annual increase in landfill tax; thus a trade recycling service was very easy to establish. The value of recyclates had not been fully understood, thus by isolating those values and showing their impact visually, it was easy to see that some investment into separating recyclates would greatly increase their value.

The service cost to continue collecting trade waste would have increased by over 9% per annum as a result of landfill tax and other pressures, however, with recyclates continually increasing in value, the actual cost to collect recyclates was likely to reduce year on year. See the simple graph below to compare impacts.

SIMPLE GRAPH TO SHOW TRADE WASTE AGAINST RECYCLATES COST

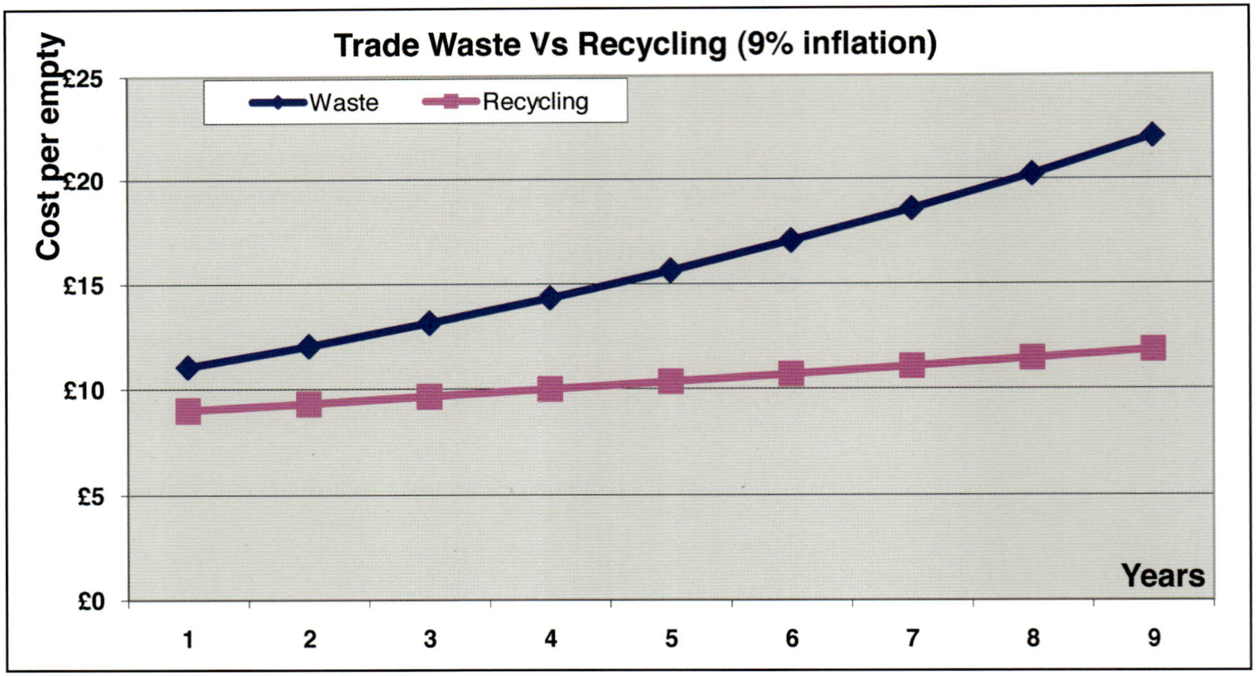

The initial target for the waste strategy was to achieve 60% household recycling for around £300,000 a year extra budget. The initial operational review for the rest of waste services was to improve the customer service element and try to halt the increase in costs.

The combined outcomes will take some while to be fully realised. In the first year accounts were improved by £600,000 revenue even after the adding in the cost of the intervention, which was considerably improved by a saving of nearly £400,000 in capital costs.

The second year revenue savings are on target for £1,000,000, there should be no reason why £1,700,000 per annum shouldn't be the out-turn savings, even in a relatively low value recyclates market. When recyclates values increase, this will get dramatically better. The domestic recycling rate should achieve around 68%, while commercial recycling should achieve over 40%.

PIE CHART FOR RECYCLATES VALUES

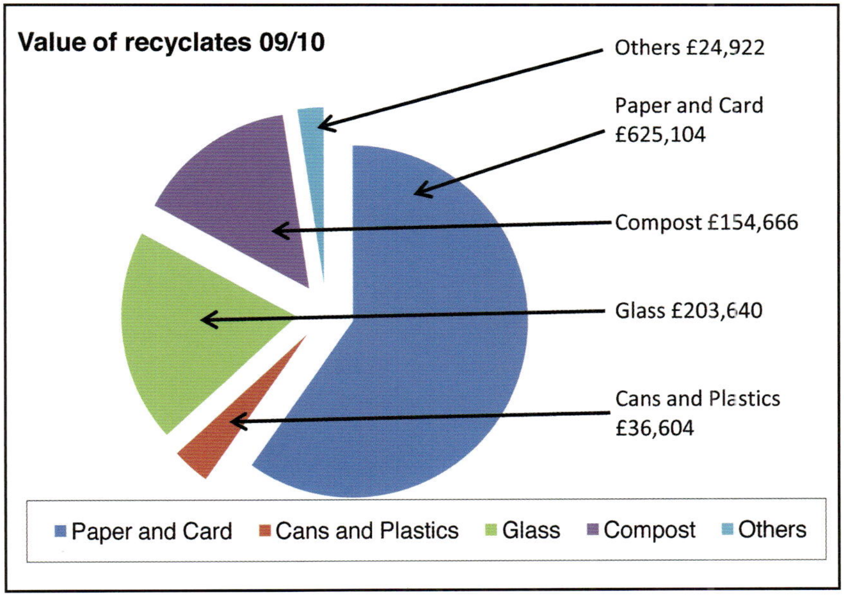

There had been no initial aspiration to divert trade waste! These two graphs enabled its inclusion.

I initially produced this chart for members and senior managers alongside the actual and predicted tonnages with values of materials per tonne, which is confidential information.

That created a great deal of interest when it was suddenly very clear that the materials were worth £1M a year and increasing. At that time they didn't have the capacity to realise the potential.

The service was, at that time, operating in such a way as to use the recyclates team far more on customer complaints and missed bins, fighting the poor IT system and doing a monthly rework of a financial budget which was more wrong than right. The amount of time a team of three had to spend on recycling development was very small; however the missed opportunity was worth nearly a million pounds a year.

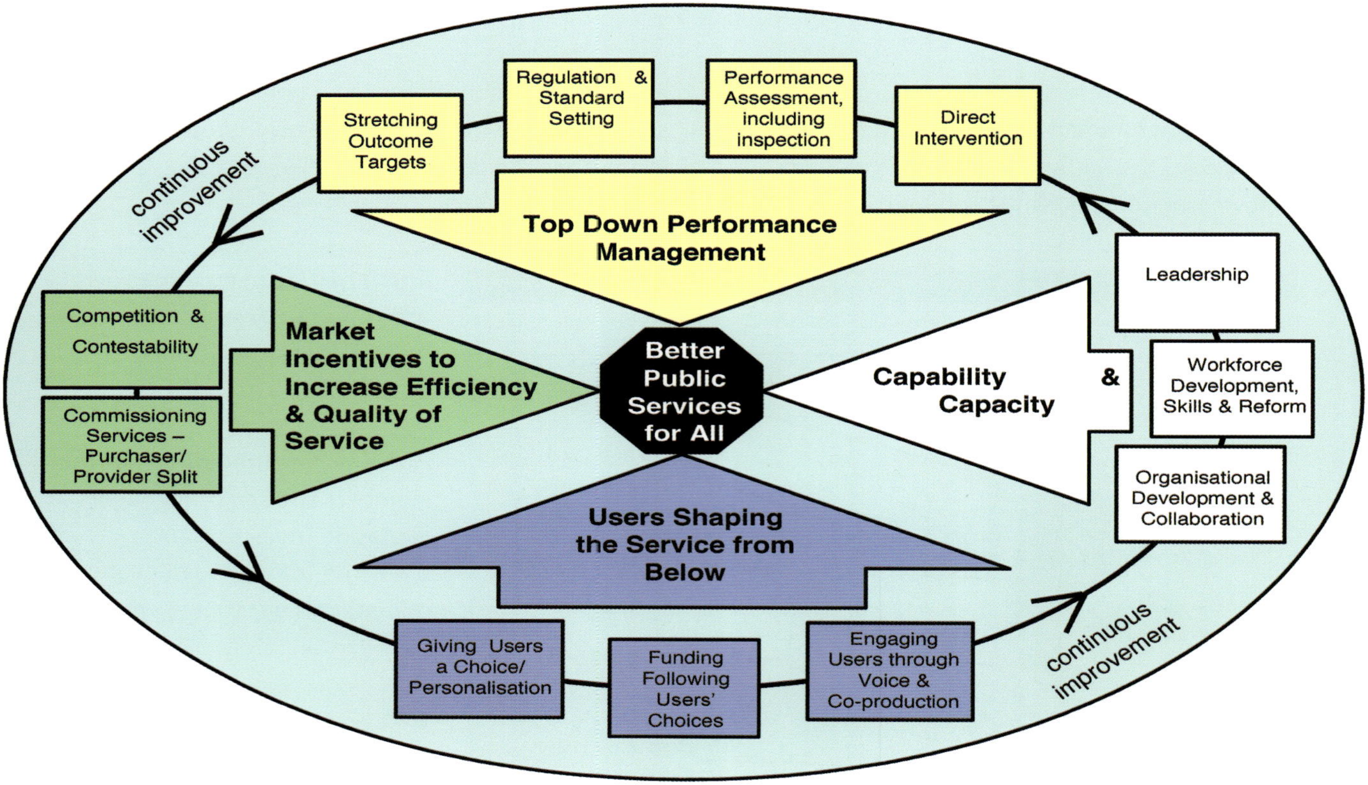

This uses the term 'continuous improvement,' but believes that quality needs to be incentivised, i.e. that you pay more for better, rather than quality improvements lead to lower costs and greater capacity. This also believes that a stretch target is good; where we have seen costs reduce from £300K to £70K while time took 2.65 days instead of 90 days (without stretch targets!). These are not the sort of targets to discuss at the outset? However, this holistic design shows that central government do not want to create designs in isolation. Note also there is no mention of information within this model.

So what transforms a reasonably challenging set of outcomes under traditional project management terms to one, that should, on its own, stabilise the council's accounts for many years? Well the first point is to understand the business you are in. If the leader of the Transformation Team hasn't got good relevant industry experience, then either the sponsor or a senior team member must have that business acumen.

REAL TIME STRATEGIC CHANGE PRINCIPLES

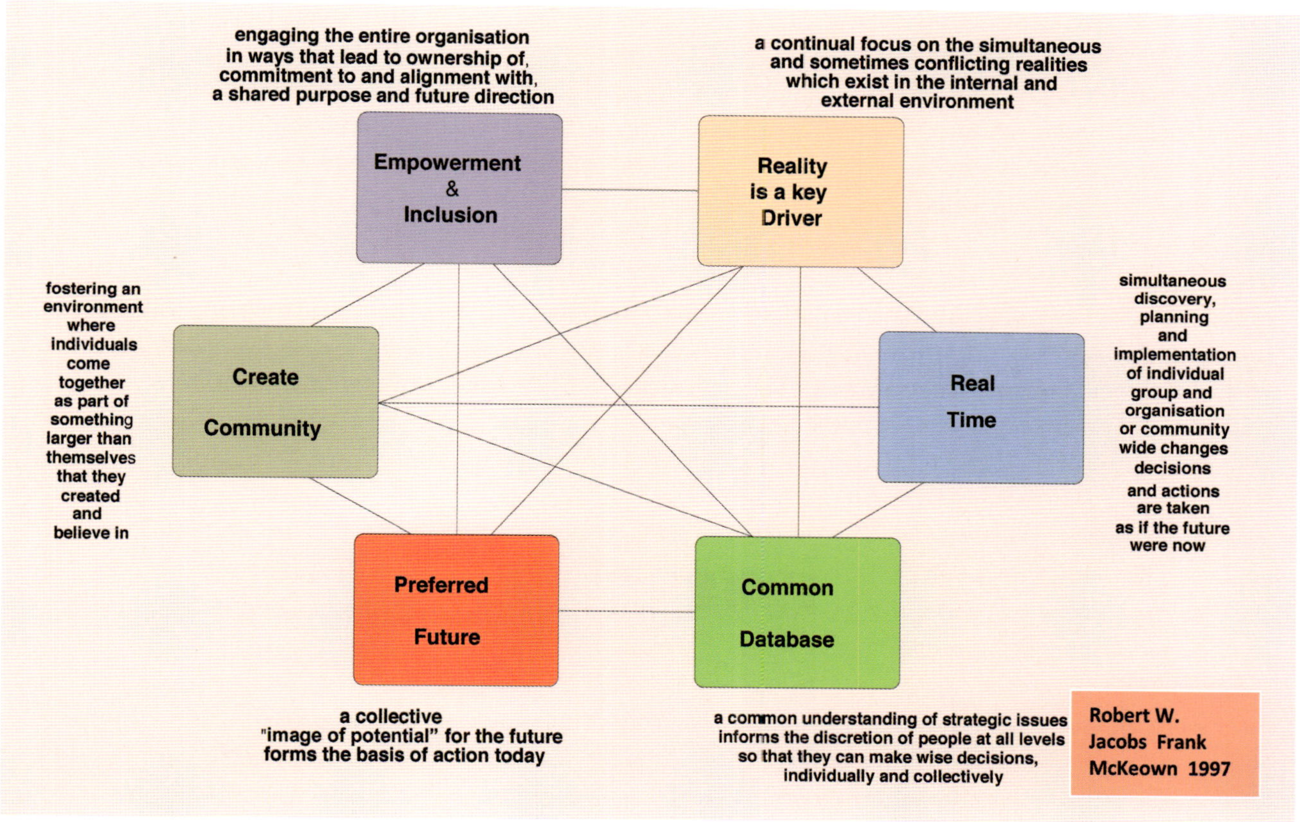

The real time model above may apply more, as corporate trust in the intervention systems develops. Visualising Transformation will create capacities; the more pragmatic the organisation becomes the more likely these capacities will enable an acceleration of improvements, rather than getting to a traditional complaint about 'death by initiative'. As stated earlier, if change management attains the same thinking patterns that apply to normal operation management, then empowerment will be more of a reality.

You need to look at the resources that are being released by the 'check plan' processes and envision what could be done with them. You need to look at the performances of the resources currently used and ask, 'Could these add even more value to the organisation?' Then return to some of the initial discussions within Check. What are the aspirations of the council, what are the strategic and operational improvements that are being sought? In addition, would a conventional SWOT analysis help with this process?

Use a wash of all the council's initiatives and values: equalities, health and safety, deprivation, supporting business, environment, carbon management, fraud, risk management, the third sector, LAA, LSP, victim support, etc. Think about how each of these could be addressed or help with the future service designs.

It's worth trying to link these concepts together in several different ways, use affinity diagrams, mind maps or cause and effect charts to see these to their best effect. Are there combinations of aspects that could come together in a better way? Look at the prime contracts which are in place – could smarter working with partner organisations enable better value for money? Could you use a unique selling point to gain strength?

In the previous cases we asked the organisations who buy their recyclates how we could add value to the products? Approach some other firms in the same business, what would they pay for these materials, what difference would it make if x and y were separated? What difference would it make if they were compacted? Look at haulage, if it takes six vehicles to take 20 tonnes not compacted, how many would it take compacted? Could you have a trailer behind that lorry to redouble your capacity again?

At another authority where a new fortnightly recycling collection had been rolled out quite quickly achieving far higher recycling rates than ever before, they had missed vital information while pushing the service to wider and wider geographical areas. This was in part due to externally imposed reductions in staff levels prior to completing the roll out.

They were monitoring all of the feedback with an array of spreadsheets and graphs. Due to the pressures and need to get to more and more properties with the service, some short-cuts were taken with their monitoring. When their data was compared to itself, via a business analyst, it was found that some impossible paradoxes existed.

We analysed the data, cleaned up some incorrect formulae, and combined data from three sources. What we discovered was that while the tonnes of recyclates recovered per fortnight were increasing, the amount of recyclates per collection per property was reducing.

There had been a reduction of staff numbers to save a budget of less than £25,000 a year, the amount of lost recyclate per annum, compared to what they had been achieving was worth £370,000 a year. The ultimate achievable would have been better than that. Key learning point: ***Savings based on cutting budgets led by accountants will often cost more in the long run.***

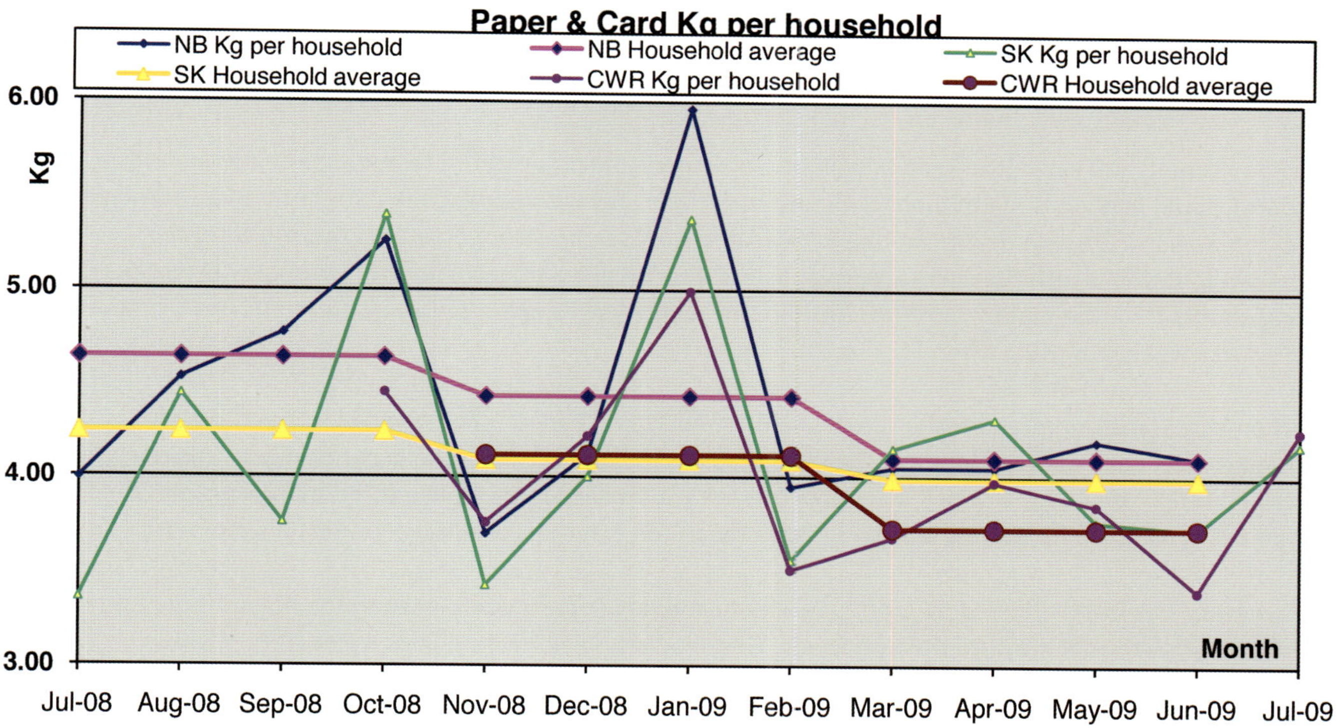

It took a trained business analyst (BA) about five days to find the opportunity to save £370,000 a year under an *Appraise* direction. Clearly this form of return wouldn't happen every week, but a BA would only cost a fraction of the sum that could be saved every year. So why were the accountants pushing for reductions in staff to save money? There needs to be a new paradigm for accounting as well. Remember also that a focus on ABC (Activity Based Costing) can reduce elemental costs but at the same time lead to considerable E2E costs. (i.e. debtor chasing versus car park total income.)

The addition of the trend lines above show the clear downshift from 4.6 to 4.1 Kg per household per fortnight. While 26 Kg per household per year doesn't sound like very much, multiply that by 160,000 households and factor in the difference in value of selling paper and card as a valuable commodity instead of paying for disposal; this then starts to create quite a large value indeed.

The same BA spent some time with the call centre staff listening to calls, checking the systems of work and logging calls. After three days work the BA was able to identify a dozen causes of system error; these would both impact on customers and operational rectification. From an NI 14 perspective the redesign, which only took another day, would save some 60 calls a month, which was around 30% of that service area failure demand calls. We also realised ways to promote some additional 'pay for' service opportunities.

By developing and actively using BAs who are inquisitive and empowered to make recommendations a council could save around ten times their cost every year. Yet I regularly speak with BAs and performance team leaders who are in despair because they can always see these opportunities but the culture of the organisation is such that they are never listened to. The council would prefer to employ external consultants from the biggest, costliest firms in the country, to listen to your staff and simply pass on the messages when you could listen for free. Strange world!

When true Transformation is achieved, those BAs and Team Leaders employed by you in your own change team will have developed an enormous ability to continue from the progress made. Their trained insight will add far more than most officers within a business. Unlike some change systems one significant measure for success is to no longer rely on the external consultants originally employed.

However, your staff will need to continue to learn and develop, so don't listen to the accountants who would try to stop their future training funds. That would be a huge long term mistake! Remember Deming's 13th point, 'Institute a vigorous programme of training and self improvement.'

Most of the above is a simple drift from traditional systems thinking work, a mixture of process analysis and redesign with attention paid to trends that are not in the host interest. There were some aspects of the interventions mentioned previously which were deliberately not related to one another at that time.

The changes to the refuse and recycling rounds structures would enable more properties to be collected per day by more efficiently designed rounds. As a direct result there should be:

- ✔ More reliable working which is easier to manage and correct i.e. less failure demand
- ✔ New properties to be absorbed onto rounds without issues as they are part of design
- ✔ An ability to show the rounds via GIS on a website, so customers can use a postcode to see collection days

- ✔ As work is far closer together there will be less travel, less congestion and less fuel
- ✔ The rounds become far more 'Carbon Effective'
- ✔ No more actual work per day than originally planned per team.

However, this is where additional business linkages are applied to the systems thinking redesigns via an *Appraise* process.

The straightforward option above is to reduce by a round, perhaps redeploying one crew member and making two redundant. There would also be a saving of £150,000 against the intended capital purchase of the next refuse compaction vehicle (RCV).

However, domestic refuse usually takes a driver plus two loaders for wheeled bin collections, while trade refuse would use a driver and loader only. If trade recycling can be started up such that it replicates the systems within domestic recycling, dealing with the same commodities, but with bigger containers, then a new market can be captured.

You already have a vehicle, fuel and crew entirely funded from your existing domestic service. If that crew could transfer over to recycling, then 90% of that additional income will be in excess of any additional costs. There will be the need for advertising and cold calling, some new bins and administration. However, administration has been released due to less complaints and more effective designs.

The costs associated with collecting and selling on recyclates is considerably less than collecting and disposing of waste, and will get less every year. So the approach to your existing customers is based on; "Would you like to save money and improve your environmental credibility?" Most businesses will jump at a new contract which is 20% less than their existing service which also has a plus factor.

However, the larger clients will often retain the same amount of bins for residual waste, thus the new recycling bins could be additional to, not replacement of, residual bins. While at the smaller end, there will be a tendency to slightly reduce the amount of residual waste containers and divert that into a slightly larger volume of transactions for recycling.

Effectively while one service is created with a growing volume of new income, the income from the previous 'waste only area' doesn't reduce much. But, as more waste is diverted from tip, the costs of disposal of waste will considerably reduce. So the cost of trade waste gets cheaper quickly while the income from trade recycling improves substantially.

The next phase is even better, because you are the only effective small volume trade waste recycler in the area, more contracts are won for both trade waste and trade recycling. Capacity will have been created by less bins being emptied on one side, while trade recycling will have lots of growth potential.

There should be a massive growth of profit, with virtually no set up costs, enabling local businesses to promote 'greener' credentials, this is a genuine win-win with a fast track to an extra quarter million pound surplus realisation.

A second phase using the spare capacity from the 'back office' recycling team who are now adding value to recyclates, is that they can promote carbon reduction services to the new 'trade recycling club', offering free site visits to assess opportunities to gain Government funding to further reduce energy costs.

This further supports the development for several NI demands which previously the council had no capacity to address, and could even enable a win-win arrangement with a contractor, or in house team, for carrying out insulation and energy efficiency work, including for the council and LSP.

Returning to that recyclates team, they could also add value to the materials being collected and sold on. For instance say the mixed paper and card is worth £40 per tonne as it is, but with a little more attention to keeping glass and plastic contamination down, it would be worth £47 per tonne. £7.00 extra for say 12,000 tonnes adds £84,000 to the income.

Another link comes in; remember the driver plus two became a driver plus one? Well, if that loader were redeployed to keeping the depot tidier and reducing cross contamination, you have 'free labour', plus extra income. The normal alternative would have been the cost of redundancy. This would create a net gain of £65,000 per annum rather than a saving of £19,000 from reducing the labour force.

The recyclates team should also be more available for recycling promotion, remember the run chart earlier where promotion led to a discernable increase in recyclates? Then there is the thorny problem of collection services for flats. If 10,000 flats were able to recycle on average 2 Kg of materials extra a week, that's over a thousand tonnes of extra recycling and a thousand tonnes less disposal. This gain was worth around £90,000 a year, increasing quickly every year due to landfill tax!

As a by-product the secondary issues of fly-tip and rats will also reduce around these flats. Flats and shops will reduce their usage of litter bins in lieu of refuse dumping, thus enabling cleaner streets. This would reduce the demands on street cleansing, the call centre and environmental health.

Cans and plastics mixed together are worth around £40 per tonne. They weigh very little when loose and cost more to transport than the income from them. Separately {that is as mixed plastics, steel and aluminium} they are worth about £170 per tonne and then they can be compacted saving depot space and reducing haulage costs. If four times the weight is taken per load, you can have the other ¾ of that haulage person feeding simple machines to separate them. {The plastics firm will supply the compacter/baler if you have enough material} This could gain a further £30,000 a year.

In addition to the project board members who gained insight and learning from the interactive processes of investigate, test and inform, we also reported to the value-for-money scrutiny committee, so the wider corporate body could be informed of progress. In general they received our presentations with delight.

The methodology of reporting to the board and scrutiny were based on the use of PowerPoint with a number of high impact diagrams, graphs and tables using colours to draw attention to certain details. These tended to be iterative, in that a story develops showing where we started, quick wins, service improvements, capacity releases, uses of that capacity and then the expanding opportunities and potentials which are being released.

The project board were given a range of potentials so they could see the projected minimum, median and maximum likely benefits from the work threads; they directed which elements to use in presenting to scrutiny or the cabinet. Sometimes they would go for a mixture of 'risk' options dependent on their view of each element. At all times support services such as audit, accountancy, IT and HR would be fully engaged and appraised of options being developed.

The final report for the major waste redesign was only 27 pages long, even with several run charts and the GIS plan for the weeks collection rounds. We added several appendices and case studies. To assist the inquisitive we created a CD with hyperlinks from the main report to the supporting documents, and even some forms of drill down from report to report.

The concept was to place stunning, compelling information into the hands of both the decision makers and those who must work in the system. Those who simply wanted a summary report had one, while those who wanted deeper information had that too. The project board agreed that this CD should be provided to the project board, the cabinet and everyone who was in the Intervention Team.

So this invaluable information was in the hands of members, directors, senior officers, drivers and union officials. All could see the plan and understand where the information was coming from. The critical path analysis (on page 37) provided the integration plan for all the threads, clearly showing interdependencies.

There were twelve appendices, which are summarised as;

- ▷ Waste and Recycling prototype designs
- ▷ A collection policy, collection operating procedure and complaints policy
- ▷ Detailed plan for the order of new ways roll out
- ▷ Completely new baseline budget
- ▷ The outcomes from quick wins and learning from experimentation.

In addition there were seven case studies detailing the added value in far more depth than the pen picture above for trade recycling. These were:

1. The restructuring of rounds, with detail of who, when and how
2. Commercial and Garden Waste development plans
3. Weights Management data (to have a single input, multiple use of information)
4. Recyclates, how to add to volumes and value
5. Linking the vehicle management system to the financial system to avoid duplications
6. Developing flats services and the gazetteer
7. Managing with information.

The overview for Visualising Transformation is shown on the next page, this shows how the continuous improvement cycle can work, how phasing of elements will be built in and how the particular thread can interface and benefit from other threads. Again this chart is available at www.supportservicesdirect.co.uk/visualisingtransformation.

Overview of Visualising Transformation

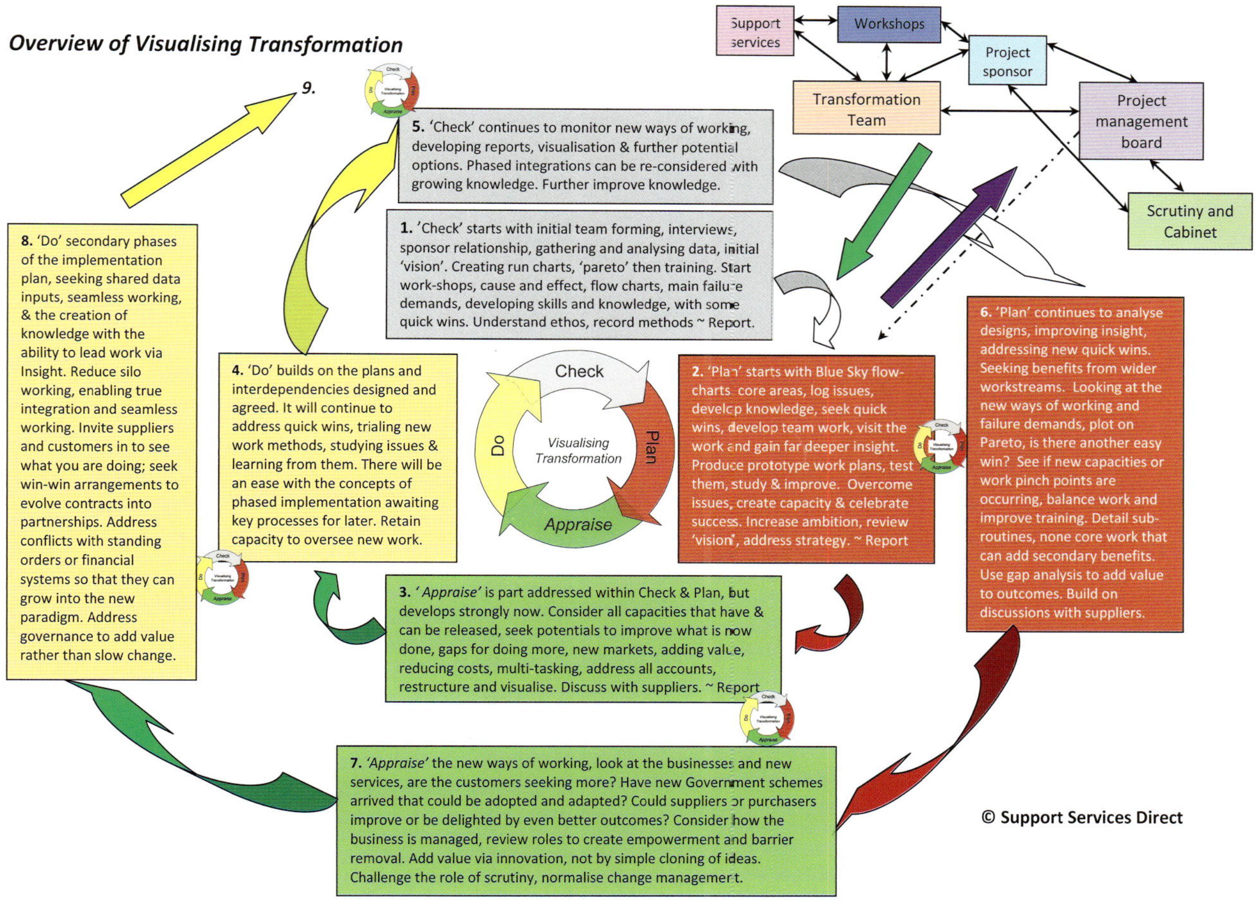

Adding value via tertiary considerations becomes easier with every review. This holistic approach is actually a great deal of fun if it's managed well and the opportunities exist in the service being addressed to add value in this way.

Applying this way of work lately has helped my hosts save £2.2M in capital (plus a number of chance conversations re IT systems), and around £10.6M a year in revenue. So far, not one intervention has led to a redundancy. They all have better customer care, better environmental outcomes and a better opportunity for the future.

The specific options discussed above were built up from an array of options to use, discard or come back to. The use of the 'Check Plan *Appraise* Do' cycle within the design phases built up the concepts of experiment and test to work out whether something would work in the current or emerging culture, how it would integrate with other options, how it could be phased in and whether there was a customer demand or need for the options.

The PRISM training included an iterative work design model which helped create a can do aspect for the team. This helps to create a team which is very comfortable in raising issues or possibilities that their previous culture would not have listened to, with a cross section of people involved in every element under consideration.

Holding the corporate culture to a 'no job losses agreement' until an array of capacity using options was achieved wasn't too much of an issue, but the financial pressures often led to a hunger for those quick capacity reduction possibilities.

The project board were excellent in many ways; they demanded wide thinking options appraisals to be presented and didn't complain when the waste strategy gave them around 150 options and sub-options to consider on a single spread sheet. (This was three sheets of A3 landscape.)

Part of the reason for no complaint was that all those options were ranked from 0 to 10 which fed into a colour coded RAG format based on 'cost, customer and environment' with a summary column also colour coded for the three combined elements.

Thus they never went through the options line by line, simply asking why one ranking was used in certain areas, enabling a rapid whittling down to 25 contenders, six main options, three best options, (with a late sub-option added) and a final presentation to cabinet of the best two distinct options recommending one as the preferred.

Details were added and scrutinised for every iteration, then challenged and improved. Without those processes from the project board, the designed outcomes would not have been so stunning. Having established this working relationship with the strategy, evolving it for the operational working and then the value for money interventions became relatively easy.

The concept of an evolving story is important within the 'Check Plan *Appraise* Do' approach, the project board were not expecting the answers at Check, but were always pleased with operational quick wins and improving insight.

The immediate resolution of the garden waste problem was manna from heaven. They knew something was going horribly wrong with a new flagship service, so good news was an ideal start to the intervention. This was a very special case of a quick win.

The analysis of the garden waste service created two elements of pro-actively overcoming unforeseen issues. The first was due to a sudden world wide lack of new wheeled bins. Much of eastern Germany was moving over to improved recycling habits and a three week lead-in for bins suddenly became horror stories of 50% dearer and four months longer. On the cusp of this becoming public knowledge the council procured the bins to meet its needs as a matter of urgency.

The design and management of the whole garden waste project was light on operational detail as previously mentioned. Unfortunately the project title had led to a lack of breadth of operational awareness. Garden waste collected on a door to door basis had been carried out for several years, every year increasing the number of customers and the weight of material to be composted.

The design of the new service was based on the experience of several other councils who had initiated a wheeled bin collection service almost as a new service, without creating an established demand pattern. However, the current service was based on a bag purchase approach, with no actual awareness of how often or where those bags could be placed out for collection. Thus we may know who has bought some of the bags, but not know how many customers may use them.

We had a service where one person could buy bags for ten others, we would have no record of where garden waste bags would be placed for collection, and then our collection teams would scour the district looking for bags placed for collection. I was none too complimentary about the effectiveness of design.

COMPOSTED MATERIAL RUN CHART, BY WEIGHT

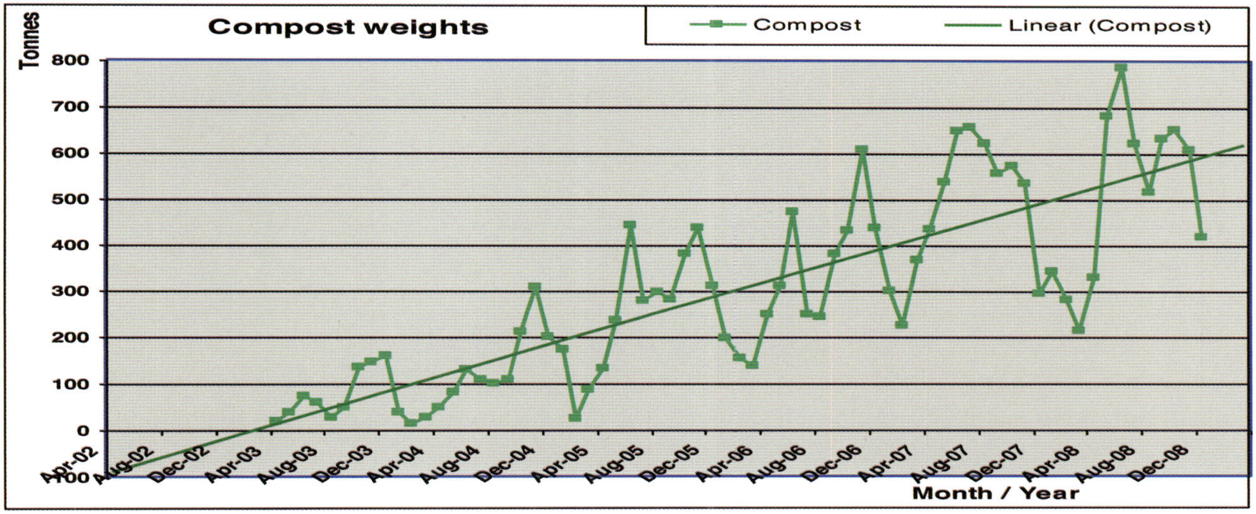

The run chart for compost weights was created after the project team had started work, from an array of spreadsheets held by the recycling team. The distinct seasonal variation was known, but no one had questioned why there was so much material in December through to February when very little material would come from the customers' gardens.

So that started me thinking where that was coming from, I then discovered the following information. Again this chart was created some time into the garden waste service design; I became very interested in the initial reduction from around 500 tonnes a quarter to nearer 300 tonnes a quarter, followed by another drop to just over 100 tonnes per quarter. The streets were being swept more often to an increased cleanliness ranking, so why was materials to tip reducing?

RUN CHART OF STREET CLEANSING MATERIALS TO TIP

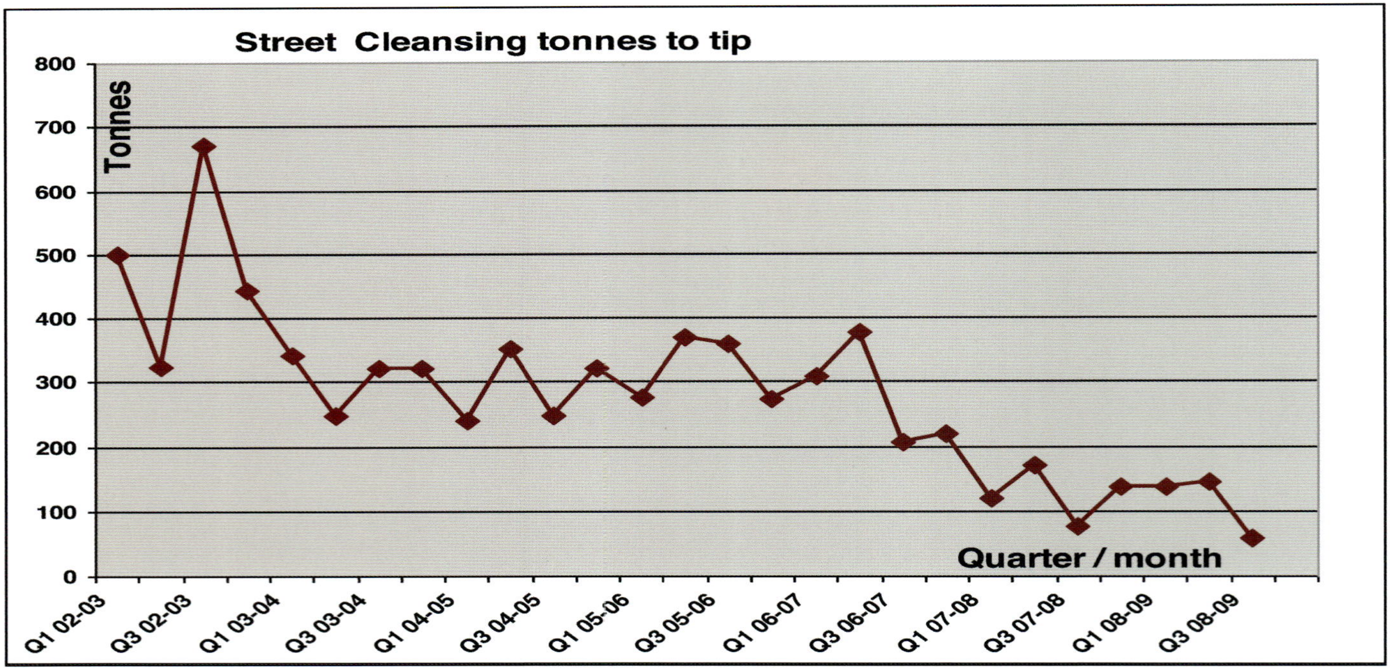

The first answer was that leaves collected from streets and public areas were being added to the garden waste material, and then it had been agreed that silt and grit swept by machine could also be added so long as they were mainly free of litter and allowed to dry off prior to mixing in with the garden waste.

Therefore, the new garden waste service design parameters were too narrow; there had been no consideration as to how these secondary materials would be dealt with. Had the additional information not been provided from outside of the 'PRINCE2' comfort zone, both the costs and environmental outcomes would both have suffered considerably.

Two other elements of monitoring are pertinent here; one was the actual weights of garden waste collected per day. The refuse manager collected the daily paper sheets from the weighbridge for all garden waste, entered them onto a spreadsheet which was then never used by anyone.

I cleaned that data, and created a run chart below to map the variation of demand, creating the weekly totals of materials collected, a trend analysis plus a cumulative chart, which is not shown.

RUN CHART FOR GARDEN WASTE TONNES

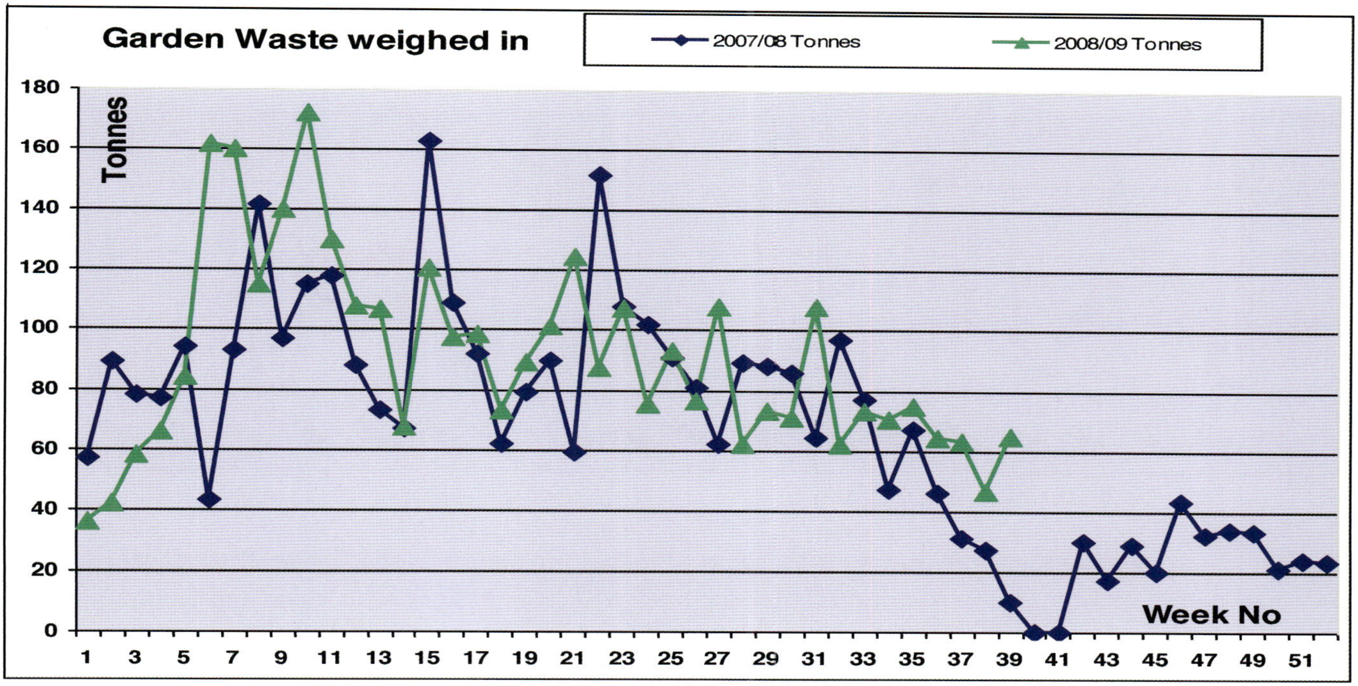

There are several reasons for volatility of service demands and outputs. These include: Temperature, rainfall, bank holidays and when the rain falls. If it rains early in a week, and is then warm and dry over the weekend, far more material will be collected. If it rains over a weekend, less material will be collected.

Notice the difference between the chart on the previous page compared to the one on page 149, for two weeks over Christmas there was no garden waste, while all compost materials shows quite a healthy output through the winter quarter. If this were considered in a control chart fashion, the peaks would most often coincide with bank holiday weekends, to show special cause.

RUN CHART FOR GARDEN WASTE AT A LARGER AUTHORITY

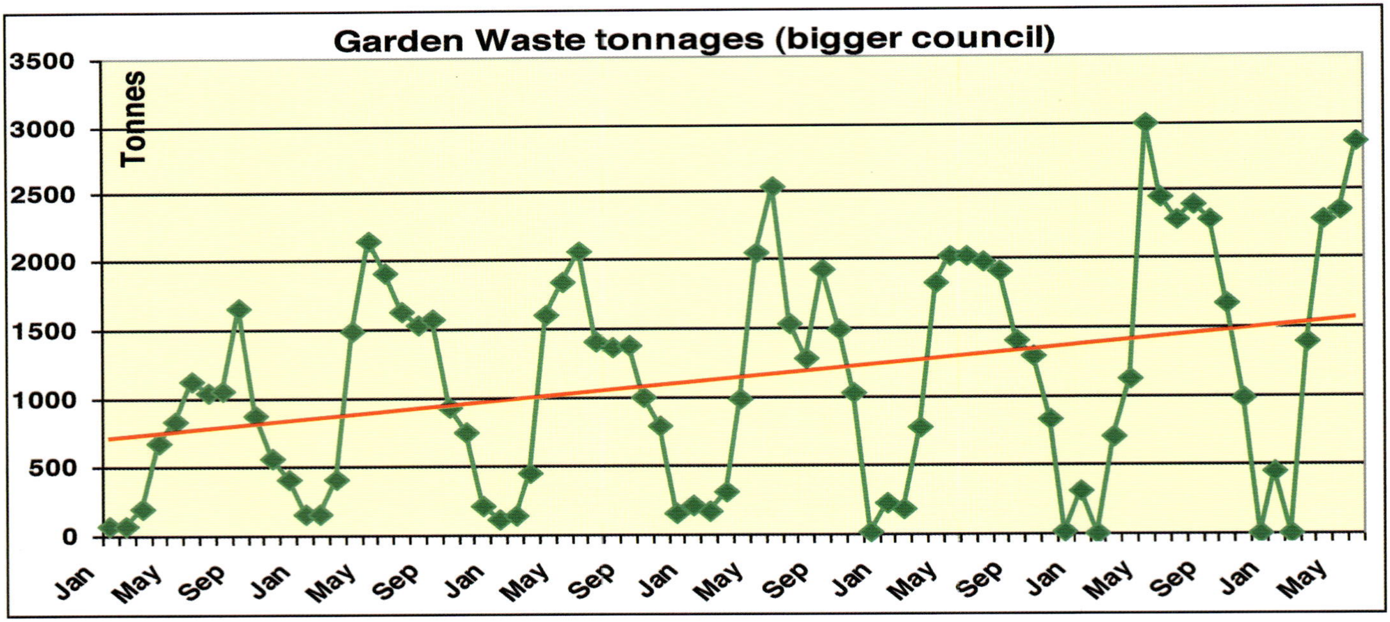

I'd like to compare the earlier run chart for compost weighs (on page 149) to this one. The first council had started collecting garden waste and realised that it had capacity to bring in leaves and silt (detritus) from street cleansing and materials from parks and gardens that they couldn't compost on site. It was a small authority where communications and opportunity were easy to work with.

In the far larger authority where this run chart was taken from, the head of waste was very good and achieving significant improvements for waste diversion, but would have been missing the thousands of tonnes a year additional and possible. That is a potential loss of around £60 per tonne between dispose of residual waste and treat to create compost. Many people believe there is an automatic economy of scale, these two graphs show that isn't an automatic relationship.

RUN CHART FOR WEATHER TO PREDICT GARDEN WASTE TONNAGE

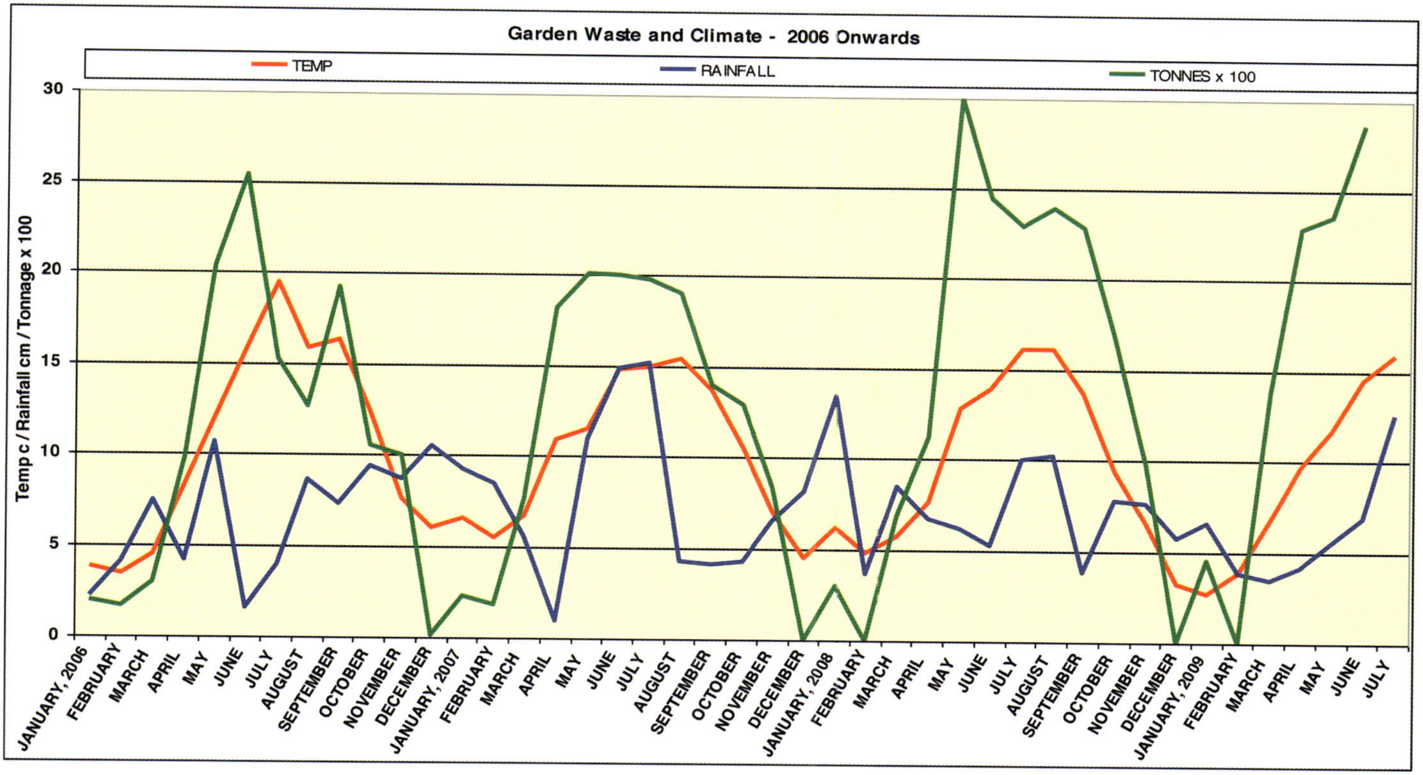

The above run chart was from the larger authority. The initiative and thinking to create this relationship to forecast demand was very imaginative and commendable. This is an example of someone who wants to create information from data – a brilliant piece of work, which would have been complimented had he also established the impact of the service being expanded to more households each year.

As can be seen above, using collected information to forecast future demand is difficult; the volatility above sends strong messages for caution[2]. The more this is summarised, the less predictable it may be, even though that flattens the spikes away. Within those parameters, forecasts are needed to ensure capacity and financial models are sound. This would be greatly complimented with automatic data harvesting and information generation. The prime focus was to predict resource demands.

In the smaller authority I used the array of graphs and supporting information to forecast the overall tonnages for recycling, compost and residual waste, factoring in initiatives, plans and background information where possible, to create a non-linear quarterly forecast for residual, dry recyclates and garden waste, for the year. I also used the daily returns at the start of the garden waste process to forecast when a re-order of bins would be needed, keeping in mind the lead-in concerns for bins.

RUN CHART OF DAILY ORDERS FOR GARDEN WASTE SERVICE

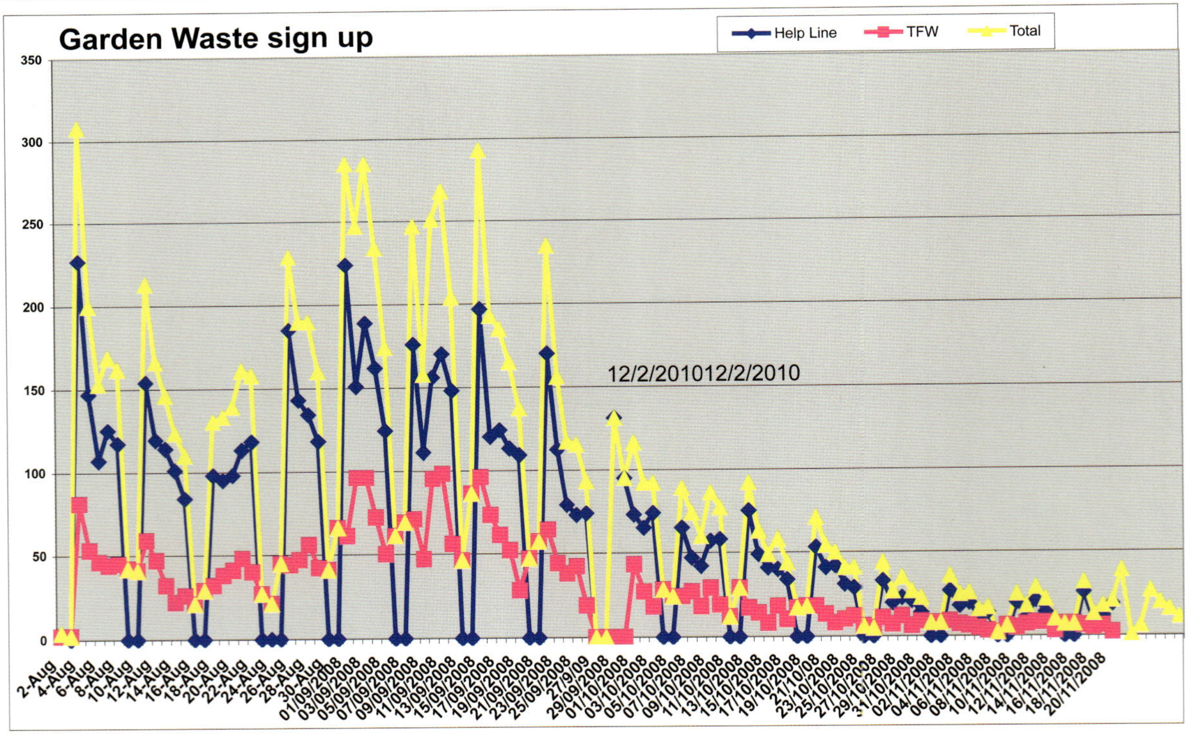

Reports of demand were registered daily, both from the call centre and via the internet (TFW above). I summarised these weekly, used the daily orders, as above, to forecast when demand was going to outstrip the original design forecasts in terms of service need and thus income returns. I was also then able to demonstrate when we would likely have calls coming in and no bins to distribute. Thus both the timing of the next order for wheeled bins and the size of it were modelled from the data we recovered.

RUN CHART FOR NEW GARDEN WASTE BINS

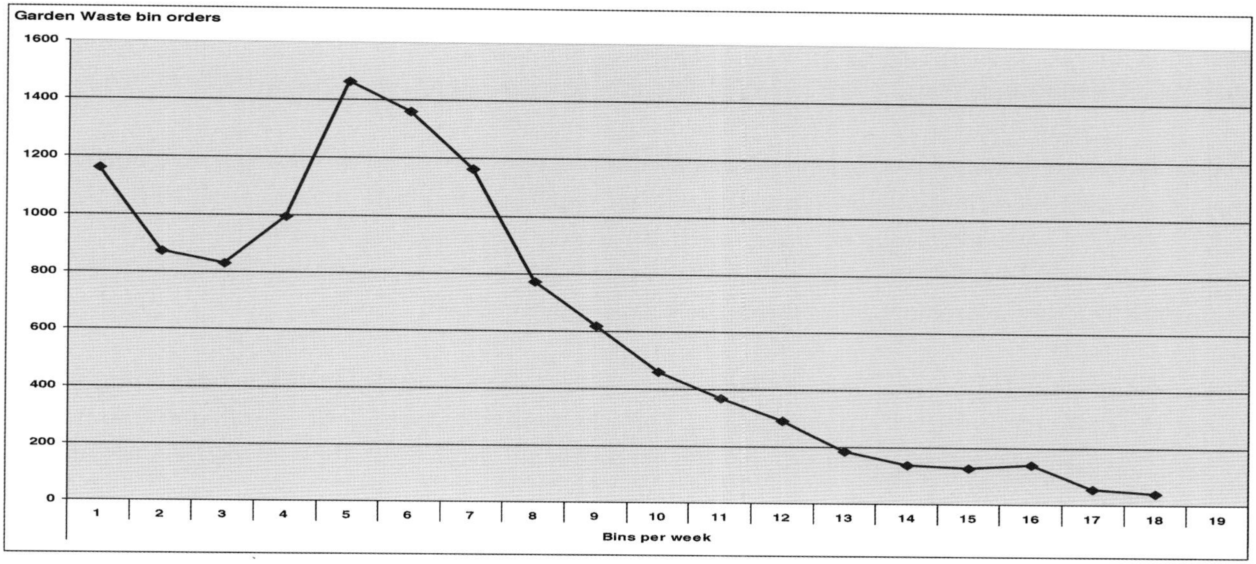

The high demand in week one came from many of the current customers and people who learned about the service from the website and customer services shops. We then carried out a mail shot campaign segmenting the district from north to south. The first year take up design which had been predicted was exceeded by the end of week 12; the need to re-order wheeled bins was before then due to lead-in time.

I have deliberately strayed from *Appraise* crossing between Plan and Do, focusing on the aspects of creating and harvesting good information and how to use that. The whole Visualising Transformation process is driven to reconsider boundaries, which is why we always listen to issues and return to them.

The design omissions within the traditionally managed garden waste project as described above; could never have occurred from a well-led systems thinking review, as that systems thinking review would be led by a genuine facilitator who knows all that they should do, ensuring great training and knowledge transfer to and from the Intervention Team at all times.

This is part of the reasoning to create Visualising Transformation as a regulated concept: to avoid charlatans and rogue businesses who bring discredit to perfectly sound systems of work. The majority of current consultants and 'lean practioners', both add value and improve service – we merely seek to guarantee this.

The *Appraise* aspects that were applied to the above intervention were to remodel forecast demand, to ensure bin deliveries were able to match demand in addition to bin procurement and to re-forecast the whole budget in a more enlightened world where the secondary issues were factored in. This was then fed into the whole waste transformation financial forecast model which follows.

The financial forecasting in a council needs to be robust, realistic and open to scrutiny. There were four main aspects to the review with dozens of sub-options, some managerial re-shaping enabled pragmatic assessment of vehicle and resources future needs. With greatly improved management information, decisions were taken with knowledge rather than instinct. This helped for instance to immediately reduce the vehicle replacement plans across the borough by £400,000.

The whole revenue budget was re-based via an agency accountant working alongside operations, whose work was then vetted by council officers. This was done from first principles so that the strategic options could predict not only what the changes would be, but move those forward in absolute clarity.

Care was taken to evaluate each new element of work on its own, and then to ensure that any potential double counting of benefits was avoided. The phasing of work, growth of capacity and timing of elements all added to the overall summary cash flow outputs. These were all agreed with operations management, the sponsor and relevant support services, prior to being reviewed by the project board.

The whole process was anchored on a single spreadsheet with additional information added as it evolved, in such a way as the components were all individually agreed. Where material was imported from previous work the visual appearance was retained so as to keep a strong link from previous awareness to the new emerging broadest / integrated plan. This is shown on the next page as the blue/ white inset box in the top right corner.

The following abstracts from that spreadsheet have had some numerical alterations as specific contract prices and sensitive information was originally included. The included impression has been designed to remain very similar to the original design outputs.

Valuation of Forward Plan (5/02/09)

Improve

1. *Seeking to commingle glass collection.*
2. *Using capacity released from commingled glass to add other material capacity.*
3. *To sell plastics to a new outlet in Lincolnshire, gaining a compactor as part of the deal.*
4. *Expanding into other plastics for recycling.*
5. *Revitalising the expansion of services into flats (using additional information from GIS)*
6. *Reducing over-servicing individual customers while improving service delivery.*
7. *Analysing the balance of round structures with a view to creating more capacity / save costs.*
8. *Considering the re-routing of all rounds to improve service delivery and align with waste rounds.*
9. *Replacing the garden waste IT system with a designed commercial waste system.*

		Tonnes	Price	Credit	Value	Improve
1	**Commingle Glass**					
	Current position	2,700	£2.00	£50.00	£140,400	
	Proposed position	2,970	£10.00	£50.00	£178,200	£37,800
	Note	Also releases 1 1/2 hours a day to commercial recycling)				
2	**Released capacity**	(mainly target paper and card)				
	Current position	1,200	£10.00	£50.00	£72,000	
	Proposed position	1,350	£10.00	£50.00	£81,000	£9,000
3	**Sell plastics to Yorkshire**					
	Current position	100	£10.00	£50.00	£6,000	
	Proposed position	150	£60.00	£50.00	£16,500	£10,500

Collected from bring sites

57 Communal, 38 School sites, 6 Micro sites

Composition	annum	Each week
Total	4,100	78.9
Paper and Card	1,090	21
Cans and Plastics	100	1.9
Glass	2,700	52
Textiles	180	3.4
Fridges	30	0.6
Others	1	0.02

Residual waste collected from household wheeled bins

From 44,000 houses and 11,000 flats.

(*Based on current properties and waste contents report)

Composition	Per annum Tonnes	Percent	*Average property
Total Weight	30,779	100%	10.76Kg
Paper and card	3,863	12.55%	1.35 Kg
Plastics	3,995	12.98%	1.40 Kg
Metals	933	3.03%	0.33 Kg
Garden waste	1,385	4.50%	0.48 Kg
Mixed Glass	1,508	4.90%	0.53 Kg
Food waste	11,157	36.25%	3.90 Kg
Other recyclable	1,287	4.18%	0.45 Kg
(Not recyclable)	6,651	21.61%	2.33 Kg

Potential all recycling (Collect and bring schemes)

Composition	Per annum Tonnes	Recycle percent	Not recycle
Total Weight	50,706		
Paper and card	12,893	25.4%	1,391
Plastics	1,357	2.7%	2,717
Cans	909	1.8%	336

The nine listed elements (top left of the above chart) all had their current capacities and prices listed followed by a scripting of the potential changes in volumes and values. This allowed the various projections of positive outcomes to be shown in red, signifying a reduction in price or an increase in income values.

The corporate base-budget document for the whole service had been based on repetitive indexation with lump sum alterations from a budget several years ago, all changes being basically shown one at a time.

The chart below shows aspirations from the interventions while still in the early stages of Plan. At that time we were showing around a £1.1M annual saving which was expressed as a simple graph.

EARLY FORECAST OF REVENUE SAVINGS AGAINST COSTS

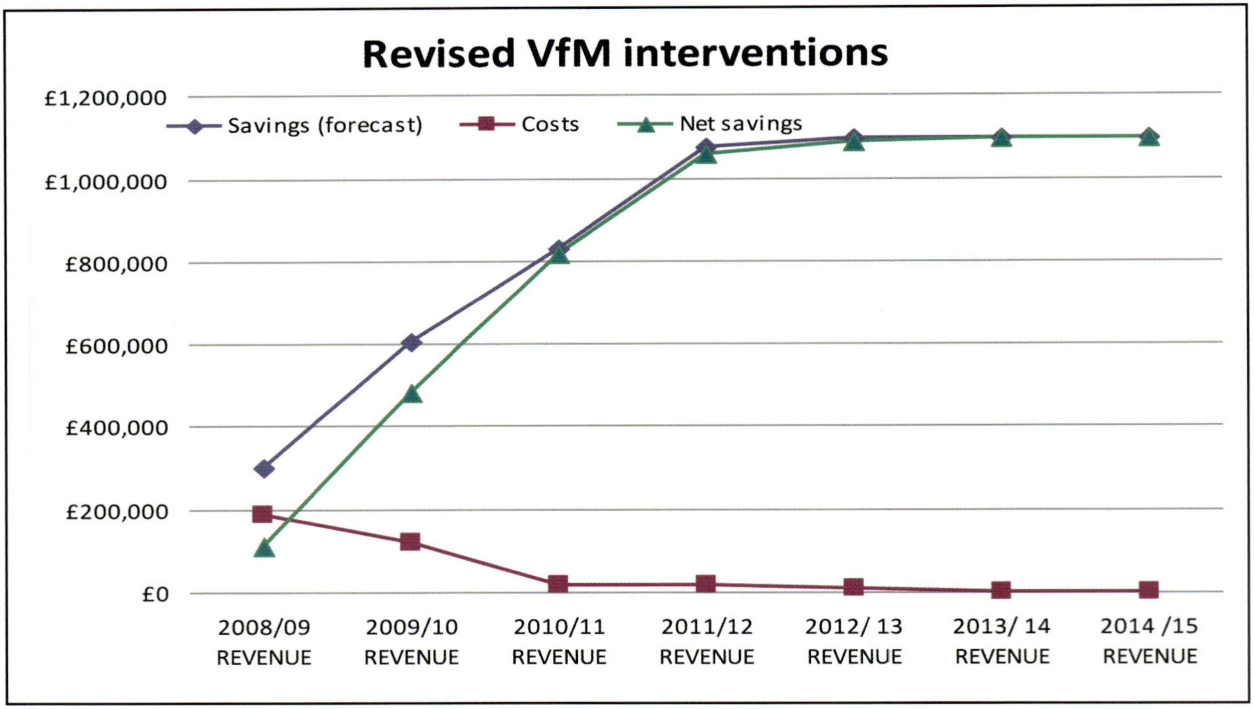

It was while we were exploring the capacities being released and some of the gaps in opportunities which could be explored that the impacts from *Appraise* started to become clear.

As previously stated we were addressing four broad review areas at the same time, the IT area was lagging behind, so its benefits were added later. We broke the IT elements down into three areas: commercial waste system, back office system and vehicle tracking (with two-way data interface to the other systems).

Elements of those systems were shown as either a cost or savings; each block was set up as a whole page for printing at that time. (These are simplified and adapted to fit onto a page here.)

ABSTRACTS OF COMMENTS AND COSTS FROM ELEMENTAL ANALYSIS

Commercial Waste System		
Cost of System	£20,000	
Benefits operational	Comment or cost?	
Round structure held in a system	Would give clarity of operations for business expansion and cross cover	
Detailed crew sheets created daily	Would give clarity of operations for business expansion and cross cover	
Clarity of who did what when	Trace-ability should be part of waste management	
Ability to record exceptions daily	Additional works and unable to gain access	
Ability to create improved costing structure	Use hire of bin plus cost per empty, would attract larger customers	
Ability to hold layers of costing (ref / rec)	Factor cost per empty between waste and recycling	
Reports for work	Weights per round, finish times, non-corrected work	
Benefits financial	Annual saving	
Automated system for billing	£4,067	Single invoice per customer, one integrated process
Loss of income from exceptions?	£8,550	1.5% of total turnover
Ability to place people on stop	£2,000	Bad debt and insolvency more likely now
Enable more surplus from service via expansion	£6,000	Improving controls will enable less resources used, than now possible
Enable more surplus from Garden Waste	£6,000	a wider service from the same overhead
Annual saving	£26,617	

This was replicated for each area under consideration with the annual savings totals hyper-linked into the final summary analysis. We addressed most threads of work in this way. Pricings were informed by demonstrations of equipment and software from various suppliers, together with intelligence gathering from neighbouring authorities and via customer enquiries.

The next stage was to evaluate the outcomes from the core work designs. We showed the first phase of this as creating capacity and through that how much savings could be achieved, then we compared that to value added.

TRADITIONAL SAVINGS MODEL FROM REDESIGN

Description	Current resources	Costs	Proposed resources	Cost	Traditional Saving £
Veh mtc / finance link	Admin 1 hour per day	£5,981	Reduced to	£2,805	£3,176
Reduced volume of refuse errors	BSO's 36 hours a week	£30,120	BSO's 18 hours a week	£15,060	£15,060
Reduced volume of refuse errors	Rec. Mgt. 25 hours / wk	£46,191	Rec. Mgt. 10 hours / wk	£18,476	£27,714
Reduced volume of refuse errors	Ref. Mgt. 18 hours / wk	£33,257	Ref. Mgt. 10 hours / wk	£18,476	£14,781
Reduced volume of refuse errors	10% of Cust Serv.	£35,000	5% of Cust. Serv.	£17,500	£17,500
Domestic Refuse rounds	8 rounds, Dr. + 2	£1,202,092	7 rounds, Dr. + 2	£1,051,831	£150,262
Collect recyclates from flats	7 rounds, Dr. + 2		7 rounds, Dr. + 2		£0
Stop over-servicing refuse	Collecting wrong side waste		Increase rec / less wst.		
Reduce double handling comm wst	7 people involved		3 people involved		
Align all weighbridge data	From 7 people		50% more data, less people		
Use vehicle tracking to reduce vehicles	Parts of many		Better use, reduces OH's		
Increase Garden Waste services			Diversify and grow services		
Improved information / dashboard	Nearly all NS officers	£48,805	BSO's , then by design	£16,268	£32,537
			Total Savings	Traditional	-£261,029

This shows from these aspects that some £260,000 a year could be saved with several aspects un-priced. It was around this time in the review that we started to harvest some GIS information. That started from only a few hours induction and training for their GIS, with basic access enabled for the BA to some newly linked data.

At this point, near to the end of our review period, we were then able to visualise the existing round structures for the first time (as per the earlier abstract on page 129).

This was very stimulating, enabling new dialogue to commence on additional opportunities where we had to rely on instinct and the opportunities from vehicle tracking previously.

ACTIVITY BASED SAVINGS, UTILISING SPARE CAPACITY TO ADD VALUE

Current resources	Costs	Proposed resources	Cost	Traditional Saving £	Value added	Third year Saving £
Admin 1 hour per day	£5,981	Reduced to	£2,805	£3,176	Grow commercial waste	-£200,000
BSO's 36 hours a week	£30,120	BSO's 18 hours a week	£15,060	£15,060	Grow commercial waste	
Rec. Mgt. 25 hours / wk	£46,191	Rec. Mgt. 10 hours / wk	£18,476	£27,714	Increase recyclates value	-£15,155
Ref. Mgt. 18 hours / wk	£33,257	Ref. Mgt. 10 hours / wk	£18,476	£14,781	Helps enable round less	
10% of Cust Serv.	£35,000	5% of Cust. Serv.	£17,500	£17,500	Capacity to expand	-£17,500
8 rounds, Dr. + 2	£1,202,092	7 rounds, Dr. + 2	£1,051,831	£150,262	7 rounds, Dr. + 2	-£137,000
7 rounds, Dr. + 2		7 rounds, Dr. + 2		£0	Sell recyclates	-£28,291
Collecting wrong side waste		Increase rec / less wst.			Sell recyclates	-£33,802
7 people involved		3 people involved			Comm waste system	-£10,067
From 7 people		50% more data, less people			Back Office system	-£16,991
Parts of many		Better use, reduces OH's			Vehicle tracking	-£93,757
		Diversify and grow services			More work same resources	-£137,055
Nearly all NS officers	£48,805	BSO's , then by design	£16.268	£32,537	Not 6 people on same job	
		Total Savings	Traditional	-£261,029	Value added	-£689,619

The previous table showed the ability to save £260,000 a year. By using the spare capacity and reinvesting it into a series of initiatives which could be developed in parallel, this shows that the third year savings could be nearer £690,000 per annum. We allowed new services to grow slowly; some would be quicker than three years, others slower. This gave some breathing space to the project, and allowed the savings to be prudent.

The art within this whole practice is to bring people along within a journey. No one involved in the review at the outset was discussing savings of this significance, the iterative stages of discovering improvements, releasing capacity, discovering gaps and opportunities enables the ambition to grow. Doing this all in parallel to developing a new policy was very important, as it allows more areas to be questioned and addressed. One of the biggest problems with the old CCT legislation was that a specification gave no opportunity to design.

FORECAST FROM LINKING ALL ASPECT OF REDESIGN AND APPRAISE TOGETHER

Original 'Budget plan'

Budget Flow		**2008/09**	**2009 / 10**	**2010 / 11**	**2011 / 12**	**2012 / 13**	**2013 / 14**
Base Budget	Expenditure	£3,345,678	£3,455,970	£3,542,369	£3,630,928	£3,721,702	£3,814,744
	Income	-1,654,321	-1,695,679	-1,738,071	-1,781,523	-1,826,061	-1,871,712
Original Net Budget		£1,691,357	£1,760,291	£1,804,298	£1,849,406	£1,895,641	£1,943,032
Changes from base budget:							
Removal of growth refuse round		-£135,678	-£152,178	-£272,678	-£272,678	-£272,678	-£272,678
Removal of growth recycling round			-£52,020	-£52,020	-£52,020	-£52,020	-£52,020
Increase in commercial waste surplus		-£75,432	-£119,121	-£187,565	-£275,432	-£275,000	-£275,000
Increase in recyclates income		-£372,781	-£410,578	-£465,778	-£465,778	-£465,778	-£465,778
Improvement in garden waste position		-£149,945	-£230,000	-£287,000	-£317,500	-£331,000	-£349,000
Improved vehicle utilisation			-£7,667	-£16,100	-£23,000	-£23,000	-£23,000
Increase plastics and values			-£8,851	-£17,702	-£46,502	-£46,502	-£46,502
Improve values of recyclates			-£15,686	-£31,529	-£47,058	-£47,058	-£47,058
Increases in recycling to flats + marketing			-£10,104	-£28,291	-£40,416	-£40,416	-£40,416
Tracking, back office and comm waste system			£20,000	£113,383	-£201,972	-£201,972	-£201,972
Recycling Plan via phasing					-£229,526	-£459,052	-£459,052
Systems Thinking intervention and training		£156,789					
Increase in haulage and collection costs		£72,020	£73,436	£77,842	£82,512	£87,463	£92,711
Unknown and contingency costs		£75,319	£55,000	£56,375	£57,784	£59,229	£60,710
Additional costs			£153,832		£100,000	£100,000	
		Revised Forecasts					
Forecast net budget		**£1,261,649**	**£1,056,354**	**£693,235**	**£117,820**	**-£72,143**	**-£136,024**

This budget has a number of alterations from the original, but is similar to the actual outcomes. The council was uncomfortable with the current cost and increasing strain that it was facing, at the time of commissioning a review. This five year plan would reduce revenue expenditure by £8.7M, while increasing customer services and environmental achievements with no redundancies. Therefore when all other councils around them are forced to increase the pressures on the recession by increasing charges and reducing employment, this council was able to work better and smarter while at the same time enabling businesses to reduce waste disposal costs. Most elements show the full value being achieved over two to three years.

In general the forecast savings were so much greater than anticipated that it was decided to report quite conservative outcomes, the spreadsheet and graph are not the best outcomes we modelled.

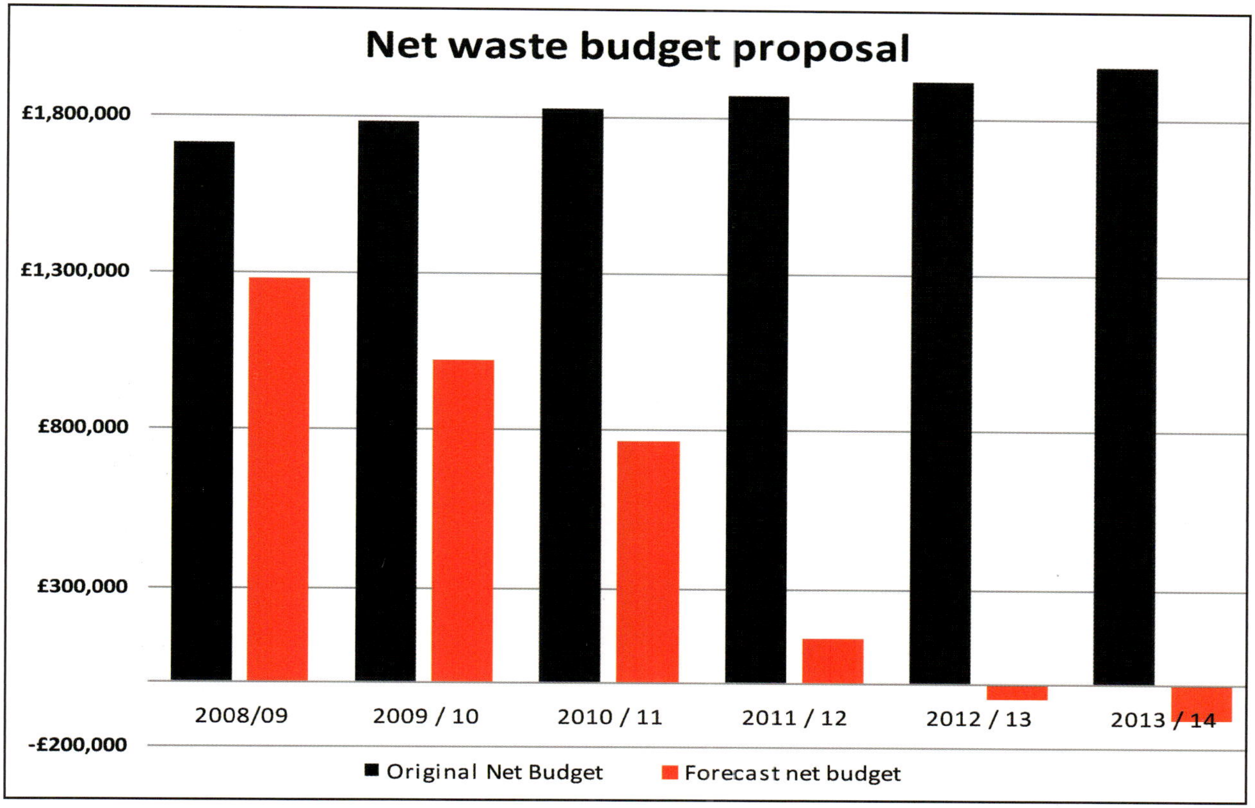

There was little discussion on whether work should go ahead or not, more about the capacity to comply with the critical path and other workstreams at the same time. As would be expected with such a plan, the host has further evolved these plans with some changes to ambitions but still on the financial course set.

The host has achieved radical changes and continued to reduce the previous issues around Christmas.

Endnotes

1 Deming never used the term Systems Thinking, he use Continuous Improvement, which translates loosely to Kaizen. In later years Deming talked about a systemic approach to management.

2 The invention of a relationship forecast between weather (rain plus heat) compared to tonnages was used to predict demand for resources (twice the tonnage from week to week greatly increases vehicle and crew time needs). The system wasn't based back to the number of properties covered by the service, as this increased the relationship would change.

"'I must do something' always solves more problems than 'something must be done'"

AUTHOR UNKNOWN

8. DO

The shortest chapter title, but ultimately this is the most important part of a transformation. There is no transformation without implementation, and certainly services will never get better unless people have the energy, skills, knowledge and authority to move forward.

'Do' now builds on all the essential foundations that have been created over the previous few months, with a significant portfolio of new skills, masses of information which had largely been invisible before, integrated teams with service designs that they have produced, tested and finalised. These people know that this way of working is not only easier to do, but it will create better customer services and less stress for all concerned.

When there are genuinely harmonious teams of people working together, with the right systems and the right tools, then going to work is going to be joyful. The fact that there are a lot of new things to learn, and that some inter-dependencies will not be optimum on day one should hold little fear generally.

So where will the main issues lie? The communications plan should have enabled the majority of customers to be aware that work is changing, and therefore some nuances of service will be different – it could be a new telephone line, a different day of the week, a different time of day, new containers, a different place to collect from, a new office location...

The one thing for certain in a massive change operation is that some people will not have registered that this week is different from last week. That will happen even if the campaign says, "Your neighbour may not have read this, please help them." Thus your plan should address this as a foreseeable issue.

If software patches have been used in the trial, prior to new systems, have they been tested to destruction? Will they take high volumes of work as well as small volumes? Does it work with all versions of Windows and Office that still exist? But, all these questions were asked in 'Plan' and all were signed off, so why is there that animal instinct of fear on the big day? Well, most likely it's because change has always gone wrong in your old paradigm, so it will now!

In many cases the planning, training and testing will have been thorough so all you need to do is start working in the new ways as if it's any other day, other than having a few extra people around who will act as guides and mentors to those who were not part of the testing.

All will have access to the work-flow plans, all will have been trained in their parts, all operations will be fully documented and it will all tie together in a cascade fashion, so that all the small details feed into processes, procedures and the strategy in a seamless way.

ILLUSTRATION OF HOW CORE WORK FLOW AND SUPPORTING DOCUMENTS INTERFACE

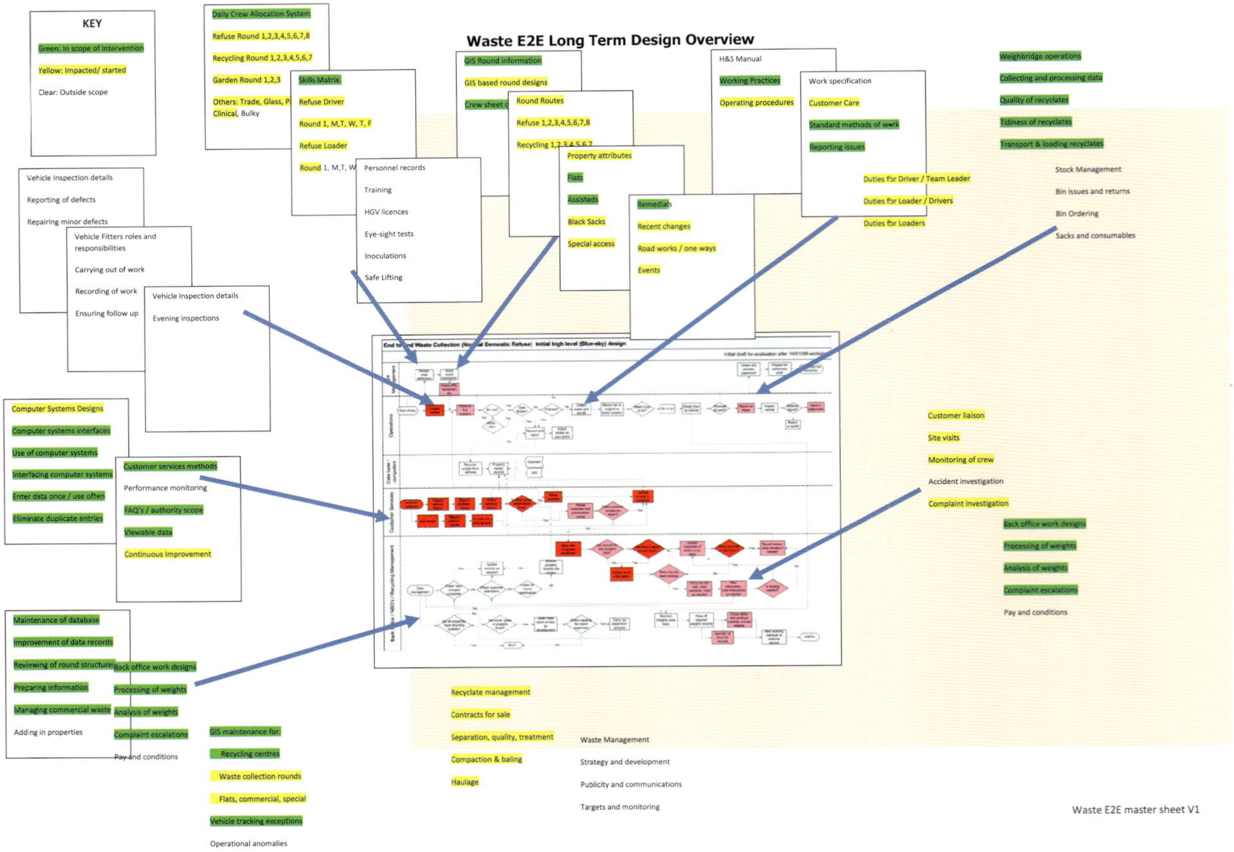

So if for the majority of cases moving to 'Do' are not big issues for the operational side of the organisation, perhaps the issues lay elsewhere? In many 'traditional' organisations power and authority rests with the executive, the cabinet and directors, these are the decision makers thus the buck stops there.

Here is where the problems with moving to 'Do' could lie in this evolving world. If the Executive have had no exposure to the training that has pervaded 'Check Plan and *Appraise*', then they will not quite fully understand that which is about to happen.

They will have fears: fears of militancy from the workers; perhaps many people won't know what they are doing, so many changes so quickly are bound to cause a melt down, or simply, we haven't the capacity to do so much change.

The diagram on page 166 is more symbolic than real, as part of an A3 communication and understanding mechanism. It shows the linkages between the work flow and the processes and controls that sit behind it. The green highlights were shown as inside the scopes of the review, yellow were affected by the review and white were unchanged.

The diagram enabled people to understand what we were working on and what had to be addressed as part of the design stages. Had we had time we were going to use it as an electronic filing system to enable aspects to be found via a couple of mouse clicks. The implementation plan did contain many of these components and they were hyper-linked on the implementation disk, to enable drill down and cross reference.

So while the design methods may be quite different to normal, and some of the business language changes, in the end people will, for example, be working with health and safety risk assessments, have procedures and work methods to comply with as should be the case for any well-designed working practices. The difference is that the designs are fully integrated and well detailed for day one.

In reality the concern is that the most influential people within the current paradigm may become distant from the emerging ethos and identity of the organisation. If there is no or very little training for the cabinet and management team, then the ability to manage and understand what is happening will be compromised. This is not a problem when there are only a few discrete threads of work under review, but it will be an increasing issue with time as full Transformation ensues.

I have also spoken with a leader and deputy leader of a council who desperately were pushing for a systems thinking based transformation to start but could not get the rest of the cabinet or management team to understand why a process-driven concept for making cars had anything to do with them!

So, 'Do' in this new emergent paradigm hasn't the great fear factor from those inside and directly affected by the change, more likely those one or two steps away.

WORK ACTIVITY FOR 'DO'

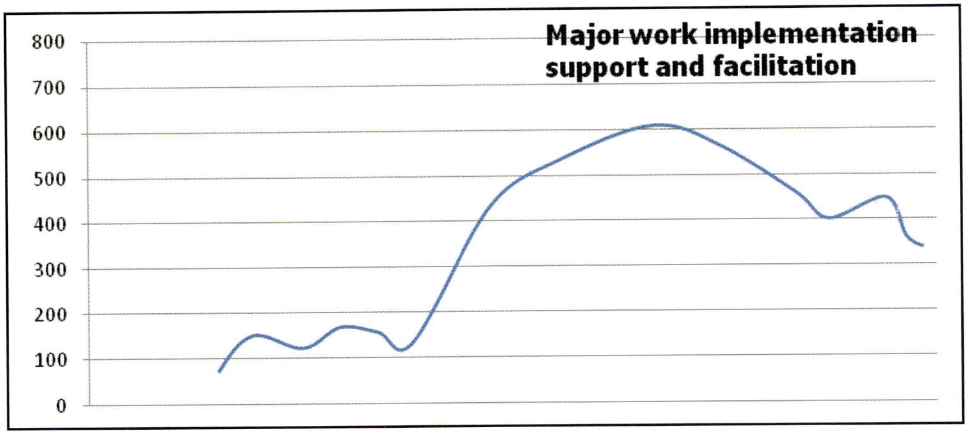

It's worth noting in the diagram above that some parts of 'Do' start quite early in the review – this will reflect the 'Quick Wins' and minor operational changes which arise naturally from cleansing and analysing data and looking at cause and effect for service failures.

The build-up to the big day will naturally include a series of minor service improvements learned from every aspect so far. Check will identify areas of duplication or gaps causing failures. Plan will show how some existing services can be standardised for better effect, and in the *Appraise* period there will be some testing of new concepts as prototype models before recommending the final plans.

The volume of activity here is dependent on the changes to be carried out; however, there should always be some real changes as a result of the reviews. This is quite unlike normal change management with a pre-occupation for resistance from within. If there are improvements to be made, the momentum of the review, and the capacity released as a result, should enable a natural flow into implementation.

In some ways 'Do' as a mark in the sand will be a variable feast, as some starts of new ways of working will be almost imperceptible other than to those directly working in the area. Shortly after someone may say, 'Heh, I just called in about my computer problem, they picked up the call straight away and resolved it in one call inside five minutes, I wonder what's happened to them?' Aside from head scratching that's the end of that impact. Later as far more calls are dealt with effectively the penny will drop, this really is better than it used to be.

Even with the largest of implementation plans, the majority of people affected may either never consciously realise that something is different, or the slight changes will be of little impact. If a waste collection service moves from one failure in 1,000 collections to say 1 in 20,000 collections, then the effect on most individuals isn't obvious. This is because a 1 in 1,000 failure rate with two collections per week still meant that on average you could have 500 weeks without a failure. So, taking this to a far better service could mean you don't need to call for several more years. Would this cause a conscious impact on your memory? No way!

However, in the call centre, the amount of complaints about that service will have reduced by a factor of twenty, so capacity has grown and the ability to address issues has also improved.

Part of the redesign for the new service would also be minded to minimise change, so the majority of customers would not have a change of day of collection where possible.

Rather than discussing complete none-issues here, I should remind you that the designs now have moved on from a 'one size fits all' concept, to a series of parallel designs, bespoke to each collection service with special provisions designed in for specified flats, assisted collections, side waste, litter bins en route, recyclate issues, bank holiday variations…

To add further value, an integrated back office system will 'talk with' the collection crews in real time, pro-actively advising of all routes, and special issues as they are on the horizon. This will now provide crew feedback of 'bins not out', or illegal side-waste via three key strokes as they do the work.

To some extent I have treated 'Do' as an anticlimax, in many ways it's because I've experienced so few problems with implementing change that actually doing the change is one of the easiest parts. The major work is in the preparation, the Army has a saying, "Perfect planning prevents p**s poor performance." Clearly that's something I can agree with.

I will use this area in the book, as a place to compare the new change management paradigm where 'Do' is often the simplest given part of the work, compared to some more traditional, 'current paradigm' area which may be in place now.

TABLE OF CURRENT PARADIGM CONCEPTS AGAINST POSSIBLE UNDERLYING ISSUES

Description	Issues that may arise, many are invisible presently
Governance	Governance is a relatively new concept in terms of its corporate importance. It should be the methodology that ensures the delivery of professional services in a reliable manner. Unfortunately it is often a restrictive force in that it is based on what I call "Management by distrust". The majority of members and staff are honest and committed to doing a very good job; Governance tends to use processes that assume dishonesty.
Risk Management	This was a good concept in many ways, more often than not failing to meet the original concept of creating a decision methodology based on balance. The majority of audits that I have seen, and have been told about, focus on minute possibilities of fraud, with additional actions to ensure that doesn't occur. Each wash of this approach actually makes it harder to do work, thus audit has become one of the prime causes of inefficiency.
Governance and Risk Management combined re Change Management	The combined impact of these two areas creates forces to retain systems as they are. For every one force to change these create nine forces to not change. I raised the concept of a positive mindset prior to going into a meeting. If the directed intention is to achieve a positive outcome a change which hasn't happened for five years can be agreed in 40 minutes. In one authority who ostensibly wanted to 'transform' they lost 60% of their potential to move forward because of red tape and the defence of the status quo at the level below directors. Thus the hired consultants and a number of senior officers were taking 2 ½ days for every productive day possible, costing thousands of pounds a day as they talked about talking about work. If consultants are happy to waste time constantly in this way, is their prime interest to sell consulting days or add value to the host?

<table>
<tr><td>Arbitrary deadlines</td><td>
There is no problem with deadlines. If something has to happen by a certain date, then the critical path to achieve that task can be generated and dependencies mapped to achieve it.
However, when this is mixed with stretch targets some interesting results occur. The corporate management team had decided to bring forward management clinics in order to look at results even earlier in the cycle so that there was more time to change outcomes.
This led to a number of unforeseen outcomes; the supply systems for the information couldn't create the right information on time. So people became inventive. Where accident records were monitored, month two information would be incomplete, containing only three weeks data, with six weeks data going into month one. This created a saw-tooth pattern of results. This had been going on for years without awareness. Other reports were slipped a month with no noticeable labelling to show that it was now later than ever before, rather than earlier as intended.
The issue is with 'arbitrary' not with targets or deadlines. The work should be designed to the capacity of the system, or the system designed to achieve the outcomes; this should not simply comply with the royal command.
</td></tr>
<tr><td>Mixing data, information and knowledge</td><td>
Many monitoring reports show a great deal of data, some information and espoused knowledge. The problem is if there is doubt about data, give notes to say why there is doubt. Incredibly finance departments appear to be the worst culprits for this. They produce monthly and quarterly accounts and give it to the people in power as information.
Without a full-blown commitment accounting system, accounts are a wicked mixture of stuff that has happened and is recorded (fact), stuff that has happened and is part recorded (estimate), stuff that may have happened and has some corporate awareness (estimating estimates) and guesswork on the rest.
Accounts do not give you the reliability rankings of the data, because the Audit Commission would mark them down for being aware of what they don't know. I have experienced many accounts with so much guesswork in them that it's frightening. Yet, people are sacked, services suspended, or the great March additional 'spend it or lose it' rush is caused by poor financial information.
</td></tr>
</table>

Integrated corporate business systems	I firmly believe that unified business systems across an organisation is the right thing to do, when it's done well and done consciously. However, I have seen numerous systems that meet the majority of the organisations needs, but not all. I've also seen people who have bought 'future systems' that will meet their needs, but then never do. From a Visualising Transformation approach, any corporate system needs to meet all the essential requirements of the authority and most of the desirable ones. I've seen HR and Finance systems that cannot, and never will be able to, meet the needs of service areas with lots of part time staff, or where inhouse trading is their prime work. The systems go in, destroy the competitive edge of those parts, later the services are forced to be externalised because they are not competitive. The reason? Because of poor corporate decisions three years prior, not because they are badly run areas. It is these areas where an array of sub-systems are needed to run the businesses offline from the corporate systems, that there is a regular extra exercise to align data in several systems, needing: compare, contrast and force fit one set of data with others. Equally I've seen stunning integrations, where high-level conscious design has been supplemented by systems thinking detailing bespoke to each function affected. The result, a financial and management information system that links to all HR modules, to the corporate CRM and GIS, enabling data handling to give real-time knowledge.
Specialist functions held and delivered centrally	There needs to be professional guidance and insight into how the whole organisation is run, but it is very important that access to that insight is truly available within the areas actually doing the work. In just the same way that BAs can work on an E2E process to review opportunity and capacity, accountants and HR staff should be embedded in the services to work with the front line, understand issues and add value, rather than create numerically correct or individual low risk decisions. If those people are part of the process, both sides of the equation will be committed to the outcomes of decisions. This in turn will create more empowerment and value for money.

Activity based costing or budget cuts in isolation	ABC has a place within an organisation, as should some form of benchmarking. However, this can be an issue where decisions are taken in isolation. I cited earlier that debt collection would only chase car park fines once and then give up. If you compared an holistic car parking enforcement strategy with a fragmented one where work is parcelled, queued and eventually processed, the holistic one may create 20% more income per parking space than the latter. In some councils where I've managed car parks, that's another million a year. The arbitrary process of budget cuts is also interesting for accountancy and HR; they've got to lose 10% of people, and so they cut the people working in the work and retain the HQ staff. In the work areas sickness levels go up by 30% and those services are blamed, even though you can show that most of that is now due to a new queue waiting for occupational health (due to HQ cuts), or because non-accountants are now doing a great deal of bookkeeping as well as their day job. Central cuts are most often a double whammy, as the services shed staff and inherit central work as well.
Batching work and economy of scale	This is an extension of ABC; people slice up work into many sections, and then show that a central unit can do nineteen of these activities in the time it takes the works unit to do twelve. The centre gets the work, the work unit loses capacity. Unless there is a fully integrated information system, the works unit still needs to do half of what it used to do, and deal with thornier issues. The new integrated team will cause some of the most complex issues to be ignored, so eventually the works unit has to resolve them. Batching of work often leads to lower success rates. It also leads to doing all the easy work to achieve arbitrary targets, leaving the hardest ones for later. The saving from mass production is then exceeded by the additional costs of monitoring and fault resolution.
Shared back office and call centres	There is no doubt that in very badly run organisations, either of these can save money. Sometimes the theory and projections are positive, the start-up will be harder than expected, taking longer to settle down, staff retention adds costs, and increasing separation of the workers from the customers causes increased failure demand and costs. Contact with the call centre increases due to more work going wrong and thus more call centre staff are needed. Even with award-winning call centres, they may create better initial customer contact, but invariably they will add to failure demand and costs. For waste collection, they will be a major part of the reason for additional rounds, which again will be blamed on those services, rather on the causes of customer service deterioration with costs increases. Councillors: Think back, before the public sector was split up into so many factions, why didn't we need a shared back office? Oh yes, because we were a single body and didn't need to share. Why did we not need to attempt to share information between so many organisations? That's right, there weren't so many. And before we had call centres did you have so many issues that are now so difficult to resolve? No, the service was integrated and able to resolve at day one when you called them!

Performance Management	Again under the post-BV paradigm PM has become an easy area to use and create new terrors for the working man. In one assignment I worked for a fairly poor director who was perceived by nearly all his staff as being a bully. He would set arbitrary targets and then use these to beat up his staff. 'Right I want to see Joe, I need to performance manage him'. I quickly adopted a process of running interference, 'I've taken that aspect on directly with Joe, he's working with me on that.' One previously good middle manager had had a mental breakdown. All his colleagues tried to featherbed him, but his outputs were pathetic. By getting between him and the director, I helped raise his self-esteem considerably, and his outputs increased about fivefold in that time. He still wasn't a top performer, but he was starting to perform. At the same time the director reduced an already stretched division by an addition (vacant) post and didn't tell anyone he had done this. We had the post out to advertising before we discovered it had been culled. Also watch out for cascaded targets. Most often these are set with no design attempt to enable a reality. Achieve a 10% increase in car park surplus! If the corporate body cannot know how to achieve this, why does this system believe it should increase pressure with no opportunity for empowered design? (Consider the negative pressures of governance and risk management and the speed of the decisions process.) If you can ask the five whys and use cause and effect, sub-optimised systems, ABC implications, bullies will become quite obvious. Look at the system as an E2E whole, not as a series of widgets. The other issue with performance managers is their constant monitoring of systems to meet the Audit Commission needs at the expense of the worker and customer needs. First of all ensure you can add value to the system, then find how you serve others who add no value.
Efficiency gains	Following on from performance managers, start to redefine efficiency! Does what they suggest help balance the books by creating better, more effective outcomes for the customers, or does it in fact reduce the service to customers? Push back, services reductions by any other name is a scam.

Cloning benchmarked designs from elsewhere	This is a great scam for certain consultants and performance managers. They go to another authority which either has a charter mark or is held up as an exemplar organisation, so you clone their visible systems and expect instant pudding results. Visualising Transformation spends a great deal of time and effort to understand the host and ensure all solutions match culture, systems and aspirations. Cloning a solution will miss most of these aspects. It's a bit like slicing the top of an iceberg which is visible in the water and assuming that is the whole entity. If your consultant cannot understand the whole proposed process and be fully aware how it works in your current paradigm to move you to the next paradigm, what assurance does that give you?

The examples of adding value and service specific outcomes in chapters nine and ten may help bridge the gap from now to soon for those sceptics who still believe that Transformation can only be achieved by making service delivery worse in the short term and destroy the morale of the staff as it occurs.

These are symptoms of badly managed change! If that always happens where you are, then perhaps, change has always been badly managed.

"Insanity, Doing the same thing over and over again and expecting different results"
ALBERT EINSTEIN

9. OUTCOMES

In just the same way that there is no point in starting a Transformation programme if you don't address 'Do', there is little point of initiating a Transformation unless positive outcomes are achieved. The chapters up to Check provided thoughts as to what a positive outcome may look like. How can you achieve a good outcome unless you have some awareness of what that vision will be?

For the purposes of this book, I'm using the term outcomes to represent the attributes attained after the first full cycle of 'Check Plan *Appraise* Do'. We created a 'Vision' together, refined and increased the aspirations during Plan and *Appraise*, then started to realise them as part of Do.

Within this chapter I'll run through some of those positive outcomes from work carried out, and then in the next chapter I'll address the characteristics of various services which I have some degree of 'expertise', giving pointers to project sponsors and team members for ideas already addressed.

Unlike most traditional change methodologies, Visualising Transformation can create positive outcomes in the first few days of the intervention. The rescue of the garden waste service discussed earlier was quite exceptional, in that even before the intervention team was formed, there was awareness of the emerging issues, and I had been involved in a different role, so could see the attributes of the problems even though I wasn't close enough to it, nor had the capacity to intervene.

To start an intervention on Monday and have positive results on Tuesday is testament to the simplicity of analysis. Ask the five whys, analyse data, seek information and use Pareto to see main issues, create a little insight and cure the worst case. This is exceptional and not a recipe for instant pudding.

However, there is a technique within the breadth of Systems Thinking called Kaizen Blitz, where a team is assembled on Monday, goes through a steep learning curve through the whole week, dissecting and modelling the data that they are addressing with some future designs and plan for the implementation created by Friday (see chapter eleven).

Quick wins are common in an intervention, these aid three aspects: customer care improves, morale improves and capacity is gained. This occurs in the early days of Check; you collect data for failure modes and use various analysis tools to find exceptions and trends. Then by discussing those with all the people involved in the service you can head those issues off. If this is Pareto related, you could make several telling savings very early indeed.

Returning to the main waste intervention, the outcomes included:

- ✔ Reducing missed collections, throughout the intervention via various step changes
- ✔ Reducing ad hoc extra fault rectification resources not needed once faults reduced
- ✔ Resolving the garden waste service meltdown in a matter of days
- ✔ Greatly improving communications and operations to nullify most of the Christmas blip
- ✔ Created a waste strategy which exceeded requirements at a reduced budget
- ✔ Identified major IT software and systems issues previously not recognised at the centre
- ✔ Created a far more genuine all one team approach, replacing a fragmented sparring culture
- ✔ Identified a wide series of additional services which would both add value and save budget
  - ⇨ Designed services for flats and high density housing
  - ⇨ Adding value to recyclates
  - ⇨ Gaining more recyclates from the waste stream
  - ⇨ Introducing trade recycling services
  - ⇨ Fully integrated IT systems for all function
- ✔ Highlighted the capability to reduce current resources to rounds, using spare capacity for new services
- ✔ Reduced capital spend in year one, and thereafter.

Overall this saved more than £1M in both years one and two, even after the cost of the intervention and latter specialist restructuring support. Service delivery in terms of missed bins improved during the intervention, from over 140 misses per hundred thousand collections, to only 17 within the trial services.

So if we returned to the 'Motivation' chapter, this shows improvements in service almost from the first day of the review, continuously improved on aspirations and achievements through the review and delivered stunning service improvements with financial and environmental step changes.

I'll discuss other intervention outcomes to give a range and a flavour for what can be done. Car parking is a service which can be difficult to describe as a useful, unless people understand the benefits that can be derived. I've directly managed and helped improve two large parking services one which was changing its contractor to manage 25,000 parking spaces, the other which was introducing decriminalisation of parking, to take 'on street parking' from the police.

The latter was in a partial meltdown scenario, the PRINCE2 led project was way behind schedule, key tasks were not being achieved on time, and morale was low and finances foundering. There were fundamental issues between the parking manager and call centre manager, with a perceived lack of resources from other support areas.

The very detailed project plan looked very impressive. It had been drafted after many weeks of debate by a consultant who then didn't have the skill and determination to keep it up to date and refreshed. The project manager was managing several projects, but this one didn't seem very important to her, as there was no drive or ambition; the easy answer was to allow it to slip and complete it later than planned.

I created two documents to share with the project team and discuss with support services. One was a mind map for the project, showing all the interweaving aspects, with the main areas being identified as:

- Development of software and hardware with communications links
- Role separation between contractor, back-office, call centre, engineers and legal
- Review and improvements to signs and lines
- Operational details for the new contractor.

We also agreed a very simple project plan with key dates to achieve critical path tasks, which we called drop dead dates. The majority of the details that were being crawled over fortnightly prior to then were shelved, only of importance if we were discussing a contractual issue.

The engineers (who dealt with Signs, lines and Traffic Regulation Orders) had their own issues with a demoralised workforce, who knew they were under-resourced, badly managed and facing increased service demands with reducing resources. I led the development of a resource allocation plan, identifying all the work that had to be done, who would lead and who would do the work, also gaining far more professional support from their consultant engineers who had been paid good money for poor work for years.

The team became more focused on doing what they could do, while duplicating work areas less. As a by-product of the parking process we procured a file server to run both parking and GIS, enabling all the other GIS processes to take about 1/3rd of their previous run time, thus creating additional capacity immediately.

All aspects of the parking plan were delivered inside the original budget, on time with little issue. On the way we resolved some operational issues, sacking one parking attendant for theft and shaking up some dubious practices which the council was hoping the incoming contractor would solve.

Inside three months we reviewed the parking enforcement delivery, finding that 80% of parking appeals were successful, which is exceptionally high. We ran a small workshop to create some simple post-it based flow charts and cause and effect charts. From there we gathered data and created a simple Pareto analysis for causality of appeals won. Most were simple pencil on A3 sketches with no need for high tech solutions.

We then fed back this information into operations, ensuring (penalty) tickets had the right: date, location, registration number, photos, offence… Overall we improved the parking budget by £400,000 per annum.

Inside three months we transformed a failing service into a winning service, as they were successfully defending 80% of appeals, rather than losing 80%. As a direct result of that primary work we enabled the parking attendants to have more drive and ambition, so the strength of the enforcement improved, with more PCNs issued per day, and quite noticeably, more tickets being purchased every day in the car parks.

There is a direct relationship here which I will describe from a negative energy point of view, and then a positive energy point of view.

NEGATIVE ENERGY:

Most parking appeals are successful, some legitimate tickets are asked to be over-turned as a favour for councillors or directors, processing officers are aware that they are not likely to be supported; parking attendants know that many tickets are not processed or finalised. Some officers are among the worst offenders, often supported by well meaning managers. Car park users know that many excuses work, friends and office colleagues will buy one or two tickets between them, and then hand over these tickets to someone else who can then claim that the ticket must have fallen on the floor.

Services were segmented; admin staff were not committed and didn't bother to provide good services, so all that was important was that 1,000 cases are moved forward per month. Most are carried out at the end of the month, thus the difficult or contentious ones are always left out. People complain that this happened three months ago, so they are excused. People argue repeatedly that they are special, the teams responsible for escalating to even higher value fines are contacted, but the cost to move forward ostensibly is greater than the income to achieve, so on a simple activity based costing approach, it's not worth doing, so the case is closed.

The result a continuing negative spiral and melt-down to lower and lower income in all areas.

POSITIVE ENERGY:

An holistic approach is taken to parking services as a whole, linked to accident reduction, safer routes to school, city centre congestion easing via urban traffic control, differential access to parking for long term, short term and disabled parking. There is positive attention placed on people who experience problems from others illegally parking around them, or for businesses who are looking to increase financial turnover, via easier customer access.

The whole design is based on an E2E review, seeking opportunities and redesigns where appropriate. Causes of service failure are examined and addressed with a mixture of quick wins and segmented highest impact to transformation being assessed.

Causes of failures are investigated with various cost benefits being considered, seeking closed loop solutions[1] where possible. Representatives for all aspects of the work come together once every quarter to share good solutions and emerging important issues.

Causes of failure are learnt from and addressed, with a constant sharing of information and celebration of success. People pass on good practice to one another and causes for failure are rectified quickly. The outcomes will include:

- ✓ Very high collection percentages against PCNs issued for all cases
- ✓ Absolute clarity of who does what, and what the internal tolerances are
- ✓ Very high enforcement for non-payment at all sites
- ✓ Repair of defects to maximise available chargeable parking locations
- ✓ Variety of options for parking which has good communication
- ✓ Best use of technology to save fraudulent use of tickets
- ✓ Very high ratio of payments in right locations
- ✓ Easier investment to add further value for the future
- ✓ Continuous improvement financially and operationally, including positive re-investment.

Typically the income per parking location will be 20% greater than a low enforcement ABC based service. As a result, there will be less congestion, safer critical locations, safer school parking, better turnover for shops and key locations and a far higher value for money of the whole service.

The same prospects of negative energy to positive energy would apply to recycling, housing maintenance, street cleansing, highway maintenance and highway potholes. I'm also certain that health provision and old age 'at home' living would be far better if the E2E process was properly addressed.

The following examples are included to show how initial debates can start and how bringing various concepts together can enable significant win-win options, delivering better services to customers with no loss of employment to save money.

MIND MAP FOR OPPORTUNITIES TO IMPROVE INCOME GENERATION

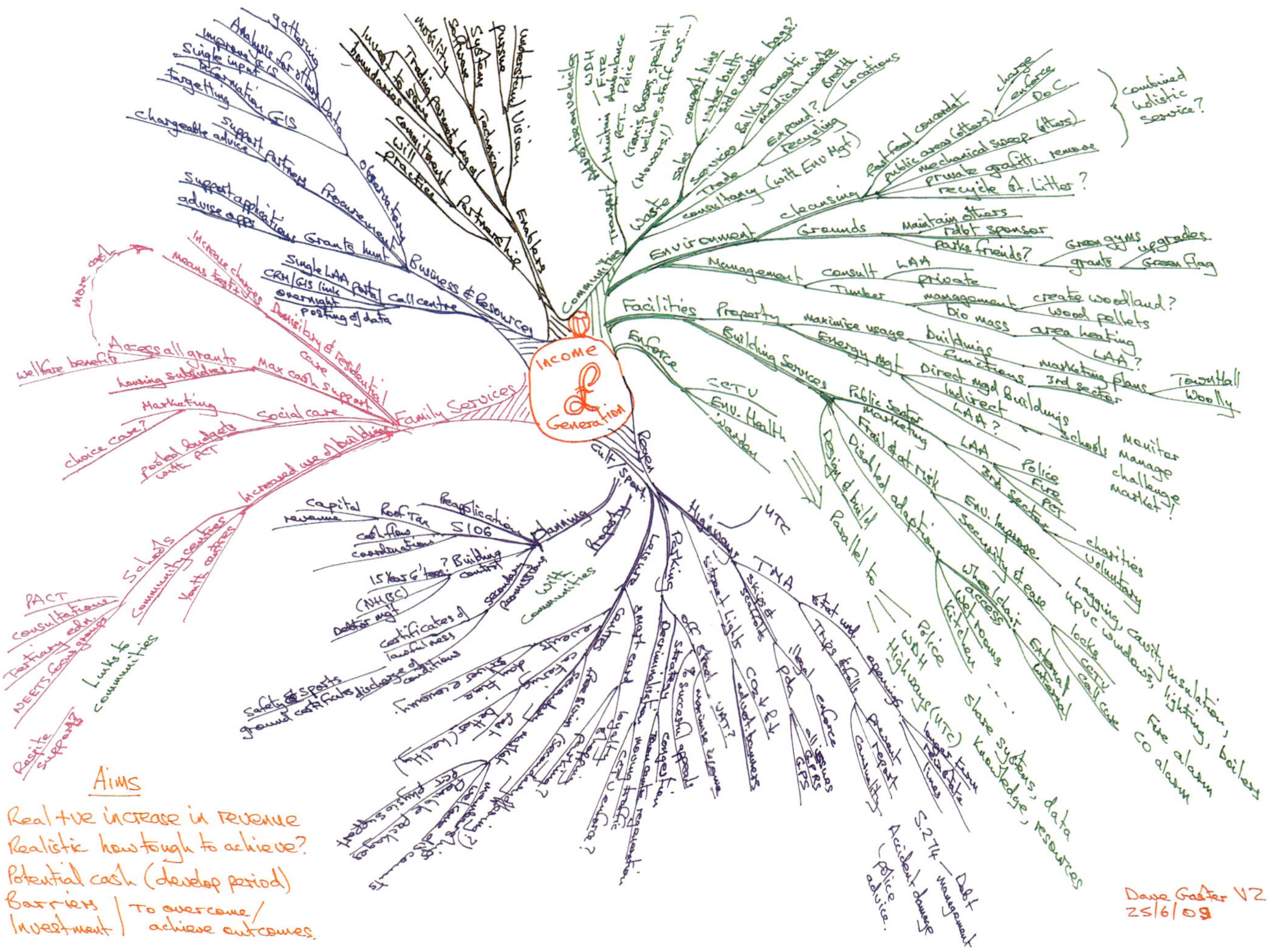

This mind map was designed to enable initial discussions to reduce costs in the current year with a combination of various concepts for continuous future improvement rather than simply reduce services as had previously occurred. The hand drawn ideas were scanned and circulated with a series of workshops carried out to not only discuss specific focus areas, but a so see if other concepts were possible.

These discussions led to a single directorate reducing net costs by £2M in that year, with a doubling of that to over £4M proposed for the next year, with no losses of service or employment. Other directorates took a more positive renewed approach to matters in most cases.

Whole service issues have been shown for the inner London review for cleaner safer places where a thirty five million annual budget needed no further monies, but achieved a series of award winning service integration and customer focus awards over the next three years.

The environmental interventions for a large county council addressed an array of highways improvements. There were dozens of inter-related services under review, some staff cuts had previously taken place without systems improvement, six separate district based areas all worked in different ways and a central call centre was being created.

The work to address trips and falls reduced the time to prepare a report from 90 days to 2.65 days, from 21 people involved to 2 full time plus part of one manager, and from an annual cost of £300,000 to £67,000. The PiD had only targeted a £25,000 a year saving.

Analysing home to school transport gained phenomenal momentum, the simple review of the use of taxis to get special needs children to and from school showed that using GIS to visualise current journeys could enable a 10% reduction at each school via better planning. The budget was £10M per annum – £400,000 per year has already been saved as a result of the first phase work.

However, that visualisation also showed that a 12-year-old was being transported 18 miles each way each day from X to Y, while another 12-year-old with very similar issues was doing the reverse journey. The intervention enabled a simple offer to both families, which could save those journeys for the next four years.

The very simple visualisation of information enabled an immediate 10% gain with at least the same again possible prior to even using traditional systems thinking tools.

This also identified work load variability throughout the day, with a massive peak from 7.45 in the morning to 9.15 and from 3.15 in the afternoon to 4.15. Outside of those times there were coaches, mini-buses and taxis plus drivers with capacity but little demand. So we started working on the whole prospect of using that capacity, in schools, for the health sector, for old people's homes, for interest groups and even for individuals who didn't qualify for free transport.

By visualising the options, opportunities and capabilities to achieve win-win outcomes, a project which was relatively narrowly designed started to free up over two million a year in costs which could be re-invested in better schools, care and support for an array of customers.

The following diagram, for obesity, has a beauty of its own and was not created by me. It certainly reflects parts of my own direction of travel, as affinity diagrams enable very complex issues to be discussed from a wide array of view points. There are a number of core clusters points where there are strong alignments of key interest issues.

If a number of parties are involved in a scheme, it's likely that they will only discuss their direct responsibilities and ignore many others. Obesity will not just be of interest to the local PCT, it will impact on schools, school meals, leisure centres, adult services and the private restaurants and shops in the area.

This affinity chart enables all these organisations to engage in dialogue to move forward. Sometimes it will take months of hard work to establish broad, meaningful discussions for such groups of people, would this act as an ice breaker?

It definitely can help to positively impact on the lifestyles and aspirations for various sectors of the community, dealing with an array of socio-economic elements.

If you can, spend time tracing how each element relates to the other, you could achieve three stages of learning:

- ▷ For you and your family, how could you make some slight changes that improve your future health?
- ▷ What value can you add to longer term debate via new insight?
- ▷ What other aspects are there which are not on this affinity diagram?

It's quite amazing to me that my specialist knowledge of this area is quite light, and yet I can immediately see where an authority can add value and what else could also be considered.

Foresight

Obesity System Map

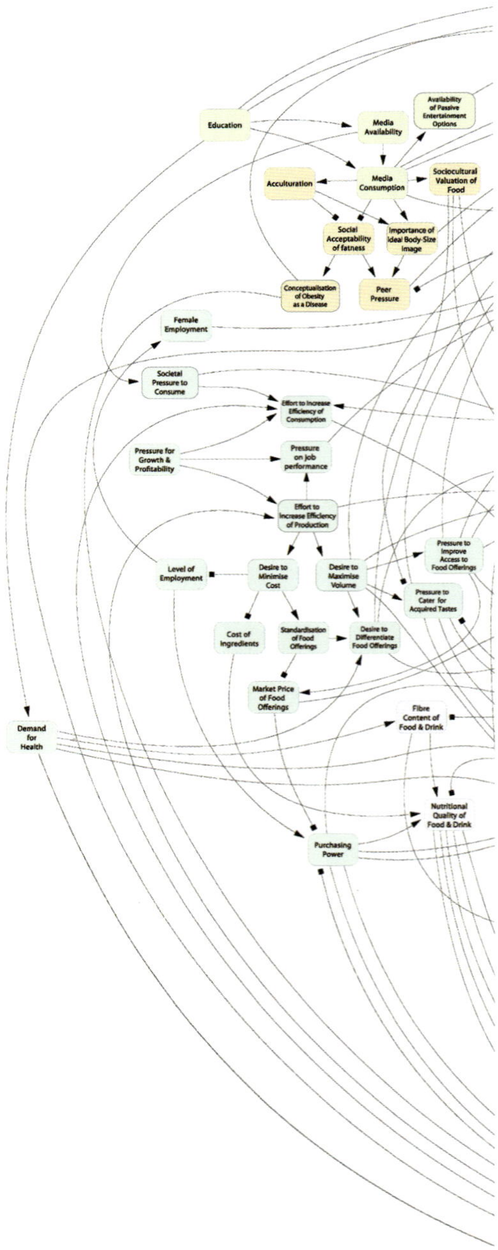

Note: This diagram is available via www.supportservicesdirect.co.uk/visualisingtransformation

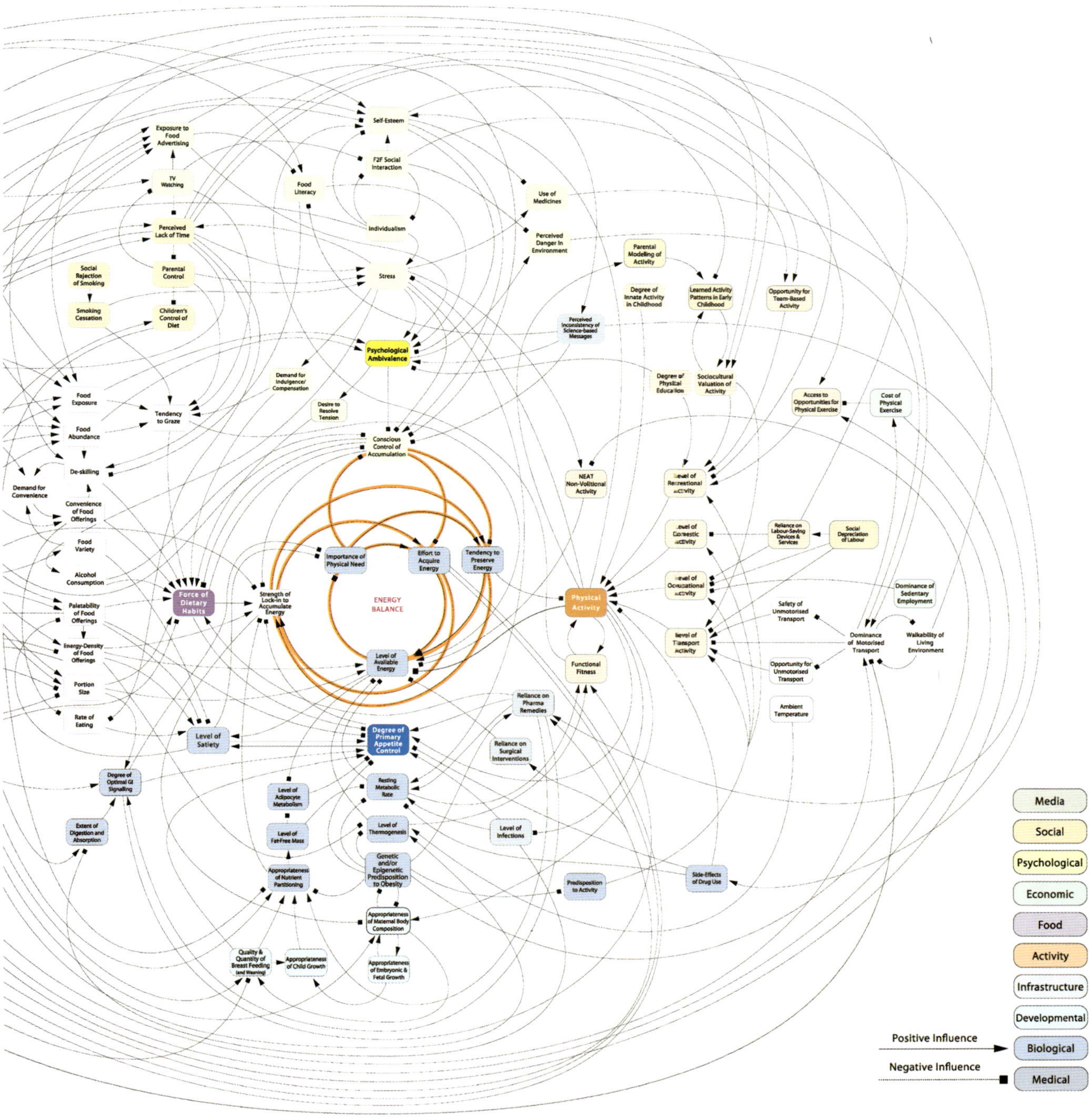

Self-Esteem
Exposure to Food Advertising
F2F Social Interaction
TV Watching
Food Literacy
Use of Medicines
Individualism
Perceived Lack of Time
Perceived Danger in Environment
Social Rejection of Smoking
Parental Control
Stress
Parental Modelling of Activity
Degree of Innate Activity in Childhood
Learned Activity Patterns in Early Childhood
Opportunity for Team-Based Activity
Smoking Cessation
Children's Control of Diet
Perceived Inconsistency of Science-based Messages
Psychological Ambivalence
Demand for Indulgence/ Compensation
Degree of Physical Education
Sociocultural Valuation of Activity
Food Exposure
Desire to Resolve Tension
Access to Opportunities for Physical Exercise
Cost of Physical Exercise
Tendency to Graze
Food Abundance
Conscious Control of Accumulation
De-skilling
Demand for Convenience
NEAT Non-Volitional Activity
Level of Recreational Activity
Convenience of Food Offerings
Food Variety
Level of Domestic Activity
Reliance on Labour-Saving Devices & Services
Social Depreciation of Labour
Importance of Physical Need
Effort to Acquire Energy
Tendency to Preserve Energy
Alcohol Consumption
Force of Dietary Habits
Strength of Lock-in to Accumulate Energy
ENERGY BALANCE
Physical Activity
Level of Occupational Activity
Dominance of Sedentary Employment
Palatability of Food Offerings
Safety of Unmotorised Transport
Energy-Density of Food Offerings
Dominance of Motorised Transport
Walkability of Living Environment
Level of Transport Activity
Level of Available Energy
Functional Fitness
Opportunity for Unmotorised Transport
Portion Size
Reliance on Pharma Remedies
Ambient Temperature
Rate of Eating
Level of Satiety
Degree of Primary Appetite Control
Reliance on Surgical Interventions
Degree of Optimal GI Signalling
Resting Metabolic Rate
Level of Adipocyte Metabolism
Level of Thermogenesis
Level of Infections
Extent of Digestion and Absorption
Level of Fat-Free Mass
Genetic and/or Epigenetic Predisposition to Obesity
Appropriateness of Nutrient Partitioning
Predisposition to Activity
Side-Effects of Drug Use
Appropriateness of Maternal Body Composition
Quality & Quantity of Breast Feeding (and Weaning)
Appropriateness of Child Growth
Appropriateness of Embryonic & Fetal Growth
Media
Social
Psychological
Economic
Food
Activity
Infrastructure
Developmental
Positive Influence
Biological
Negative Influence
Medical

Lastly from a customer point of view on outcomes, every intervention has worked on improving service delivery for the significant majority of customers. Where there were failures previously, these become less likely; where homes were left vacant for seven weeks and often turned down, they were occupied in less than three weeks and rarely turned down; where recycling was not very positive for a community, it improves massively.

So the outcomes meet financial, customer and environmental demands, moving forward ambition and frequently delighting the hosts!

For me, that's quite a good start!

Endnote

1 A closed loop solution refers to the whole end-to-end process being within the boundaries of control for the team involved. So for instance if the yellow lines were inspected and maintained by the team, then as better lines were in place, more fine income (or indeed car park space income) would accrue, enabling the initial costs of line painting to be funded.

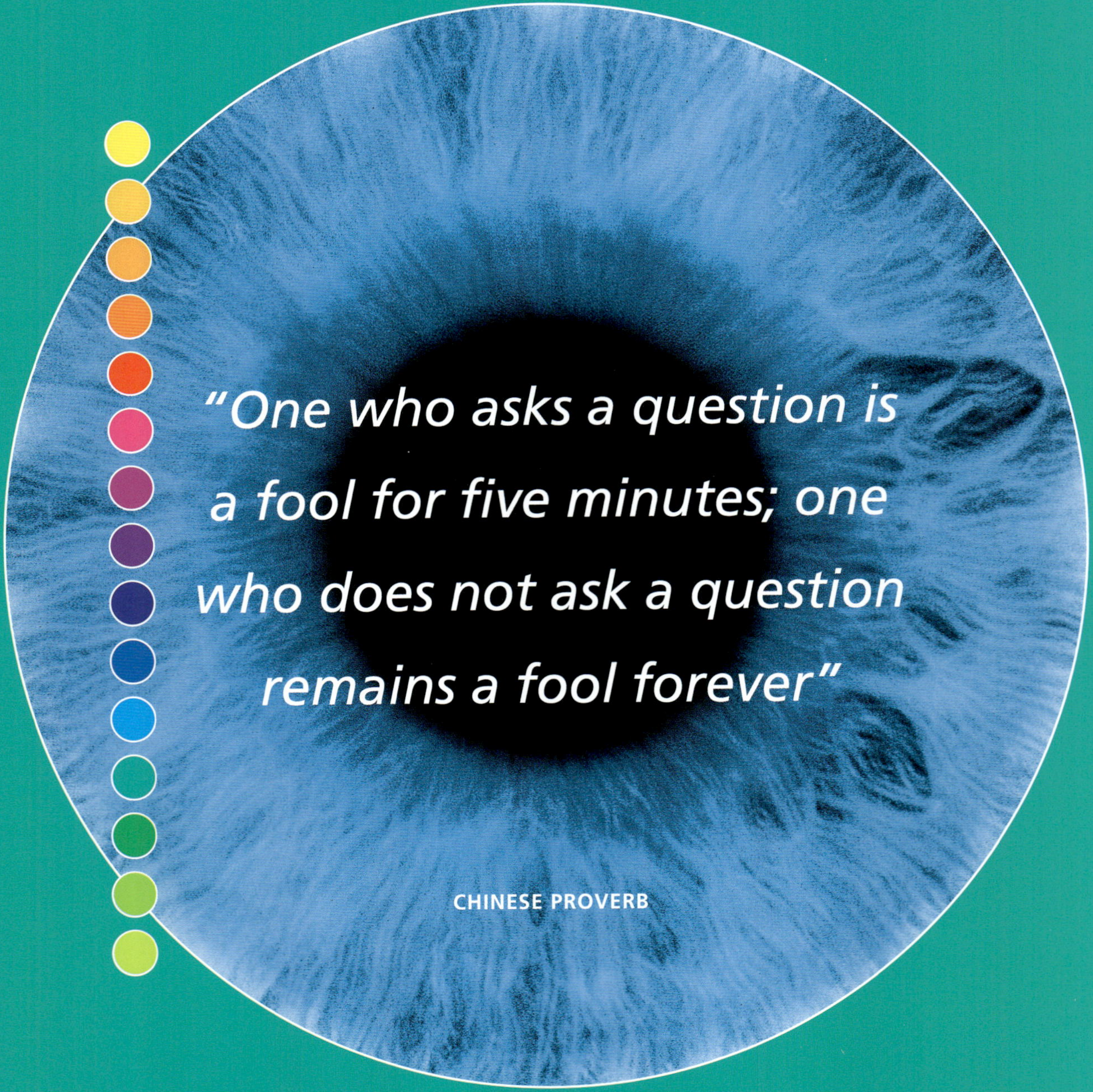
"One who asks a question is a fool for five minutes; one who does not ask a question remains a fool forever"
CHINESE PROVERB

10. ADDING VALUE TO SERVICES

If you were looking for a distinctive difference between Systems Thinking, Six Sigma and other approaches compared to Visualising Transformation this would be where the telling differences are. For instance, a six sigma black belt is described as a person who will 'focus entirely on every aspect of performance … to achieve enhanced performances, customer satisfaction and profitability…'

There is no mention of creating and developing strategies nor diversifying into secondary markets. The entire raison d'être of a six sigma black belt, 'is to reduce defects in products and services', which is a major emphasis for Visualising Transformation but not the sole approach.

Six Sigma is also very target driven. If the target is to reduce time or costs by 25%, once that is achieved no more will be sought.

In all the following examples there were mixtures of data cleansing and analysis, together with graphical and tabular representations. Every case also has a degree of business acumen included, using financial, legal, marketing and HR skills to add a considerable extra advantage.

Similar case studies are not repeated; learning threads starting from one case may help shape the opportunities for another thread, but the host determines what will work and what will not.

The majority of this chapter provides a listing of what has been improved, with some ideas of how it was improved using what approaches plus some outcomes. There are many more case studies on the website at www.supportservicesdirect.co.uk . These should be seen as 'high level markers' to assist the shaping of work for the future. This demonstrates that virtually all forms of service can be made more effective, more efficient and have considerable added value for both the host, and more importantly the customers.

Brief description	Achievements	Areas addressed / Actions taken
Waste collection customer service improvement in a Large D.C. (Phase one) Reducing failure demand	Reduced from over 1,000 misses per week to less than 50 inside three months and then continued to improve. Saved contract from termination.	Root cause of issues: Round structures, contract design, work methods, T&C of employment, vehicles, warranty, downtime, maintenance, data / information. New vehicles, restructured rounds (minor), team creation / development, improved knowledge and training. No extra budget!
Phase two: Improved same service to among best in Britain	Reduced missed collections to less than three a week. Reduced resources to meet new budget constraints.	Continued above, used business modelling to move to nine hour day, producing 18% improvement in daily productive time ratio. Increased daily value work by reducing failure demands. Added recycling services to reduce tonnages with no additional overheads. Eliminated need for a client as there was only value demand.
Introduction of new edge of property bin / box waste and recycling service. Very small D.C. Design, specify and enable new services	Moved from 4% to 19% recycling within the same net budget. Improved service delivery. Excellent support from a hung council. Created new waste strategy, future planned partnering with VCS for composting.	Started genuine team working for the first time. Used GIS to gather data and model. Built simple database to design new services and run the contract. Balanced rounds consulting with employees. Designed work methods, redefined sizes of wheeled bins, bought new vehicles. Established and ran communications plans. Door knocking support to answer questions. Ran demonstration caravan and public meetings with a very positive feedback. Step increase in Trade Refuse, special designs for weekend home owners.
Improve recycling returns and resolve contract dispute. London Boro. Contract resolution	Recycling improved from 4% to over 7% via successful challenge of tip data, nearly doubling outcomes. Proved contractor claim costs were overstated by £600K and settled without legal costs.	Deep analysis of contractor information to compare data from several sources to prove inconsistencies and errors. Negotiated more probable / favourable recyclates solution. Proved (from data provided) that vehicles and staff which were supposedly unused were largely in use all the time to reduce a £750K plus costs case down to a £150K settlement without legal costs. Improved trade refuse controls and viability, created 'ghost tender' enabling £2M saving on waste contract.
Step reduced failure demand for waste services. London Boro. Linked Client, Contractor and Call Centre to design out issues.	Immediate 40% reduction in missed bins, followed by gradual further improvement. Led to easier working relationships and restored trust. This saved costs for all parties while radically improving customer services.	Flow charted system in place to prove where errors were started. Most problems were caused by poor IT alignment and an attempt to save money. Instigated minor changes to link CRM with contractor properly. Used CRM outputs to map issues generated due to poor questions and many cases of customer untruths. Created capacity to improve customer service and trust between parties to actively further improve there-after.
Integrated waste and recycling service intervention. New strategy and operations plans to transform services.	Saved £1M in each of years one and two, final saving of nearer £2M per annum. Increased recycling plan to 68%. Easier work methods, no loss of employment.	Deep analysis with excellent probing by the council. Strategic and operational reviews in parallel enabling mutual improvements to both. Deep extensive training. Good motivational drivers in place to seek environmental, customer and cost improvements, healthy balance between pushes to cut costs and or improve services.
Carbon reduction plans for large Met. Translate, adapt and develop carbon reduction plans to enable fast track adoption.	Large integrated invest to save program started, replacing existing heating and lighting with more efficient equipment. Achieved EDI (Electronic Data Interchange) billing saving 20,000 invoices per year.	Sought balance of opinions and attitudes to environment, the works needed and savings sought. Restructured bid and finances to make the decision very easy and clear. The speed of return, especially when 50% grant funded, on initial savings would pump prime the second and future phases (also grant funded) enabling a true quick return, self sustaining, invest to save project.
Integrated plan to reduce fly-tipping in a large Met. Reduce causes of fly-tipping and side waste, faster resolution of issues.	60% reduction in complaints, in four months, whole team approach created faster resolution and fewer instances. Enabling ambitious strategic plans to be introduced. Big impact for NI14.	Initial training for data analysis looking at issues from a joined up approach. Using CRM and GIS better with five sections working in harmony. Step improvement after first discussion leading to a complex interactive strategy, owned by the wider teams and council to address all the elements via the public engagement. New service and LSP strategies to create genuine joint working.

Brief description	Achievements	Areas addressed /actions taken
Addressing highways trips and falls to reduce issues. Large County. Redesigned services to radically reduce the claims pressure / improve operations.	Costs reduced from £300K to £67K, days to create report from 90 to 2.65. All reports to a good standard first time. Also analysed prime cause back to utilities for better enforcement for second phase improvement.	We examined all highways claims against the council, in order to radically reduce a growing negative pressure. The redesign went to a full council trial due to the small original workload which was later adopted as the final solution. Identified heavily fragmented approach to work design had caused most issues. Secondary action showed how similar savings could be made elsewhere in the service including for statutory undertakers control and the LTP designs.
Reduction of third party claims arising from pot-holes. London Boro. Quick win sought to overcome significant annual budget increases.	Set up for labourers plus small vans with very simple technology and high value material, dealing with eight times the pot-holes per day compared to previous. No extra budget, claims reduced straight away.	We started with a quick analysis of road repair controls and processes, compared demand to capacity. Research by walking around compared to options. We sought a less bureaucratic approach with high outputs and empowerment / self audit. The resulting plan arrested an 18% annual increase in self insured costs, to being a fast reducing issue. For trips (not exceed 25mm), simply angle grind off the leading edge prior to permanent repair.
Street lighting management to reduce costs and CO_2 emissions. Large unitary.	Establishing far tighter control on actual energy usage, introducing a low energy estate lighting replacement using 400 year life columns with central switchgear to gradually dim or increase light intensity.	The increasing use of energy had been projected as considerably less than reality and energy costs were climbing fast. After research the new designs were agreed and implemented with an ability for global light level reductions in late evening through the night, with a switch up if some form of ASB occurred to disperse and record better on CCTV. Grant funded, with significant energy savings.
NRSWA now Traffic Management Act. Improved controls. Met council.	Self financed inspector appointed funded entirely from additional fees and penalties for the inspections. Saved costs of latter repairs, roads were safer and parking income improved.	Inadequate road repairs or safety control during works often leads to complaints, accidents and the long term deterioration of roads and paths. I proved that £6,000 worth of fines could be issued on one evening walk. I also proved that over 50% of Trips and Falls had a trench or opening as the initial cause. Some 10% of parking excuses started from incomplete works. The post was self funded in terms of 'fines' only, in addition safety increased and parking appeals reduced. Win-win-win!
Improvements to parking management, enforcement for shopping and work place prosperity.	Reduced appeals success from 80% to 20%, improved signs and lines, increased valid patronage in car parks, reduced nuisance parking. Annual income improved by £400,000. (This was helped with a strategic price increase) Traffic congestion started to ease. More spaces were paid for and yet more short stay spaces were available to park in.	The service had been fragmented, appeals proliferated, so parking attendants didn't issue enough tickets, (no point if they don't pay!) Admin went through the basics, then debtors wouldn't strongly chase debt, low volume low value! We started improvement in admin, flow chart, cause and effect, why did appeals succeed? Stop the causes! We improved signs and lines, the quality of tickets issued by individual PAs, made a better IT base with bad debt separately dealt with. We chased staff who habitually wouldn't pay, stopped ticket sharers. Even got the Police to stop an alleged cloned car. We finished up with more of everything: Spaces, tickets, fines paid, happy shop owners...

HOUSING MAINTENANCE, SAFETY AT HOME

Brief description	Achievements	Areas addressed /actions taken
Overall service delivery for one stop shop with an appointment on time. Small Housing Association.	All general, urgent and emergency repairs carried out within due time, to increasing customer satisfaction, with most jobs via a single visit. Costs reduced, staff and customers far happier.	Replaced four sets of T&C's with one set which embraced multi-skilling, appointments and quality of work. Refreshed IT systems to correctly record work and create meaningful reports to future manage. Replaced ageing fleet with cheaper one and enabled enforced depot closure to be replaced with day shed and fully integrated supplies contract with local suppliers.
Step increase in work demand without TUPE transfer while improving service delivery. Large DC.	Eliminated 1,000 overdue jobs plus doubled workflow in eight weeks. Improved overall customer satisfaction for north area in the first quarter with improvement there-after. Dealt with quantum shock as just another part of the process.	A contractor withdrew from an unsuitable contract (for them), causing a 110% increase in our work with no transfer of labour, equipment or vans, and a backlog of 1,000 overdue jobs. The fast-track recruitment process was problematic partly due to Jurassic HR support. The backlog grew for three weeks and was eradicated inside eight weeks. Phenomenal support from the whole team, all trained in continuous improvement concepts. We created new teams and field promoted staff, created new IT controls to micro-manage work flow. Including this blip we were still in the upper quartile for BV jobs on time for the whole year.
Step improvements to the quality and letting times for void properties. Small DC	Transformed a 45 day letting achievement to 12 working days, while carrying out condition improvement to revised standards. Nearly all homes became first time lets.	A series of issues were overcome to achieve this: Partnership working, joint inspection of property, key safe bolted to the property side, uniform standard of specification, communications between operatives, sub-contractors, suppliers and inspectors. Final clean and flowers left by professional cleaners.
Opportunities for business growth, security improvements and environmental improvement. Large Met council.	Trading with small housing associations, the elderly and at risk to carry out professional, value adding services to avoid cowboys and other contractors who are always top of the Trading Standards issues pages. A win-win solution.	Councils generally are overly worried about their freedoms to trade, but they have duties to safeguard the public, to reduce CO_2 and to reduce the relative impacts of poverty. Thus the concerns and responsibilities need analysis via an affinity diagram, if authorities can enable or carry out home safety, maintenance or environmental work, that will strengthen income while reducing the fear of crime and concerns about cowboy contractors.
Street-scene, integrating services to reduce gaps and duplications in services. Creating a safer cleaner environment. (Four very different councils)	Eradicated boundaries of work invisible to customers. Enabled seamless working, intuitive enforcement and rectification. Reduced issues that caused disquiet quickly and routinely. Reduced the demand for rectification thus enabled more proactive improvement.	It takes huge effort to be able to model a complex town centre as a system. Once that starts, designing in all the services who clean, collect, cultivate, regulate, maintain and construct to a coherent approach in locally self managed units across cross sections of contracts and budgets can be surprisingly easy. What needs to be remembered that there isn't a single solution, there needs to be an array of designs, each capturing a group of issues, such that all together they will improve services and cost no more than the former problematic solutions had cost.

OTHERS

Brief description	Achievements	Areas addressed /actions taken
Step reducing the cost of vehicle provision via better management. Small D.C.	Five times the average life span of tyres, for the whole fleet, achieving around a 70% cost saving. Industry leading methodology adopted by one of the largest HGV fleet tyre providers.	My transport manager applied operational learning post Deming training to vehicle management. One incredible piece of lateral thinking was applied to tyre management. Tyres on 26T refuse lorries are scuffed and scraped, always subject to accelerate and braking and go on tip twice a day. There are usually ten tyres per vehicle costing several hundred pounds each. He 'managed' the tyres to check pressures, alignment, turn them, re-cut and re-tread them, increasing the average lifespan from around 6,000 miles to nearer 30,000 miles while only adding 50% to costs. Thus a saving of over 70% on tyre costs was achieved.
Turn-round of sickness levels in a department of 2,500 employees. Large Met.	In less than six months the average sickness levels reduced by 40%, many areas becoming far better than industry averages.	The sickness levels in a very large council were very poor with no real prospects to improve. Central resources had been reduced; advice was ultra cautious, reporting more than two months late and woefully inadequate. Control had been lost. We improved information creating run charts, sub-analysed to worst locations, briefed HR that they would be less cautious, more positive to take action, engaged additional occupational health nurses to deal with the backlog, discussed the balance and role play with the unions. Were in every sense more pro-active. We took 'taking a sicky' out of the sickness management system, and declared it as fraud.
Addressing the fear of crime, creating a safer street-scene with an emphasis on housing association areas. Complex LAA.	First time holistic alignment and coordination of resources. Several 'first' uses of joined up powers, increased prevention and detection rates. Aligned websites with operational hyperlinks for connectivity. Local area engagement and empowerment of the public started to become a reality. Structure for area based liaison designed.	In an extremely complex, very varied area, the existing paper strategies were exceptionally good, lauded by the Audit Commission; however the nuts and bolts of working together in harmony were absent. We opened our doors to practicable partners, worked with the Police to align to their PACT areas, discussed operational issues with the Police and Housing Association, and linked with the probation and fire services. Aligned internal departments to speed work through. Greatly improved the use of GIS, created 44 operational sub areas to fast track response. Introduced shared ward walks, with several modules of strategic / operational planning to rapidly address social inclusion.
Business to business re-engineering. (Insourcing company within a unitary council)	Unstructured department with 22 direct reports reduced to 4 section heads. 4% loss transformed to 21% profit. All KPI's taken out of the red (failing) with virtually all taken out of the amber as well. No redundancies.	An in-sourcing contract with a prestigious council had created a department of 78 individuals 22 of whom reported to one senior officer. The role took a 37% financial risk of the whole contract (of 600 staff) and nearly half the KPI's to manage. Adding value by design, linkages, GIS, CRM and commitment accounting. Structure, improvement, positive energy, challenging internal audit and creating a more effective place to work.

These twenty two examples give an idea of application and practices available within this broader philosophy. There were a multitude of small wins on the way, enabling happier staff to work more effectively with less effort and far less repeating the same problems over and over again.

Many of the twenty two examples overlapped, most operational reviews included strategic development, re-writes and challenge.

New designs often created a blurring of boundaries. In the inner London borough, the post CCT work methods involved lots of 'invisible boundaries' that the public couldn't see, between housing estates and highways or open spaces. Litter picking to the edge of one land type would be immediately affected by wind blown material from the next.

Poor management and enforcement of markets caused litter everywhere else, while ignoring minor ASB and drug offences in underground car-parks, caused fear all around them.

By showing all these issues in a simple diagram, and thinking about them as a customer who cannot see the contractual, or operational boundaries, allows those boundaries to be designed more sensibly.

Consider the role of the park keeper; they cut grass, edge paths, pick up litter and glass, check play equipment for safety, remove dogs' muck, trim trees and hedges, empty litter bins, remove weeds, put up goal netting…

In general they look after a designated area, ensuring a safe, appealing landscape for the public, with an ability to report dangerous trees, pot-holes, play equipment and so forth, if more specialised support is needed.

Yet, in the streets most of these maintenance aspects are separated, different people collect the litter, from those who cut hedges, to cut grass, inspect lights (OK they need to do that after dark), inspect pot-holes…

From a design point of view, this is where the consideration of boundary conditions should be used. Separation of duties for large, repetitive and intensely occurring work makes sense, however in small towns and villages, a 'street-keeper' much the same as a park-keeper, may be a far more efficient and effective solution.

This goes back to a very early observation in this book, a prime design may be good for ninety per cent of the needs, yet dealing with the other ten per cent, can make the difference of more than twenty per cent of the costs.

At one host there was an extremely charismatic recycling manager (I'll call her Erica) whose prime role had gravitated to dealing with 'problem customers'. She was great at dealing with people, it was the systems she worked with that she hated.

Despite an excellent attitude to work, a caring nature to support those around her and a willingness to put in the hours when needed, she absolutely hated Monday mornings. It produced a gut-wrenching dread in her.

So, within the intervention, a well discussed, but never formally written desired outcome for the intervention, was for Erica to actually look forward to coming to work on a Monday morning. At first she, and others around us, thought that this was a flippant one off statement from us that would go away that day. However, the Transformation Team all kept Erica's Monday morning firmly in the plan for the final outcomes.

Deming understood the psychology of self motivation, taking the concept beyond those of Maslow in my mind. Among his 14 points seek: at 8, to drive out fear, at 9, to break down barriers between departments, and at 7, to institute leadership … to help people do a better job.

Why should Erica be personified as an example of what needed to be part of the prime focus of the intervention? As I said she was charismatic, she was also able to communicate well and wore her heart on her sleeve. Her job should have been to lead a team to add value to recyclates; we eventually showed this could reduce the council's costs by £1M a year, if they had time to do this. Yet most of her time was dealing with customer escalations, and then petty administration, most of which should be generated automatically from the systems.

Most of the problems being raised to her should have been dealt with by many people before she saw them. There was a considerable amount of data, but little knowledge. The Call Centre/Operations/Back Office segmentation with a useless IT system caused failures, inaction and internal arguments.

By the time these failures came to Erica customers were in despair and most people involved in denial. The IT system was basically totally wrong for the task in hand; to call a case file up in a very expensive database took an average of six minutes, then it often then gave quite spurious information.

Work had to be traced back – who did what initially? Why didn't this get resolved? Were the operations comments taken on board? Were they even directed to the right property?

In addition to this repetitive agony, the systems to record waste and recyclates weights were flawed and the vast majority of the annual budget had a pasting of last year's financial (but not operational) changes on the previous years, with little view of the truth other than the bottom right hand cell.

So effectively, nothing that she worked in was efficient, effective, fit for purpose or met business needs. Thus holding Erica's plight up and saying 'part of the vision for this Transformation is to make Erica look forward to coming to work on a Monday', may have seemed flippant, strange or even callous, but it was genuine and well worth aspiring to achieve.

If you have happy workers, able to do their work via well designed and integrated effective systems, more work will get done, fewer errors will occur, more value can be added, less sickness will occur, stress levels will reduce and customers will be happy.

This 'personalised' option will not occur at every intervention, but it's a really good litmus test for direction of travel. And yes, Erica started to find that Mondays weren't so bad after a while!

As a last opportunity within this book I'll have a little focus on equipment. It's invariably part of the cause and effect charts, and often an area where IT professionals take that same well-meaning approach to cutting costs that accountants espouse within their ABC paradigm.

A PC or laptop costs less than an average week's pay, the difference in costs between Office 2003 and Office 2007 is frankly peanuts, so why do these apparently intelligent senior officers nearly always act in a penny wise pound foolish way?

Excel 2007 can do many operations that 2003 cannot do; it will save time, data space and add value. In nearly every assignment I have worked within, resources are skimped on and opportunities wasted. If the host will not allow me access to the right kit I buy it myself, and get on with it and will not compromise! I'm there to add value not have potential clipped by small minded bureaucrats. (Yes my fuse here is shorter than most other areas.)

When we were discussing the 'six minutes for a report' as above, the IT senior officers asked how long was acceptable, my reply of, 'a couple of seconds', was taken as a joke. But I had taken the operational officers to a previous employer, where we had had total control of the IT, so my staff said 'we were at XXX last week, all these reports came up within the time of the screen refresh, there was no delay.'

In virtually all cases, scrimping on the hardware and software is a false economy. Get what is needed, ensuring that the system can work to your needs, not you have to bend to its functions. Remember for twenty thousand pounds we have had systems that out-performed £250K ones.

So cash isn't king, functionality is. Data security is a real issue with so many laptops going missing with valuable data in them, however, the prime role is to work smart and that should come ahead of being secure. Make sure you don't put the cart before the horse. That is, make sure that operational systems work, and then can be secure, rather than pinning down the security in such a way that operations are compromised.

So as part of the value for money aspect of the final reports, look at this with a fresh pair of eyes, what is the cost per hour of a senior officer: waiting for a report to run, a system to refresh or to create what should be an automatic report.

Let's say their costs are £30 an hour and they waste only 1½ hours a week. That's £45 per week, so four weeks pays for a faster machine, three weeks pays for the better software and twenty weeks buys the all signing database and report writer. The machine will last for around three years! So why are so many places pound foolish? Beats me!

This moves full circle to the Transformation Team, every BA and team leader needs access to fast laptops, Office 2007, Access, Visio and Winchart (or equivalents). Most will need PowerPoint, all will need internet access. If they are handling loads of data they need fast processors and large high quality screens.
If GIS is likely to be featured strongly there should be at least a 21" high quality screen for the mapping plus a 15" screen for the commands. A 32" screen in the main ops room makes team meetings and minor workshops far easier.

They'll also need: A3 colour printer, high volume A4 printer, scanner, projector, 3 no flip pads and stands, access to a plotter (for A0 plans and diagrams), pens, markers, post-its, pencils and a roll of brown paper plus sticky tape. They'll need a base camp with a notice board and white board, with internet and intranet access.

Meeting rooms should be fairly large to allow break outs, with an ability to eat and drink throughout the day, so that energy and tastes are all dealt with well.

This investment is so small compared to the value it will enable!

"The problem is at the top, management is the problem"
W. EDWARDS DEMING

11. SYSTEMS THINKING OPTIONS

I will start with a generic name of Systems Thinking[1], even though I don't believe that this is the correct title[2]. I have previously pointed out that this is not intended to be an academic book, although it is quite possible that an academic book with the same substance should follow.

While I enjoy research, I am not fanatical about 'crossing every T and dotting every I' when trying to expand my knowledge. Like many people I'm happy to get the gist of understanding where useful and only seek total immersion where essential. So here I drift from one zone to another. I have not tried to totally understand every way that a scientific approach can be taken to deal with change management.

Within the IDeA discussion threads for Systems Thinking which were started by me four years ago, I have 'met' and discussed various ideas and concepts that help me to improve, what I have now discovered to be a very limited knowledge of the 'Systems Thinking universe'. The more that I learn, the more that I realise that I don't know!

This is a very genuine statement. I've attended many training courses, seminars, workshops, and webinars plus educated meetings. I learn something new all the time, and do my best to file the information to add to possibilities next time. I had been told that I should be rated as 'Master Black Belt[3]', despite the fact that I have passed no quality based tests (other than ISO 9000 which shouldn't count) and am starting this chapter with trepidation. However, my colleagues now advise that my ranking would be 'Head of Six Sigma' or 'Head of transformation'. Martin Gibson was Head of Six Sigma at Motorola UK but was never a Black Belt – he had all the experience and qualifications required before Black Belts were even invented.

The main reason for concern is that my research will be thin in many ways in the areas of 'soft systems' approaches. I read some papers on these six months ago and they may as well have been in Urdu. I can survive in a bar or café in several European languages, but my command of languages is poor.

Nearly two years ago I attended a class on soft systems and liked all the clouds, but gained no insight at all. So with a little hard work and much reading I'm approaching a novice capability in this area. My attempts to talk with both / various camps of Systems Thinking at the same time (on and around the IDeA discussion threads) have caused problems, so my translation skills are still woefully out of tune.

So without any more hesitance or prevarication… you'll get the idea!

CONTINUOUS IMPROVEMENT

Most people cite Dr. W Edwards Deming[4] as being the initiator of quality management, although Walter Shewhart[5] was his mentor. Deming first went to Japan in 1948; it is understood that Deming had a deep respect for the Japanese culture. It was in 1950 that the Japanese Union of Scientists and Engineers wrote and invited him to lecture to them on statistical methods for industry. Later, through JUSE, Deming was able to give seminars to over 500 Japanese presidents, chief executives, and senior managers, as part of an American support after the Second World War. This represented eighty per cent of the capital value of Japan at that time.

During these lectures Deming showed business as a flow on blackboards, in August 1950, it was almost forty years prior to these being in his books. The Japanese employers and businesses took to Deming and soon were listening and acting on what he had to say.

This led to continuous improvement based on statistical process control[6] (SPC). Please refer to chapters 2, 3 and 4 of 'Quality or Politics' which deals with the development of SPC theory and practice. This shows how Deming wove together the two fundamental arts of science and psychology. Even in 1950 Deming was talking about boundaries to systems; in 1950 the boundary was the whole of Japan.

In time the Plan, Do, Study, Act cycle became common place as a basis for change management, Deming's chain reaction to expand market growth and employment by improving quality was very different to the American concepts. By 1970 the re-birth of the Japanese manufacturing position led to a few businesses in America adopting most of his principles, which eventually started into Europe in the 1980s.

Visualising work as a flow was shown within *Out of the crisis* in 1988 and in *The New Economics* in 1994. By this time Deming had discussed a Theory of Profound Knowledge (see page 47) where you need to understand: Systems, Knowledge, Variation and Psychology to be able to have a rounded understanding of how a business works.

He ran many four-day workshops around the world in order to discuss, model and challenge ideas. He ran statistical based games such as the red bead test and the funnel experiment. These both show how current management techniques not only damage a business but can ruin an economy.

Many people have learned from, adopted and adapted the methods and learning from Deming. One of the most heralded is Taiichi Ohno. Ohno worked for Toyota and was the lead person developing what has become known simply as TPS, the Toyota Production System[7].

TPS has strong resonance with Deming, it's highly dependent upon variability reduction and waste prevention, further developing SPC with measurements at the place of work, with analysis and constant probing to improve systems. In developing this chapter I have been in discussions with individuals with quite differing views on TPS.

Many people associate TPS solely with Lean / Kaizen / Continuous Improvement while others say that this is the production side of Toyota only. The extreme view is that TPS includes over a hundred tools for product and service improvement, all of which get used where they will add value. I can relate to this, my initial training as a Civil Engineer involved a very wide array of technical, mathematical, management, project management, computing and statistical elements. A good professional uses the right tools and techniques at the right time, blending them and balancing them as needs be. Toyota would not be a great company by making the best cars alone.

What wasn't so clear from the majority of my research until recently is that there are several methods of change going on at any one time, even with a business like Toyota which is a world leader in product reliability. TPS (production) is based on what I am calling hard systems approaches, however, the management of the whole of Toyota as a business is more likely to be managed via what have been further developed to be known as soft systems within my terminology for this book.

Production /transactional systems can be described as closed 'Deming based' systems of work within defined boundaries. Toyota also operates as an open systems cybernetic system and may employ all the wide breadth of methods, e.g. SSM, VSM, TSI, CAS etc. An open system reflects 'Ashby's law of requisite variety' and also the resource based view of the firm. Whether or not Toyota adapt an emergent or divergent strategy is another issue.

The 'hard side' is based mainly on minimising variation so that reliable products are produced, while the 'soft side' will often seek to embrace variety, seeking boundary conditions and grouping of issues.

So in the current world market is the future vision in the production of large gas guzzling cars, or smaller, safer environmentally efficient ones? Should we solely use petrol and diesel or should other energy sources be used? Should we stay in Formula One or have some more appropriate world image?

The soft systems approaches were using the term 'Systems Thinking' some thirty years ago, while the use of the same term for hard systems seems to have started within the last decade via the work of John Seddon. The following are abstracts from various sources to give an idea of the breadth of the subject.

LEAN SERVICES

This is the application of the lean[8] manufacturing concept to service operations. It is distinct in that *Lean Services* are not concerned with the making of 'hard' products.

To date, lean principles of continuous improvement and respect for people have been successfully applied to call centre services, health care, higher education, software development, plus public and professional services. Conceptually, these implementations follow very similar routes to those in manufacturing settings, and very often make use of the same tools and techniques. Two key distinctions however are differing types of wastes, and the distinction between value demand and failure demand.

Large IT software systems are better developed via soft systems approaches discussed later in this chapter. Again people from the differing backgrounds have strong views on which approaches are most appropriate.

Understanding of Service

'Service' in this context is not limited to 'the office' or 'administration' that have been the focus of several publications, but also wider service situations that are not necessarily repetitive, where 'takt' time is not applicable, and where task times may be both long and variable. Service in this context could mean anything from a hospital to a university, from an office process to a consultancy, and from a warehouse to field service maintenance.

It is important not to confuse 'service operations' with the economic definition of service sectors (as distinct from manufacturing sectors), since many 'service sector' organisations have manufacturing-like operations in that they produce regular outputs along value streams. In both cases there will be customer facing services and support services such as sales, procurement, marketing, after-sales, finance etc.

Instead, 'service' refers to the 'service concept' or 'product service bundle', which are all the activities that provide value to the customer along a value stream.

The Service Wastes

The original seven wastes (Muda) are based on and predated by Therbligs, which are 1940s industrial engineering techniques. It is worth noting that Shingo at Toyota was an industrial engineer and employed 100 or so quality tools and techniques; these were further defined by Taiichi Ohno, the father of the Toyota Production System. While these waste categories have been applied to service operations, their manufacturing heritage can make this difficult in practice, and leads to redefinition of these wastes for service operations.

The seven Service Wastes can be defined as:

1. *Delay* on the part of customers waiting for service, for delivery, in queues, for response, not arriving as promised. The customer's time may seem free to the provider, but when she takes custom elsewhere the pain begins.

2. *Duplication*. Having to re-enter data, repeat details on forms, copy information across, answer queries from several sources within the same organisation.

3. *Unnecessary Movement*. Queuing several times, lack of one-stop, poor ergonomics in the service encounter.

4. *Unclear communication*, and the wastes of seeking clarification, confusion over product or service use, wasting time finding a location that may result in misuse or duplication.

5. *Incorrect inventory.* Being out-of-stock, unable to get exactly what was required, substitute products or services.

6. *An opportunity lost to retain or win customers*, a failure to establish rapport, ignoring customers, unfriendliness, and rudeness.

7. *Errors in the service transaction*, product defects in the product-service bundle, lost or damaged goods.

Value Demand and Failure Demand

One of the central concepts that distinguish lean services from lean manufacturing is the concept of *value demand* and *failure demand* (Seddon, 2003).

Value demand is the demand for service from customers, while *failure demand* is the demand caused by a failure to do something right for the customer. Failure demand is thus demand that only exists because initial demand was not satisfied properly. For example, a large proportion of calls that call centres receive are either chasing up enquiries made earlier, or to correct earlier work that was not done properly. As one of the key aims of lean is to eliminate waste, failure demand represents a first and obvious type of waste in service organisations.

By treating failure and value demand alike in statistical analysis, failure demand can help give a quite false impression of greater productivity. There may be 14,000 transactions, but only 9,000 add value, or are value-enabling. This merely reinforces the need to look at this all from the customer's perspective, and ask what he or she might think of the service.

We should also take some caution here, in that most call centres are built on a seven layer ETOM architecture where the process is embedded in the technology. It is believed to be cheaper to generate another call than train all operators to answer all queries right first time especially with an average contact centre annual staff turn-over rate of 30%. (UK average)

Care should also be taken not to design all call centres based on one belief, narrow based, high repetition centres need a very different design from a local authority centre where there is very broad demand, for an array of totally different services.

DG comment: I have introduced the Lean Services aspect prior to Lean Manufacturing and Six Sigma, due to the affinity to the Public Sector. Researching this chapter largely via Google and Wikipedia produces interesting questions regarding, 'who said what first' and 'who developed one area compared to another'. What is obvious is that some books and references are clearly wrong; a collaboration between several learned bodies to establish an agreed truth is being sought.

I will not attempt to fully detail what 'Systems Thinking the Vanguard way is' as I believe that John Seddon enables his consultants and customers to evolve with time and experience. There is a link to the Vanguard web site from www.supportservicesdirect.co.uk which has many excellent stories to tell. The differentiation of failure demand from value demand exhibits one area where ABC is so wrong in counting all activities. Vanguard are producing a book of case studies at the same time as this book.

TPS (TOYOTA PRODUCTION SYSTEM)

TPS is an integrated socio-technical system, developed by Toyota, which comprises its management philosophy and practices. The TPS organises manufacturing and logistics for the automobile manufacturer, including interaction with suppliers and customers. This is a major precursor of "Lean manufacturing." Taiichi Ohno, Shigeo Shingo and Eiji Toyoda developed TPS between 1948 and 1975.

Originally called Just In Time Production, it builds on the approach created by the founder of Toyota, Sakichi Toyoda, his son Kiichiro Toyoda and the engineer Taiichi Ohno. The founders of Toyota drew heavily on the work of W. Edwards Deming and the writings of Henry Ford and F.W. Taylor. When these men came to the United States to observe the assembly line and mass production that had made Ford rich, they were unimpressed. While shopping in a supermarket they observed the simple idea of an automatic drink resupplier; when the customer wants a drink, he takes one, and another replaces it. The principles underlying the TPS are embodied in The Toyota Way.

The main objectives of the TPS are to design out overburden (muri) and inconsistency (mura), and to eliminate waste (muda). The most significant effects on process value delivery are achieved by designing a process capable of delivering the required results smoothly; by designing out inconsistency. It is also crucial to ensure that the process is as flexible as necessary without stress or overburden, since this generates waste. Finally the tactical improvements of waste reduction or the elimination of muda are very valuable. There are seven kinds of muda that are addressed in the TPS:

1. over-production
2. motion (of operator or machine)
3. waiting (of operator or machine)
4. conveyance
5. processing itself
6. inventory (raw material)
7. correction (rework and scrap).

The elimination of muda has come to dominate the thinking of many when they look at the effects of the TPS because it is the most familiar of the three to implement. In the TPS many initiatives are triggered by mura or muri reduction which drives out muda without specific focus on its reduction.

This system, more than any other aspect of the company, is responsible for having made Toyota the company it is today. Toyota has long been recognised as a leader in the automotive manufacturing and production industry. Following staggering growth over the last three decades, it also has fallen foul of the world wide recession. The next few years will determine which companies have the inner capabilities to achieve new positive stabilities.

While low inventory levels are a key outcome of the Toyota Production System, an important element of the philosophy behind its system is to work intelligently and eliminate waste so that significant inventory is no longer needed. Many American businesses, having observed Toyota's factories, set out to attack high inventory levels directly without understanding what made these reductions possible. The act of imitating without understanding the underlying concept or motivation may have led to the failure of those projects (similar to seeing only the tip of an iceberg).

The underlying principles, called 'The Toyota Way' are outlined as follows:

The right process will produce the right results

1. Create continuous process flow to bring problems to the surface.
2. Use the 'pull' system to avoid overproduction.
3. Level out the workload (heijunka). (Work like the tortoise, not the hare.)
4. Build a culture of stopping to fix problems, to get quality right from the first.
5. Standardised tasks are the foundation for continuous improvement and employee empowerment.
6. Use visual control so no problems are hidden.
7. Use only reliable, thoroughly tested technology that serves your people and processes.

Add value to the organisation by developing your people and partners

1. Grow leaders who thoroughly understand the work, live the philosophy, and teach it to others.
2. Develop exceptional people and teams who follow your company's philosophy.
3. Respect your extended network of partners and suppliers by challenging them and helping them improve.

Continuously solving root problems drives organisational learning

1. Go and see for yourself to thoroughly understand the situation.
2. Make decisions slowly by consensus, thoroughly considering all options; implement decisions rapidly.
3. Become a learning organisation through relentless reflection and continuous improvement (Kaizen, 改善).

The Toyota Production System has been compared to squeezing water from a dry towel. What this means is that it is a system for thorough waste elimination and waste prevention. Here, waste refers to anything which does not advance the process, everything that does not increase added value. Many people settle for eliminating the waste that everyone recognises as waste. But a considerable amount still remains that simply has not yet been recognised as waste or that people are willing to tolerate.

People had resigned themselves to certain problems, had become hostage to routine and abandoned the practice of problem-solving. This going back to basics, exposing the real significance of problems and then making fundamental improvements, can be witnessed throughout the Toyota Production System.

DG comment: The Toyota Production System has helped to revolutionise the production world, reducing the costs of goods while increasing their quality enormously. It has been the inability of much of the western world to realise that the attention to design and process to carry out work is paramount to survival. This applies to services just as much as it did to production. ***This is a key learning point: the failure of American business over the last thirty years to change has led to recession and unemployment, so why use their way of work to manage services?***

KAIZEN 改善 (AND KAIZEN BLITZ)

While kaizen (at Toyota) usually delivers small improvements, the culture of continual aligned small improvements and standardisation yields large results in the form of compound productivity improvement. This philosophy differs from the command and control improvement programmes of the mid-twentieth century. Kaizen methodology includes making changes and monitoring results, then adjusting. Large-scale pre-planning and extensive project scheduling are replaced by smaller experiments, which can be rapidly adapted as new improvements are suggested.

In modern usage, a focused kaizen that is designed to address a particular issue over the course of a week is referred to as a 'kaizen blitz' or 'kaizen event'. These are limited in scope, and issues that arise from them are typically used in later blitzes. The original kanji characters for this word are: 改善 which in Japanese is pronounced 'kaizen'. 改 (kai) means change or the action to correct and 善 (zen) means good.

Kaizen is a daily activity, the purpose of which goes beyond simple productivity improvement. It is also a process that, when done correctly, humanises the workplace, eliminates overly hard work and teaches people how to perform experiments on their work using the scientific method and how to learn to spot and eliminate waste in business processes. The philosophy can be defined as bringing back the thought process into the automated production environment dominated by repetitive tasks that traditionally required little mental participation from the employees.

People at all levels of an organisation can participate in kaizen, from the CEO down, as well as external stakeholders when applicable. The format for kaizen can be individual, suggestion system, small group, or large group. At Toyota, it is usually a local improvement within a workstation or local area and involves a small group in improving their own work environment and productivity. This group is often guided through the kaizen process by a line supervisor; sometimes this is the line supervisor's key role. Kaizen on a broad, cross-departmental scale in companies, generates total quality management, and frees human efforts through improving productivity using machines and computing power.

DG comment: Being aware of the meaning of Kaizen is sufficient within this book, the TPS would embody the philosophy of kaizen. While a kaizen blitz may help an organisation get better, it may not have the rigour or longevity of a more traditional Kaizen intervention. The 'succeed or fail' concept with a blitz is sufficient cause for concern in my opinion to avoid them. If a service is poor, which most are, a blitz will improve it, but not as much as a more rounded approach would achieve. You could however argue that the rescue of the garden waste service was a form of blitz?

LEAN (MANUFACTURING) ABSTRACT TO COMPARE

Lean manufacturing or lean production, which is often known simply as '**Lean**', is a production practice that considers the expenditure of resources for any goal other than the creation of value for the end customer to be wasteful, and thus a target for elimination. Working from the perspective of the customer who consumes a product or service, 'value' is defined as any action or process that a customer would be willing to pay for. Basically, lean is centred on creating more value with less work for the customer.

Lean manufacturing is a generic process management philosophy derived mostly from the Toyota Production System. It is renowned for its focus on reduction of the original Toyota *seven wastes* in order to improve overall customer value, but there are varying perspectives on how this is best achieved. The steady growth of Toyota, from a small company to the world's largest automaker, has focused attention on how it has achieved this.

Lean manufacturing is a variation on the theme of efficiency based on optimising flow; it is a present-day instance of the recurring theme in human history toward increasing efficiency, decreasing waste, and using empirical methods to decide what matters, rather than uncritically accepting pre-existing ideas.

For many, Lean is the set of 'tools' that assist in the identification and steady elimination of waste. As waste is eliminated quality improves while production time and cost are reduced. Examples of such 'tools' are Value Stream Mapping, Five S, pull systems and error-proofing.

There is a second approach to Lean Manufacturing, which is promoted by Toyota, in which the focus is upon improving the 'flow' or smoothness of work, thereby steadily eliminating unevenness through the system and not upon waste reduction per se. Techniques to improve flow include production levelling, pull production and the *Heijunka box*. This is a fundamentally different approach to most improvement methodologies which may partially account for its lack of popularity.

DIFFERENCES FROM TPS

Whilst Lean is seen by many as a generalisation of the Toyota Production System into other industries and contexts there are some acknowledged differences that seem to have developed in implementation.

1. **Seeking profit** is a relentless focus for Toyota exemplified by the profit maximisation principle (Price – Cost = Margin) and the need, therefore, to practice systematic cost reduction (through TPS or otherwise) in order to realise benefit. Lean implementations can tend to de-emphasise this key measure and thus become fixated with the implementation of improvement concepts of 'flow' or 'pull'. Toyota often used target costing values rather than seeking to maximise profit. However, the emergence of the "value curve analysis" promises to directly tie lean improvements to bottom-line performance measurements.

2. **Tool orientation** is a tendency in many programmes to elevate mere tools (standardised work, value stream mapping, visual control, etc.) to an unhealthy status beyond their pragmatic intent. The tools are just different ways to work around certain types of problems but they do not solve them for you or always highlight the underlying cause of many types of problems. The tools employed at Toyota are often used to expose particular problems that are then dealt with, as each tool's limitations or blind-spots are perhaps better understood. So, for example, Value Stream Mapping focuses upon material and information flow problems (a title built into the Toyota title for this activity) but is not strong on Metrics, Man or Method. Internally they well know the limits of the tool and understood that it was never intended as the best way to see and analyse every waste or every problem related to quality, downtime, personnel development, cross training related issues, capacity bottlenecks, or anything to do with profits, safety, metrics or morale, etc. No single tool can do all of that. In order to surface these issues, other tools are much more widely and effectively used.

3. **Management technique rather than change agents** has been a principle in Toyota from the early 1950s when they started emphasising the development of the production managers' and supervisors' skills set in guiding natural work teams and did not rely upon staff-level change agents to drive improvements. This can manifest itself as a Push implementation of Lean rather than Pull by the team itself. This area of skills development is not that of the change agent specialist, but that of the natural operations work team leader.

Although less prestigious than the TPS specialists, development of work team supervisors in Toyota is considered an equally, if not more important, topic merely because there are tens of thousands of these individuals. Specifically, it is these manufacturing leaders that are the main focus of training efforts in Toyota since they lead the daily work areas, and they directly and dramatically affect quality, cost, productivity, safety, and morale of the team environment. In many companies implementing Lean, the reverse set of priorities is true. Emphasis is put on developing the specialist, while the supervisor skill level is expected to somehow develop over time on its own.

DG comment: There are certain aspects of Lean which do not work well for me, there are some that say 'A tidy desk is a sign of a tidy mind.' Well when I'm into a large project I like to have loads of papers and graphs to hand. If part of lean is having a tidy desk, I fail! Frequently I will plaster a wall in graphs, diagrams and flow-charts, keeping records of superseded charts with a simple S/S and date written on the version, with the new version retained over the top of it.

However, Lean was the basis for the renaissance of Porsche from a failing 'massive rework company' to the relative minnow who are buying Volkswagen. One of John Seddon's most frequent concerns has been about 'tool heads'. People who have the kit, but not the notion! I consider some people to be far too mechanistic, unable to use the right ideas at the right time. Change should become second nature, with the surety to move forward in harmony.

SIX SIGMA

Six Sigma originated as a set of practices designed to improve manufacturing processes and eliminate defects, but its application was subsequently extended to other types of business processes as well. In Six Sigma, a defect is defined as any process output that does not meet customer specifications, or that could lead to creating an output that does not meet customer specifications.

Bill Smith first formulated the particulars of the methodology at Motorola in 1986. Six Sigma was heavily inspired by six preceding decades of quality improvement methodologies such as quality control, TQM, and Zero Defects, based on the work of pioneers such as Shewhart, Deming and Crosby. Deming once dismissed Six Sigma as 'A nostrum that misses the point!'

Alternatively Six Sigma can be described as a cut down version of TQM with a reduced tools set, using only six tools, with an approach centred on SPC. The 3.4 defects/ million opportunities is said to be fundamentally flawed. See properties of normal distributions, the 1.5 sigma shift is not proven. In these cases how would you define short and long term process drift? This is meaningless, 'as long term drift' on a milling machine can be one day or could be one year or so for a different process. Run /control charts cannot be used for non-normal distributions, ie for service processes where variable work content is involved.

Like its predecessors, Six Sigma doctrine asserts that:

- ▷ Continuous efforts to achieve stable and predictable process results (i.e. reduce process variation) are of vital importance to business success.
- ▷ Manufacturing and business processes have characteristics that can be measured, analysed, improved and controlled.
- ▷ Achieving sustained quality improvement requires commitment from the entire organisation, particularly from top-level management.

Features that set Six Sigma apart from previous quality improvement initiatives include:

- ▷ A clear focus on achieving measurable and quantifiable financial returns from any Six Sigma project.
- ▷ An increased emphasis on strong and passionate management leadership and support.
- ▷ A special infrastructure of Champions, Master Black Belts, Black Belts, etc. to lead and implement the Six Sigma approach. *(There is no standard to define these grades, and thus no rigour to prove competence.)*
- ▷ A clear commitment to making decisions on the basis of verifiable data, rather than assumptions and guesswork.

The term Six Sigma comes from a field of statistics known as process capability studies. Originally, it referred to the ability of manufacturing processes to produce a very high proportion of output within specification. Processes that operate with six sigma quality over the short term are assumed to produce long-term defect levels below 3.4 defects per million opportunities (DPMO). Six Sigma's implicit goal is to improve all processes to that level of quality or better. Even their statistics are challenged! *While Six Sigma is marketed as the level at which 3.4 defects occurs, statistically this should be 4.5 sigma. From a marketing point of view four point five sigma isn't too clear.*

Don Wheeler says in *The Six Sigma Practitioner's Guide to Data Analysis* (speaking about DMAIC models) 'The fact that so much progress has been reported (through the use of DMAIC) is either a tribute to the ability of Six Sigma Practitioners to identify things that have escaped the notice of previous generations of process engineers, or else it is a commentary on how completely disorganised everyone was to begin with.'

Six Sigma is a registered service mark and trademark of Motorola Inc. As of 2006 Motorola reported over US$17 billion in savings from Six Sigma.

Methods

Six Sigma projects follow two project methodologies inspired by Deming's Plan-Do-Check-Act Cycle. These methodologies, comprising five phases each, bear the acronyms DMAIC and DMADV.

- ▷ DMAIC is used for projects aimed at improving an existing business process.
- ▷ DMADV is used for projects aimed at creating new product or process designs.

DMAIC

The DMAIC project methodology has five phases:

- ▷ ***D****efine* the problem, the voice of the customer, and the project goals, specifically.
- ▷ ***M****easure* key aspects of the current process and collect relevant data.
- ▷ ***A****nalyse* the data to investigate and verify cause-and-effect relationships. Determine what the relationships are, and attempt to ensure that all factors have been considered. Seek out root cause of the defect under investigation.
- ▷ ***I****mprove* or optimise the current process based upon data analysis using techniques such as design of experiments, poka yoke or mistake proofing, and standard work to create a new, future state process. Set up pilot runs to establish process capability.
- ▷ ***C****ontrol* the future state process to ensure that any deviations from target are corrected before they result in defects. Control systems are implemented such as statistical process control, production boards, and visual workplaces and the process is continuously monitored.

DMADV

The DMADV project methodology, sometimes incorrectly termed as DFSS (**D**esign **F**or **S**ix **S**igma), features five phases:

- *Define* design goals that are consistent with customer demands and the enterprise strategy.
- *Measure* and identify CTQs characteristics that are **C**ritical **T**o **Q**uality, product capabilities, production process capability, and risks.
- *Analyse* to develop and design alternatives, create a high-level design and evaluate design capability to select the best design.
- *Design* details, optimise the design, and plan for design verification. This phase may require simulations.
- *Verify* the design, set up pilot runs, implement the production process and hand it over to the process owners.

DG comment: There is no doubt that Six Sigma is a powerful set of practices to improve products and start new product designs. The creation of Lean Six Sigma may have enabled enough deviation from the registered methods to enable others to claim proficiency without the control. But there is also a strong argument to say that the control placed on Six Sigma actually builds in waste with people receiving weeks of instruction in techniques they will never use, and the sheer governance of Black Belt projects holding back the bigger gains in much the same way as for PRINCE2 in earlier chapters. The categorisation of capabilities for people within the system are good, although the linkage to martial arts is not always helpful.

VALUE MANAGEMENT

Value Management uses a unique combination of concepts and methods to create sustainable value for both organisations and their stakeholders. Some tools and techniques are specific to Value Management and others are generic tools that many organisations and individuals use. Detailed below is a summary of some of the main tools and techniques.

In terms of Value: Value = Function or Objective / Cost, i.e. you get what you require for what you pay. This is one of the better defined and controlled approaches in the UK with an institute to be a member of and progress through learning. The table below summarises most of the approach.

Tool	Description	Benefits
Brainstorming or Mind Showering	Idea generation that focuses on creation of ideas by volume (no judging)	Allows a large volume of ideas to be generated in a short period of time. Also strives to ensure all parties are involved – no ideas are discounted initially (later evaluation and filtering undertaken)
Cost Benefit Analysis	Used to analyse the costs of implementing something compared to the benefits to be achieved. Assists business case submissions.	Often used in VM on procedure or process type projects. Can be combined with other tools e.g. process mapping, option selection.
Criteria Weighting Technique	A tool used to assist in option selection. Uses functional drivers (or objectives) that are weighted for scoring options against.	Enables option selection and alternatives to be reviewed in order to support decisions being made.
Excursion/ Metaphors	A tool used to take delegates on an outward and return journey (possible excursion). Moves delegates away from a problem to somewhere where creativity flourishes. The return journey often releases such creativity and ideas that would not normally be evident.	Very effective in bringing creativity to the forefront. Often used as a precursor to brainstorming or other idea generation tools.
Function Analysis System Technique (FAST)	Identification of functions (at the heart of Value Management) of products, processes, projects or services. Focused on client needs and wants.	Determines what functions are delivered i.e. what they do or must do, not what they are (avoiding solution mode). The FAST diagram works by asking how the functions (primary and secondary) relate to each other by ask How and Why questions to check the logic work. Later costs are added to functions to assist in identifying any VM mismatches or areas of over-engineering.
Objectives Hierarchy	Diagrammatic process for identifying objectives in a hierarchical manner. Often used in conjunction with functions.	Assists in focusing input where the key objectives are as the diagram is constructed in descending order.
Issues Generation and Analysis	A way of eliciting many issues connected with a problem or opportunity. Team members write down their issues on post-it notes and they are displayed on the wall under appropriate categories or groupings. e.g. Requirements, Constraints, Problems, Opportunities, Assumptions, Uncertainties, Risks	Voting of the top 10 important issues follows. Actions to address issued then explored.

Tool	Description	Benefits
Process Mapping	Uses basic flow charts to review steps in processes	Identifies processes in a diagrammatic format in a step by step manner. Often used in manufacturing of system type processes. Used to identify omissions or superfluous items in the process for correction.
Risk Analysis	A structured approach to identifying risks that could affect project, product, process or service success. Risks are identified, evaluated (in terms of cost, time, and other impact) and robust action planning applied.	Often used in parallel with Value Management as there are genuine links. Assists decision making or option selection.
SCAMPER	Used as a checklist to develop ideas by applying separate verbs to chosen ideas singly or together with others. E.g. Combine, Amend, Modify, Put to other use, Expand, Reverse/Reduce	This could help with moving an idea from a creative thought to a more practical use, expand on the concept behind ideas, find different ways of expressing the idea, provoke new ideas, etc.
Stakeholder Analysis	Identifies those key stakeholders (groups of individuals) with an influence or interest in a project, product, process or service.	Can assist in focusing attention where the priorities are required i.e. satisfaction of key stakeholder interests.
SWOT Analysis	Identifies strengths, weaknesses, opportunities and threats. A tool used in many organisations to assist in focusing activities where required and minimise those items that can impact negatively.	Assists in understanding strengths, weaknesses, opportunities and threats that can impact on an organisation, individual, product or process.
Value Analysis	Structured team based approach to identifying functional requirements of projects, products, processes or services.	Optimisation and maximisation of value to the client or customer. Optimum balance between function and cost without detriment to quality.
5 W's & H	A technique for exploring problems which provokes further depth of questioning about the dimensions framing the problem or opportunity.	Who - e.g. is responsible? Why - e.g. is the end date important? What - e.g. what would happen if the scheme were delayed? When - e.g. must the work start? Where - e.g. might the problem occur? How - e.g. might we do this seemingly impossible thing?

DG comment: I am very supportive of the concept of having an Institute to regulate Value Management and by extension any service provider. VM has many similarities to other approaches discussed elsewhere in this chapter. While they use cause and effect and some other imagery, I naturally prefer a less prescriptive approach than I believe that VM uses.

There are some aspects of Value Management that seem similar to Quality Function Deployment (QFD), and I could have considered QFD as an entry of its own. There is a QFD Institute and it carries its own accreditation system with Green and Black Belts.

SOFT SYSTEM METHODOLOGY

Soft Systems Methodology (SSM) was developed by Peter Checkland, Brian Wilson and others at the University of Lancaster in the late 1960's. Originally it was seen as a modelling tool, but in later years it has been seen increasingly as a learning and meaning development tool.

At the heart of SSM is a comparison between the 'world as it is' and some models of the 'world as it might be'. Arising from this comparison should be a better understanding of the world 'research' and some ideas for improvement 'action'.

The researchers begin with a real-world problem. They study the systems which contain the problem. Following this, they develop some models of that system that generate insights into the way the 'real-world' problem might be addressed. As this is a systems methodology, the models must be formed using systems rules and concepts which are shown as being in seven stages.

1. ***The problem situation unstructured.*** The problem situation is first experienced, by the researcher. That is, the researcher makes as few assumptions about the nature of the situation as possible.

2. ***The problem situation expressed.*** In this step the researcher develops a detailed description, a rich picture, of the situation within which the problem occurs. This is most often done diagrammatically. In addition to the logic of the situation, the rich picture also tries to capture the relationships, the value judgments people make and the feel of the situation.

3. ***Root definitions of relevant systems.*** This is where the root definitions, or essence of the relevant systems, are defined. There are two aspects, the logical analysis and the cultural analysis. For the logical analysis, Checkland provides the mnemonic CATWOE as a checklist for ensuring that the important features of the root definitions are included:

   Customers............................who are system beneficiaries
   Actors..................................who transform inputs to outputs
   Transformation....................from inputs into outputs
   Weltanschauung.................the relevant world views of ALL the actors, players and owners
   Owner..................................the persons with power of veto over the system
   Environmental constraints..that need to be considered

The transformation element is one of the features that signal this as a systems approach. Checkland encourages you, and indeed virtually insists, that you develop several root definitions. Each root definition will have different elements in CATWOE. You are expected to be creative.

For instance think of a professional football match. What root definitions flow from seeing it as a means of keeping hooligans out of shopping malls, police training for crowd control, a means of keeping 25 people fit and well paid, a way of entertaining 30,000 people in one place, an exercise in product advertising?

A root definition could be 'A system that permits police recruits to be more highly trained in the humane control of a large excited crowd, allowing them to keep within current legislation and out of the Sunday newspapers and the Police Station.' Here the Customers are the police recruits, the actors are the crowd, the transformation is the ability to control crowds, and the Weltanschauung is humane: for evaluation terms the value or worth, the owner is the Police Inspector and the environmental constraints are legislation and the Press. Not all root definitions have to be this cumbersome.

The cultural analysis has three parts:

i. A role analysis, focusing on the intervention itself. This seeks to identify the client, the would-be problem solver (the researcher), and the problem owner (roughly, stakeholders). In the terms that we used earlier, you could think of this as the diagnostic part of entry and contracting.

ii. A social system analysis. This identifies for the problem situation, three sets of elements: roles, norms, and values.

iii. A political system analysis. This identifies the use of power in the problem situation.

4. ***Making and testing conceptual models.*** This is a critical and rigorous step. The task now is to develop a systems model using only those elements of the root definition, in a way that flows logically from that root definition, which has all the properties which define a system (Checkland has his own definitions of key system components). Other systems theories may also be used to test and reframe the conceptual model. The researcher now draws upon their knowledge of systems concepts and models. They develop descriptions, in system terms, of how the relevant parts of the situation might function.

5. ***Comparing conceptual models with reality.*** The purpose is not to implement the conceptual models. Rather, it is so that models and reality can be compared and contrasted. The differences can be used as the basis for a discussion: how the relevant systems work, or might work, and what the implications of that might be.

6. ***Identify feasible and desirable changes.*** From step 5, certain possible changes are identified. They are likely to vary in desirability and feasibility: Is it technically an improvement? Does it fit the culture?

7. ***Action to improve the problem situation.*** The most desirable and feasible changes identified at step 6 are now put into practice. In the past decade, Checkland has modified this basic structure into four core activities:-

   i. Finding out about a problem situation

   ii. Formulating some relevant purposeful activity

   iii. Debating the situation using the models; seeking from the debate desirable and feasible changes which would improve the situation, and accommodate conflicting interests

   iv. Taking action to improve the situation.

A brief review of the systems approaches shows several layers of modelling, as shown below for instance;

DIAGRAM SHOWING THEORETICAL BOUNDARY CONDITIONS

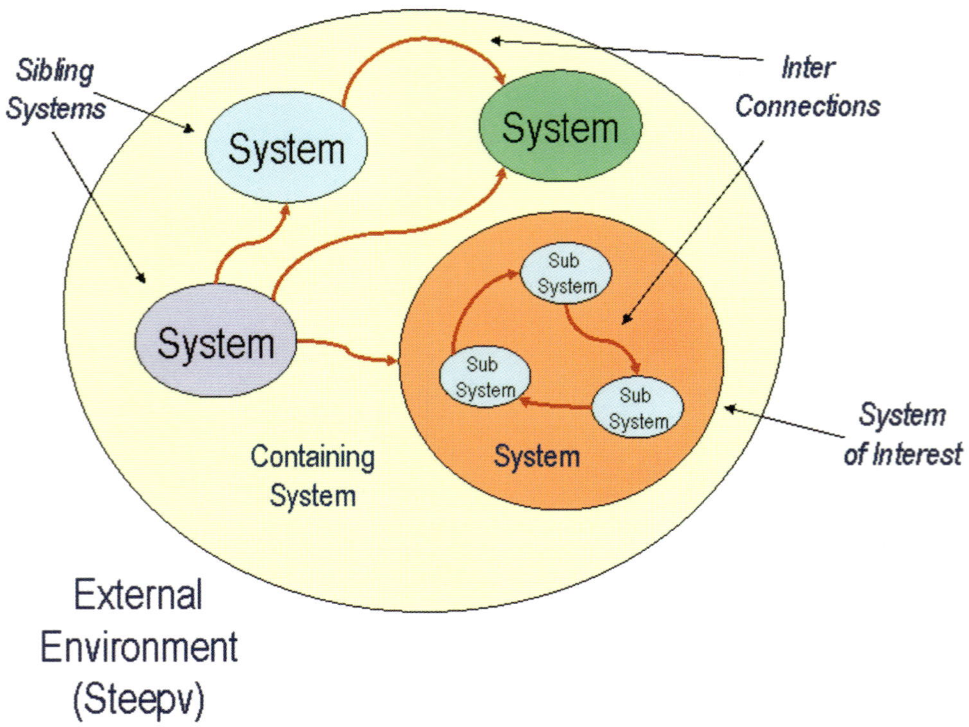

DIAGRAM SHOWING THE BOUNDARIES AND INFLUENCES ON A DESIGN

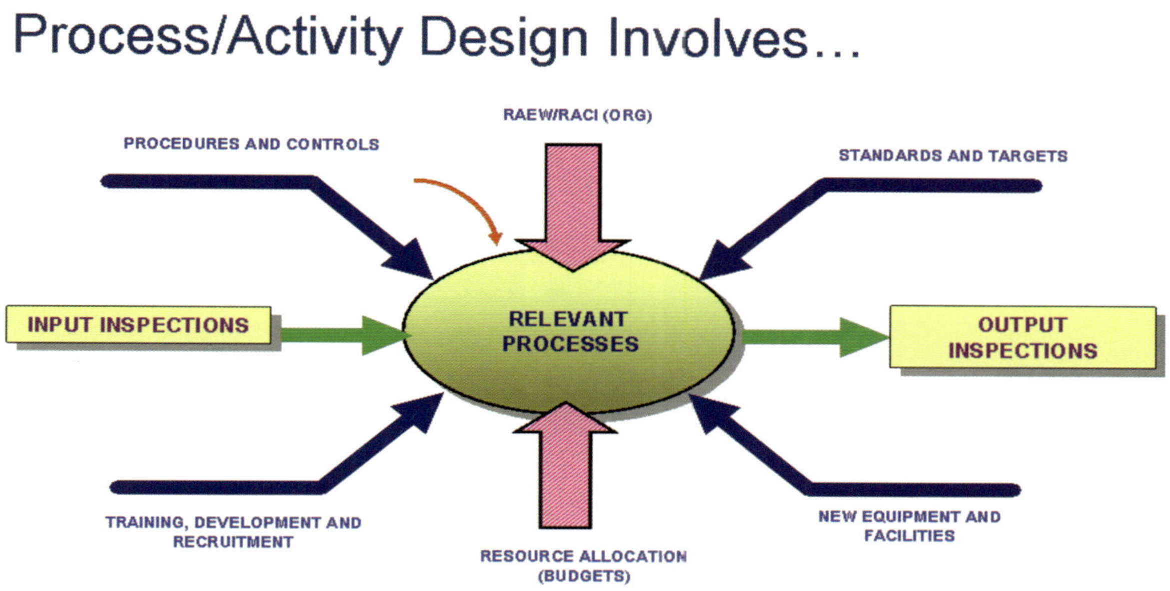

DIAGRAM TO ADDRESS HOW SOFT SYSTEMS CAN HELP DESIGN SYSTEMS BOUNDARIES

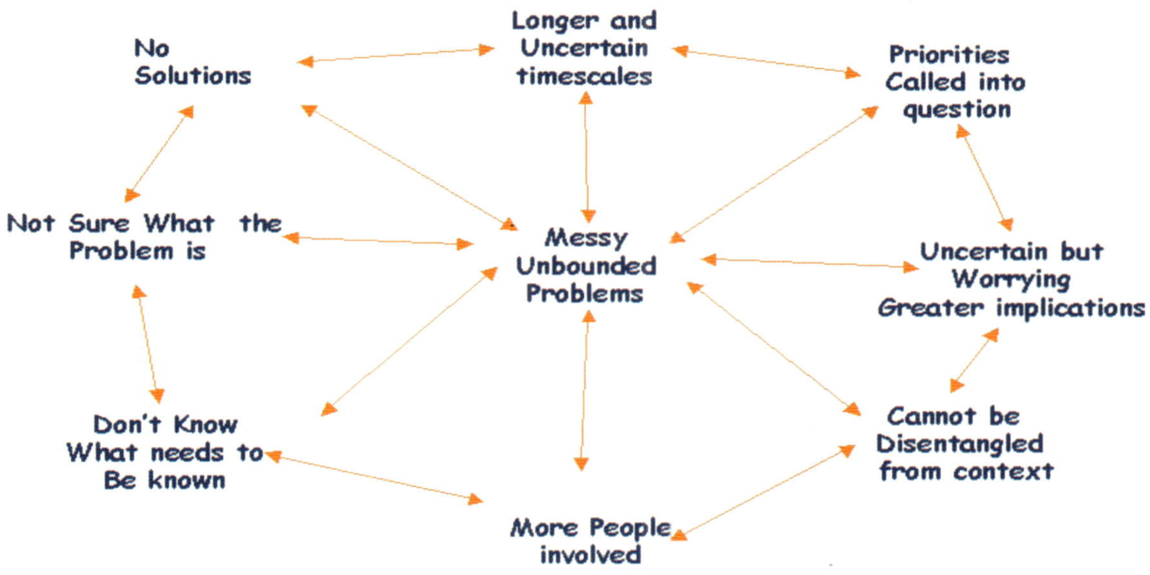

DIAGRAMS DEMONSTRATING BOUNDARY CONDITIONS FOR A WHOLE SCHEME WITH NUMEROUS SUB-SCHEMES

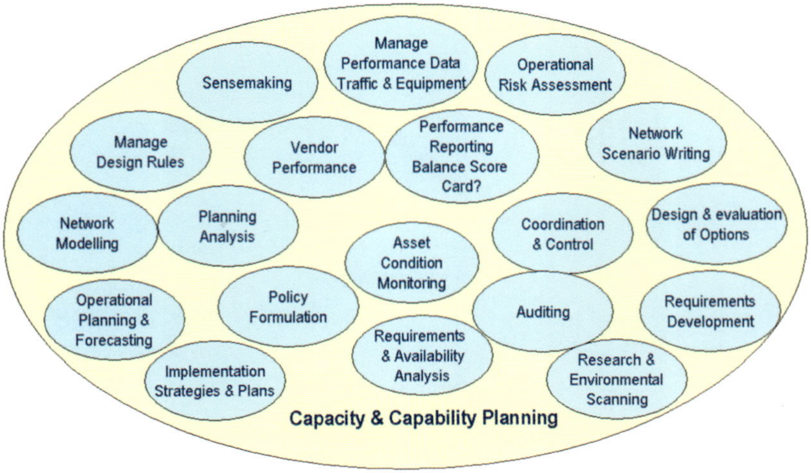

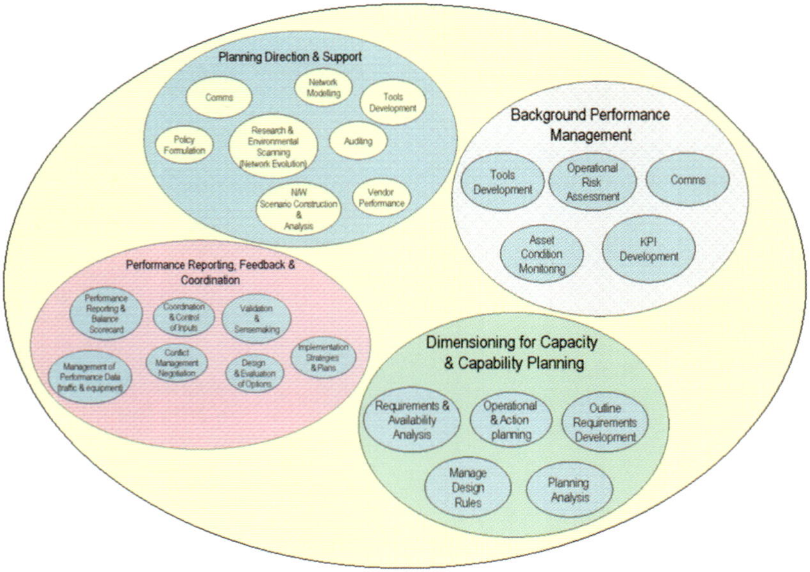

First of all I would like to thank Geoff Elliott for his time to introduce me to concepts and talk me through these and for his generous donations of materials to help me with this section.

This pair of diagrams shows the initial assembly of areas in consideration, and then how they can be detailed, combined and grouped to enable relationships of the design to move forward.

It is necessary to start at the conceptual level as this gives one an indication of all the internal and external relationships which have to be maintained. Just drawing an activity flow diagram at the transactional level often misses a key relationship.

Note. There also are several types of process modelling and mapping which may be useful. For example:

IDEF (0) levels 0 and 1
Role activity diagramming
Activity flow diagramming
Materials flows
Document and data flows

DIAGRAM TO DEMONSTRATE VALUE STREAM MAPPING

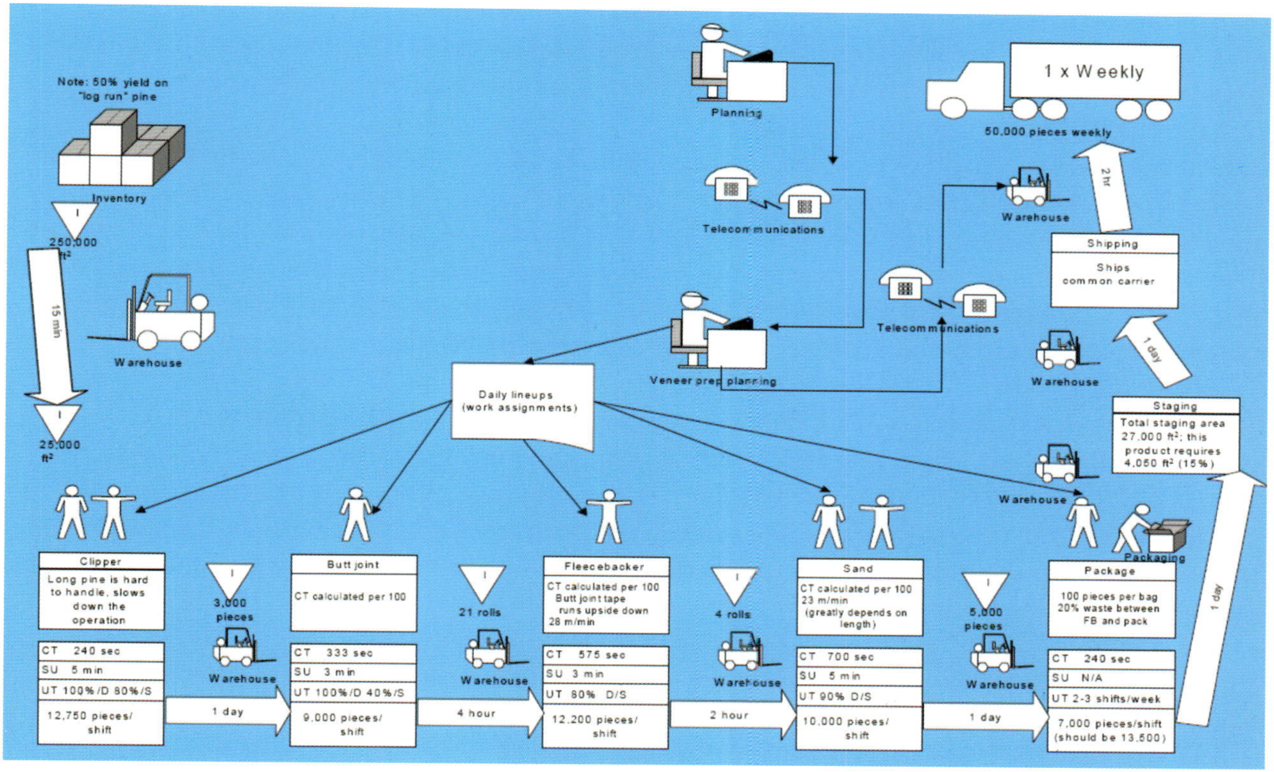

DG comment: I've never trained adequately in these concepts, so I believe that there is far more to understand than can be found from the brief word picture. The concepts to me are good from stage 4 through to 7 where I have a more tangible lock on the perception and can relate it to a PDSA approach. The additional diagrams help illustrate the power of visual representation enabling rapid information assimilation while not needing to understand the entire context.

It is my intention to continue to learn more about these elements and create updates to the book via my website as appropriate. All larger diagrams are also available via www.supportservicesdirect.co.uk/visualisingtransformation.

SYSTEM DYNAMICS

System dynamics was developed by Jay Forrester at MIT back in the 1960s from Stafford Beer's concepts of cybernetics. It got a boost in the 1990's when Peter Senge took system dynamics, placed it alongside organisational and personal development concepts and called the result "Systems Thinking".

System dynamics is based on two notions regarding cause and effect. Firstly, in any system there is *detail complexity* – large number of potential causes and effects. Secondly and more critically, there is *dynamic complexity*. Not only does cause contribute to effect, but the effect in some way contributes to the cause. Then, most systems have complex arrays of such feedback loops. What is important here is that any delay in a process, or feedback loop, when placed alongside all the others, mean that the dynamic complexity increases to such an extent that most people will misinterpret what actually is going on.

There is a famous simulation exercise of a brewery. This is the Beer Game which is often run by a colleague, which shows the greater importance of dynamic complexity over detail complexity. In this simulation, there is very little detail complexity – it is a simple demand and supply chain, brewing beer for customers. But dynamic complexity is added by the delay caused by having to wait two weeks for the beer to brew. When asked to manage this system, even skilled managers generally perform worse than if they took their decisions by throwing a dice.

So System Dynamics focuses primarily on identifying the main variables of a system. i.e. the bits that are able to change and exploring rigorously the effect they have on each other. It therefore emphasises the dynamics of the system, perhaps described as a snapshot based on underlying assumptions and perceptions of the multiple cause and effects in the system. Systems dynamics is a process simulation model based on some basic archetypes based on one's perception of the related cause and effect variables. System dynamics has proven very difficult for me to explain what it actually is. Most descriptions describe feedback loops within computer simulations and then something extremely technical.

DG comment: One step further away from the clearer certainties of working in operations and simple strategies. From recent awareness gained something I will look at again, I need to play the beer game and work with colleagues so as to further evolve linkages between methods to enable the most appropriate 'tools' to be used at the best times.

CULTURAL-HISTORICAL ACTIVITY THEORY (CHAT)

CHAT was originally developed by Yrjo Engestrom at the University of Helsinki. According to its proponents, the theory essentially covers three things. Whilst each component is quite well known, the important aspect of this theory is that it seeks to accommodate the relationship between all of them.

It describes the factors that affect or mediate between individual behaviour, the subject, and the results of that behaviour, the object, in order to achieve the goal in the context of wider social systems. These wider factors are not merely external context, since they are part of the system – changing as a result of the system's activities.

There are three key relationships, and three mediating factors. This can be shown as a clear triangle to show the key relationship between the individual, the community of which they are part and the activity they are all engaged in. There are interrelated relationships that mediate the relationship between individuals, activities and communities. Thus, concepts and technologies mediate.

I.e. *they have an active influence upon the relationships between the individual and the object of his or her action and vice versa.*

Social rules and regulations mediate the relationships between the individual and the community, and vice versa.

A division of knowledge and labour mediate the relationships between community members and the shared object of the activity system, and vice versa.

CHAT proposes that these features can be aggregated, i.e. the individual can be a single person, a group of people, an organisation or a community. So for instance, the activity system which is a branch office of a government agency influences and is influenced by, the wider activity system which is New Zealand society.

This contains a theory of learning that explains how an individual or groups of individuals interact with these factors so that they learn from that experience. The theory of learning is based on Vygotskyian concepts of identifying and explaining patterns and puzzles or contradictions.

1. Questioning the current situation
2a. Historical analysis of the contradictions
2b. Actual empirical analysis
3. Modelling the new solution
4. Examining the new model
5. Implementing the new model
6. Reflecting on the process
7. Consolidating the new practice

DG comment: This is, in some ways, far too academic to me, with insufficient practicable reading or practioner support to give me a reasonable grasp. However, the core triangle based model is similar in context to the model used to create a waste strategy.

COMPLEX ADAPTIVE SYSTEMS THEORY (CAS) - plus socio economic systems

Complex adaptive systems have extreme sensitivity to initial conditions. In other words a very small initial intervention can have a tremendous ultimate effect. (This can be similar to the butterfly theory.)

Boundaries

The area lying between different parts of the system are critically important. These boundaries don't have to be physical: they can be differences of viewpoint, experience, expectation, or culture.

Transforming feedback loops

Information which flows across these boundaries, if it can, has a significant and transforming effect compared to simple systems.

Fractals

These are simple rules, practices, procedures, principles or values that are present in every part of the system, no matter how big or small that part of the system is.

Attractors

A complex adaptive system is made up of a large number of interdependent subsystems. The interactions between them are the effects of the transforming feedback loops which create recognisable patterns. However, these patterns can only be understood at a large system level. They cannot be used to predict the behaviour of smaller parts of the system, i.e. the whole cannot be understood by measuring the performance of the parts.

Self-organisation

When pushed to an extreme state: complex adaptive systems without an obvious plan and without the control of any single individual component, spontaneously reorganise themselves. This is a controversial aspect of CAS, since it appears to challenge the current dominant organisational paradigm of charismatic leadership, strong management systems and explicit strategy. It means we are at best influencers of the system rather than managers of it.

Coupling

Essentially this means that the relationship of the system and its environment, between parts of the system and between individuals within the system is based on notions of influence rather than control.

DG comment: CAS is apparently one of a suite of theories which surround the concept of complexity. The complexity field has developed its own set of concepts and jargon. However at the core there are some fairly simple concepts, which could alter the way we see the world and react to it. See also the work of the local government management board on systems thinking and systems ideas. They explain many of the underpinning concepts for CAS.

CONTEXT OF WHERE TO APPLY DIFFERING SYSTEMS

The systems and approaches discussed within this chapter need to be set into context; the following mind map and applications diagram attempts to show how various aspects of management and change management have evolved, and where these approaches may best be applied.

People and organisations have their own personal strengths and ways of thinking, thus with some adaptability, the applications diagram attempts to show why all change management approaches cannot be applied to all types of work being examined.

The following mind map and affinity diagram apply a different approach to their use, so that you can both reflect on their application, while you also consider their content. The mind map should help position the evolution of 'hard convergent designs' against 'soft divergent designs'.

The mind map shows the evolution of statistical based concepts at the top, with boundary based concepts at the base of the diagram. To place these in context a number of contributors and influences are included, with operational areas depicted.

None of these should be considered without 'context', thus some management based themes and contributions are also included. It may be a surprise to some, that I have included an area for 'Genius'. Without inspiration many developments over the last five hundred years or so, would never have occurred.

Major changes that impact on society used to be rare, today intellectual capital, combined with technology are transforming the world, such that, IT systems can be out of date, before they achieve mass production.

Six of the listed people in 'Genius' made lasting, fundamental discoveries, insights or development, which helped change the world for the better. The seventh, Salvador Dali, was an artist who challenged what you see, making impossible couplings of images with totally smooth interfaces. Leonardo Da Vinci was driven and inspired, an absolute master of any trade he applied himself to.

All have a special place for me, influencing my beliefs, ambitions, and ways of thinking. Einstein used mathematical insight to re-describe the physics of nature, Newton realised the forces of nature and described them in a more logical way, Darwin described evolution in a far more logical way, while Florence Nightingale was a 'mere woman' who challenged the medical profession with her crazy notion that washing stops surgical deaths. They were all challenged by their society, with ridicule and heresy risked.

Lastly I. K. Brunel, a great engineer in many ways; my family affinity to him is great, as my fore-fathers were involved in the building of the SS *Great Britain* in Bristol and then the SS *Great Western* in the east end of London. There are precious few charismatic Civil Engineers, thus someone who moved technology on so well for rail, bridges, tunnels and ships, must be good.

The second diagram attempts to show the boundary conditions for the two major approaches to systems thinking. It shows that some systems and approaches are far more effective for some areas of work than others. There is no point in trying to apply SPC to a 'one off' situation, as there is no: mean, deviation or variation.Equally applying pure boundary condition thinking to a machine that produces 10,000 bolts per shift, is far less apt, than to ensuring that every bolt is made of the best quality steel, for its purpose, within a micron of tolerance. SPC is the prime set of tools for that work.

The diagram is a conscious blend of IT created images, with pen applied after. This is partly due to the limitations of programs that I have at my disposal, but also to help people to think more creatively. Just because you don't have key components, doesn't mean that you can't do something. If I were creating these types of images every week, I would buy better kit.

What the diagram addresses, are the types of approaches that should be tackled by different change methodologies. This is definitely a case of one size does not fit all.A higher definition diagram could also attempt to model which 'tools' work best where. As above, SPC sits best in the bottom right hand corner, while affinity diagrams are best in the top left.

Now consider the host, what approaches and methods work best for them at present? If they have evolved through a TPS style, then familiarity will help, thus a waste strategy, which could benefit from a soft systems approach, would still be best addressed via TPS, with some broader use of mind maps, affinity diagrams and cause and effect charts. That is, statistical based with lots of softer edges.

However, the development of civil emergency plans should be addressed by starting with boundary conditions and interfaces, rather than thinking about the statistics first.

Equally, an organisation which is wedded to soft systems approaches, could start on operational designs for infrastructure repairs from their own stronger areas, and increase the influence of SPC with flow charts in swim lanes where that detail is needed.

Visualising Transformation is applicable to the central 90% of this diagram, with 'hard' SPC applying to thousands of widgets per hour, and purer soft systems to jet aeroplane development.

Managing Change
STATISTICS W. Shewhart W.E. Deming
Bell Telephones 1920's
1950's – 1990's
D. Wheeler
SQC Statistical Quality Control
7 Tools
SPC statistical Process control
PDSA
14 points of management
7 Deadly diseases
System of profound Knowledge
Empowerment
Leadership
A3 management
7 Wastes
Stock
Variation
time
Add value
Continuous Improvement
Six Sigma
Project Management
Black Belts
Green Belts
J. Ohno Toyota production system (TPS)
J. Seddon Vanguard
'Systems Thinking'
Design in Value
Lean
L. Services
L. Manufacturing
L. Construction
Value Mgt.
Constructive Dialogue
Last Planner
Ishikawa
H. Neave
B. Joiner
P. Scholtes
J. Juran
M. Tribus
B. Crosby
Taguchi
Ackoff
A. Kohn
Visualising Work
Total Quality Mgt.
Business Process Re-eng
Visualising Transformation
MANAGEMENT
Theory
philosophy
ECONOMICS
H. Ford
FW Taylor
De Bono
Senge
Maslow
Drucker
Keynes
Theory X/Y
Intrinsic
Extrinsic
Motivation
Control / Empower
Land
Capital
Knowledge
INSPIRE / GENIUS
Art
Science
Engineering
Health
A. Einstien
L. Da Vinchi
I. Newton
I.K. Brunnel
S. Dali
C. Darwin
F. Nightingale
Sketches
Designs
Energy
Persistence
Strength
Challenge
Mind maps
Evolution
Visualisation
Innovation
New order
Germ Theory
Global warming
5th Discipline
Socio Technical systems
Emery & Trist
CODE BREAKING
1940's – Enigma
Code breaking
Computer development
Operational Research
Management
Cybernetics
Stafford Beer
Systems Engineering
Jenkins
Lancaster
De Neufville
Stafford MIT
RAND Corp and IBM 1950's
Systems development
Circular planning (Ackoff)
Soft systems methodology (Checkland)
Hard systems approach MK1
Complex Adaptive Theory
Strategic Development
Interactive Management (Warfield)
Systems descriptions
Cranfield
Operational Designs
Critical Systems Heuristics
HSA
O.M. (UK)
CATWOE
Boundary conditions
Systems approach to failures
System Dynamics
Business System Design Methodology (BSDM)
Information Management
Informatics
CCTA
Prince 2
Project Management
COMPUTER SYSTEMS DEVELOPMENT
ORGANISATIONAL DEVELOPMENT
CHANGE MANAGEMENT
INSPIRE CHALLENGE
STRATEGY
OPERATIONAL CHANGE
Dave Gaster 3/1/10

I have shown a considerable over-lap of the middle-ground in this diagram. Neither approach is exclusive to other. In that area either systems thinking approach can, and will, work.

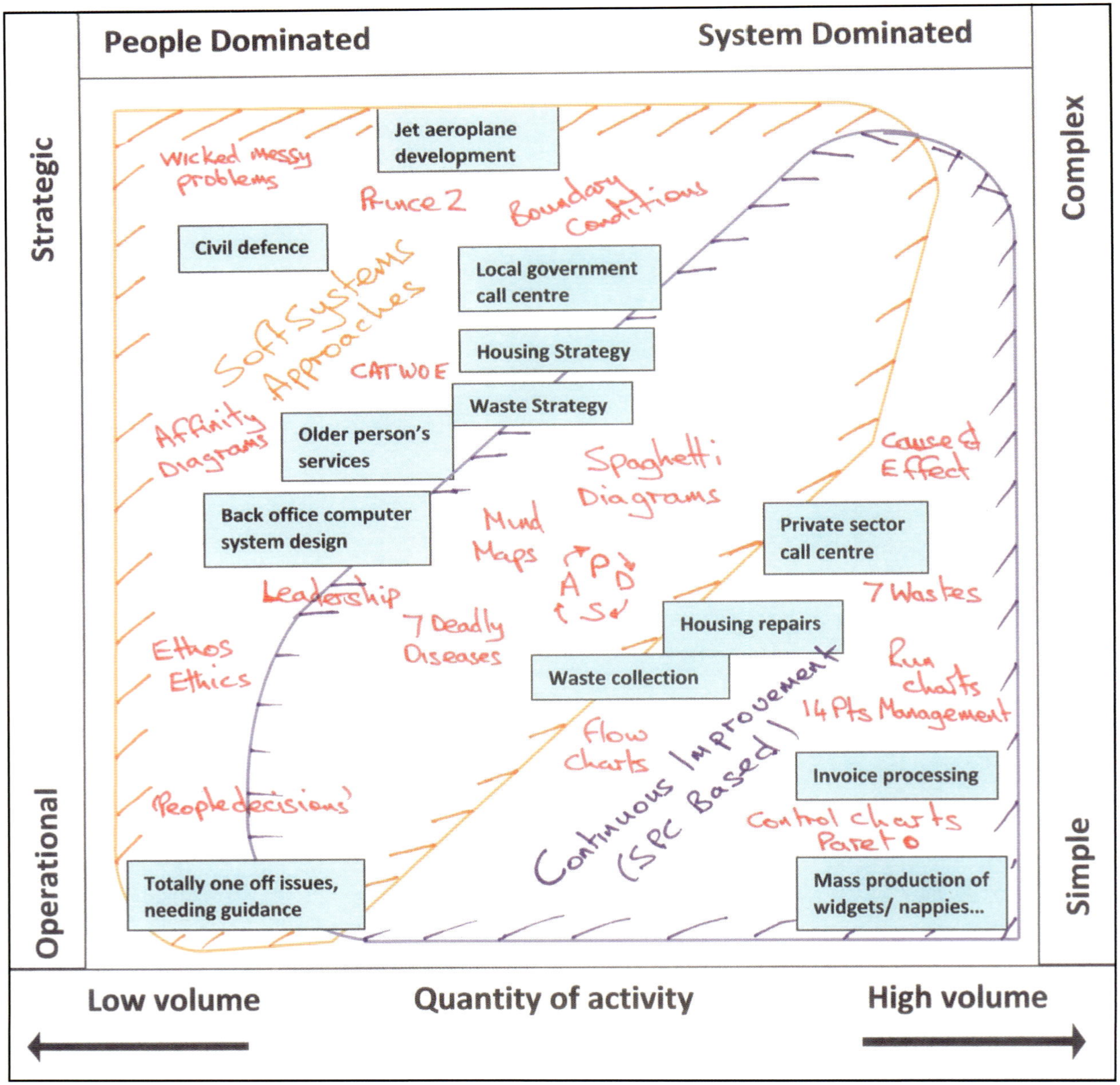

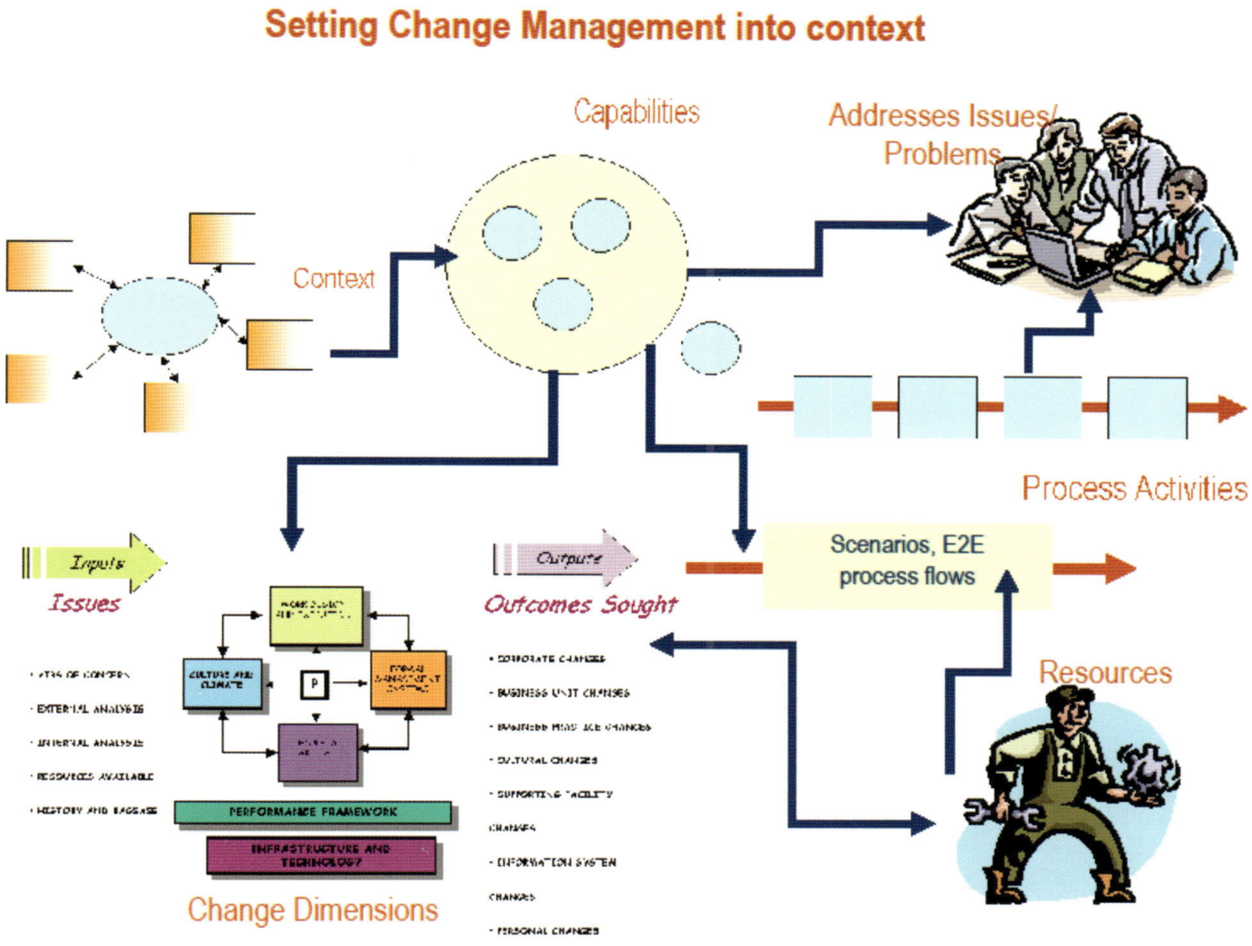

The diagram above shows how all the aspects for change management, properly addressed, can come together, as stated earlier; there is no reason why change management needs to be treated differently to operations management. Operations occur every day without the need for additional permissions or direction as they act within prescribed boundaries. In the same way change can act within boundaries enabling improvement and development, without limiting improvement through red tape.

The diagram below is based on the work of Nadler & Tushman for an organisational balance, processes 'p' are merely enablers. Change in one area will impact all other areas to begin with. This shows the boundaries for change under examination, when these boundaries are exceeded those permissions will need to be sought.

DIAGRAM SHOWING BOUNDARY CONDITIONS FOR CHANGE

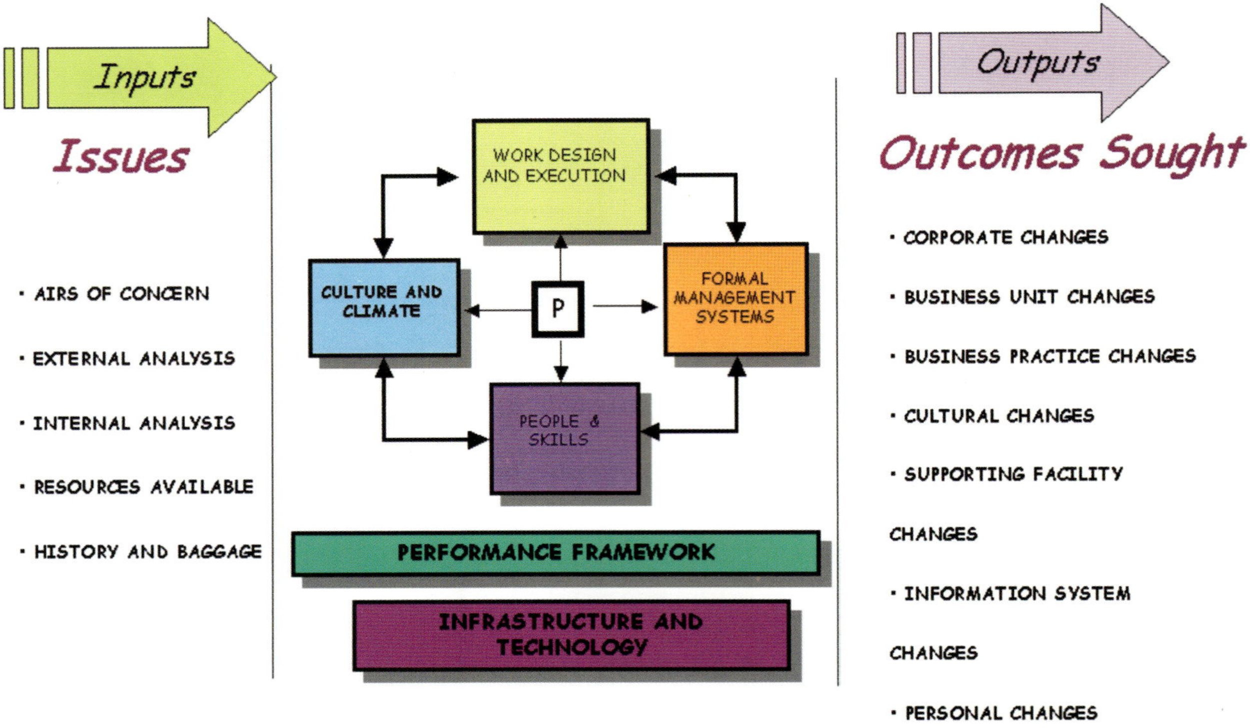

5TH DISCIPLINE

Is this systems thinking or extended change management? Essentially, Senge says that if you are to promote creative and humane institutions that are truly systemic in their approach, then you need to use five critical ways of understanding or promoting what is going on. Is this similar then to profound knowledge?

Systems Thinking
Essentially this is a repackaged form of system dynamics. Indeed some would argue that Senge rescued system dynamics from oblivion.

Mental models
Mental models are conceptual structures in the mind that drive cognitive processes of understanding. They influence people's actions because they mould people's appreciation of what they see. People therefore observe selectively. Mental models most often invisibly define our relationship with each other and with the world in which we find ourselves.

Consequently mental models used badly can undermine systems thinking by limiting the vision of what can be seen and done. However, multiple perspectives and the ability to manage a different view is the essence of Systems Thinking. In other words, we see what we believe, not believe what we see. This mental mode perspective draws heavily from the discipline of Action Science developed by two other Boston based academics Chris Argyris and Don Schön.

Shared vision

Shared visions create the energy and focus for successful endeavour. To use Ackoff's phrase it makes the system *purposeful* rather than merely *purposive*. On the other hand, Senge insists that it is not primarily what visions are that matter but what they *do* to people. By saying this, he essentially locates visioning in the cognitive psychology discipline rather than the strategy discipline.

Personal Mastery

Like many of Senge's components, this is more subtle than it appears to be. At first glance this emphasis on skill development sounds like a plea on behalf of the training and education industry. On closer inspection this is far from the case.

Indeed he implies that these industries pose as much a threat to personal mastery as an opportunity. For Senge, personal mastery is a state of mind for those who wish to gain full knowledge of themselves and the world around them; constantly deepening their own sense of personal vision. As Bob Flood says it is a calling of intrinsic desires not a purpose to pursue.

Team learning

In Senge's eyes, the purpose of a team is to create something greater than the sum of its individual members. This is achieved by creating a collective alignment between personal mastery and shared visions. The critical mechanisms Senge identifies for doing this are dialogue and discussion. According to Senge, the primary purpose of *discussion* is to win, whereas the primary purpose of *dialogue* is to understand; especially to understand the mental models of your colleagues. In dialogue, a group explores complex, difficult issues from many points of view. Individuals suspend their assumptions but they communicate their assumptions freely. In dialogue people become observers of their own thinking.

DG comment: This is more difficult for me to differentiate than other concepts, in that there are many similar concepts to profound knowledge; the aspects of mental models and shared vision are similar to Visualising Transformation in that every effort is made to jointly understand what is happening and what can be made to happen. My interpretation of communications: are you talking to overcome people's resistance, or talking to jointly agree ideas. There should be considerable emphasis on training, and all one team with some people as experts.

LAST PLANNER® – Collaborative conservations for reliable project delivery

Developed to help front line supervisors in project-based production environments produce predictably, Last Planner[9] supports the conversations, commitments and the planning required to deliver roads, schools and other projects on time and in budget. In construction it results in significant reductions in accidents and injury to workers. In the process it minimises waste of materials, time and effort.

Designing a production system to deliver what's wanted is only possible through the collaboration of all project participants from the earliest stages of a project – owner, designers, constructors, facility managers, end-users. This goes beyond the contractual arrangement of design/build or constructability reviews where constructors and, occasionally, facility managers, merely react to designs instead of informing and influencing the design so that the production system design progresses alongside the design of the project – bridge, library or housing refurbishment.

THE SIX KEY CONVERSATIONS THAT ENABLE RELIABLE PROJECT DELIVERY WHEN DONE COLLABORATIVELY

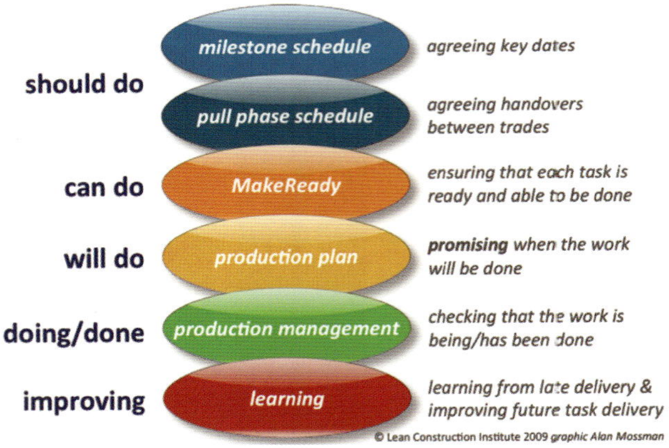

Last Planner goes beyond traditional (CPM-based) construction management approaches by requiring the *Last Planners* (trade foremen on site, design team leaders) to plan (with an eye to end-user value and awareness of what the next trade needs to do quality work) material, equipment and information flows, space use and personnel so that they all come together at the workface *when* the work is to be done.

Last Planner achieves results by:

- **optimising the whole project** through collaboration and systematic learning

- **involving everyone** in continual improvement and the pursuit of perfection
- focusing on delivering the **value** desired by the owner, client and end-user
- creating **flow** in the project by systematically eliminating obstacles to value creation and those parts of the process that create no value
- pulling production – rather than pushing it.

The priority for all construction work – and for many other project-based production environments – is to:

- keep work flowing so that teams and crews can be productive;
- keep batch sizes small to speed work up while reducing inventory of material and tools
- reduce costs.

The **Last Planner System** is a critical tool in the **Lean Construction** toolbag – it is a great way to *lower the river*, in Engineer Ohno's phrase, so that you can see the rocks more clearly. Other lean tools, many from manufacturing, can then be used to remove the rocks and help the river to flow smoothly – tools like *5S, Kanban, Kaizen*, quick setup/changeover, Poka Yoke, Visual Control and Five Whys.

Using lean tools, even Last Planner, won't make your project or organisation lean. Lean and Lean Construction are a philosophy and require a significant change in thinking compared to the way most people go about construction. As Einstein noted, doing what you have always done is no way to change the results you get. Thinking influences the behaviour that produces results. If you change your thinking, you will change the results. Lean tools used in the context of lean thinking are much more effective than when they are used on their own.

DG comment: It was the subtitle of this section that first attracted me to Last Planner. We used many of these aspects when redesigning housing maintenance and voids management, there's a great deal of translation to the public service to address these areas. Where this would really start to make tremendous difference is in programmes like Building Schools for the Future (BSF).

Both in the UK and abroad, Lean Construction and Last Planner have already shown that they can help teams deliver safer, faster, cheaper, greener and higher quality projects without reducing the scope. Failing to optimise the design early often means that additional thermal, environmental and operational costs are locked into the future when with minimal expenditure now they could be designed out.

CRITICAL SYSTEMS HEURISTICS – Extremely powerful and an absolute must in the field of Systems Thinking, along with Stafford Beer.

CSH has been recommended to me by more than one officer I have worked with, there is a very good paper by Werner Ulrich who advises the Open University as a taster which can be found at: http://www.wulrich.com/downloads/ulrich_2005f.pdf

DG Comment: I have tried to summarise it without success, my alternative would be to simply copy this here. The terms Critical and Systems should be fairly clear to us all, 'Heuristics' is a Greek word meaning to discover. One very notable quote in the paper is 'we certainly risk that others will understand something else than what we expect them to understand.' Clarity of speech is rarely as good as the clarity of a picture or diagram.

OTHER BUSINESS EXCELLENCE TOOLS AND STANDARDS

EUROPEAN FRAMEWORK FOR QUALITY MANAGEMENT (EFQM)

EFQM is an over-arching framework that, if used as a diagnostic tool, will help you put in place an improvement plan to better your organisation's results. Other tools and standards focus on specific areas of your organisation whereas the Excellence Model follows an holistic approach. The diagram below shows that there is synergy between EFQM and other tools and standards.

For instance, if you conduct a self-assessment via the Excellence Model and determine that an area for improvement is in your "People Results," you may want to use the Investors in People standard to help your organisation improve. Likewise, if your organisation's "Processes" need improving, you may want to consider implementing ISO 9000:2008.

I had access to a number of visualisations for the EFQM, I chose this one, as it is also wedded to ISOs 9000 and 14000, IiP and similar options. At a large DC, my department was forced to achieve all three of these standards. We had mature continuous improvement systems in place, but via CCT, were forced by the corporate centre, or more specifically, a procurement officer, to achieve 'recognised standards'.

OVERVIEW OF EFQM MODEL

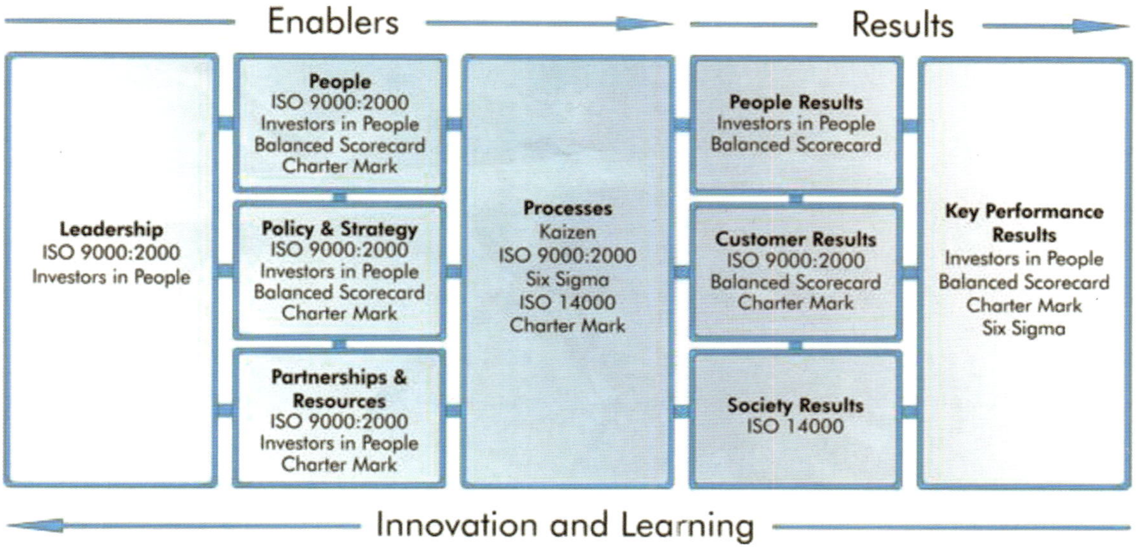

We had choices, these standards could be achieved with the minimum of effort, going through the motions of compliance, or, we could use those approaches to maximise the benefits that they may have. We did the latter, making a conscious decision to use the rigour of approach to add value.

We also did these with care, for ISOs 9000 and 14000 we mainly ensured we documented all the processes of the ways we were working, and then established audit and review routines to assist invigilators. IiP was being introduced across the whole council. I ensured that I was involved in the inner sanctum to address and design and context, ensuring this would complement our way of working, rather than conflict with it.

We found that all three added value to our services, creating some needed controls where certain officers would achieve excellent service delivery, irrespective of the costs. I am not saying do these all! Had we spent the same time and effort into more continuous improvement work, that would have been far better for the organisation, and customers, however, this does show that there has to be exclusivity of approach.

This also takes me back to the model above, and my first approaches to CI eighteen years ago. The nine boxes above do not address running the business effectively, efficiently, with a view on the future. I can only assume that if you are in a business, that that is taken as a given. However, a great deal of the public sector problem now is that it doesn't have great businessmen running it. THAT is why *Appraise* is so important.

DG comment: I have seen the EFQM add a great deal of value. One director used it as the cornerstone of moving forward, with great operational, training and development initiatives based on that together with almost obsessive use of MS Project Manager.

It will add value, but not as much as either systems thinking or Visualising Transformation.

CAPABILITY MATURITY MODEL

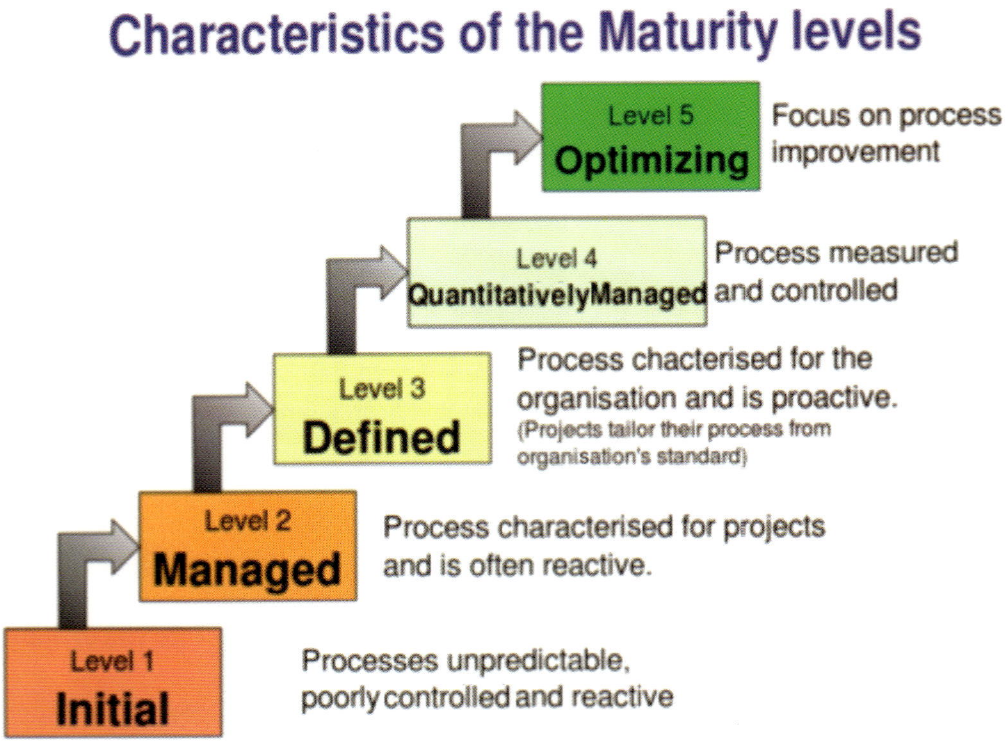

As so much of Visualising Transformation is based on data and information, I thought it quite important to show this diagram. Most councils will rank in the level one or two zones of this diagram at best. Being 'data rich – information poor' is not a good place to be.

It is very difficult to make insightful decisions based on incomplete, incorrect and suspect data, but that is what most organisations, irrespective of being public or private sector, do every day.

That is why I am convinced that transforming 'data into information' is a key part of the journey to improvement.

INFORMATICS (not part of Systems Thinking, but parallel to it)

Informatics is the science of information, the practice of information processing, and the engineering of information systems. Informatics studies the structure, algorithms, behaviour, and interactions of natural and artificial systems that store, process, access and communicate information. It also develops its own conceptual and theoretical foundations and utilises foundations developed in other fields. Since the advent of computers, individuals and organisations increasingly process information digitally. This has led to the study of informatics that has computational, cognitive and social aspects, including study of the social impact of information technologies.

DG comment: This is included here, as there are several degree courses running in this country, where exceptional Business Analysts could be trained with an incredible ability for finding information amongst data as their speciality.

MIND MAP (Not part of Systems Thinking, but parallel to it)

A mind map is a diagram used to represent words, ideas, tasks, or other items linked to and arranged around a central key word or idea. Mind maps are used to generate, visualise, structure, and classify ideas, and as an aid in study, organisation, problem solving, decision making, and writing.

The elements of a given mind map are arranged intuitively according to the importance of the concepts, and are classified into groupings, branches, or areas, with the goal of representing semantic or other connections between portions of information. Mind maps may also aid recall of existing memories.

By presenting ideas in a radial, graphical, colour coded, non-linear manner, mind maps encourage a brainstorming approach to planning and organisational tasks. Though the branches of a mind map represent hierarchical tree structures, their radial arrangement disrupts the prioritising of concepts typically associated with hierarchies presented with more linear visual cues. This orientation towards brainstorming encourages users to enumerate and connect concepts without a tendency to begin within a particular conceptual framework.

DG comment: I have used mind maps extensively since meeting Tony Buzan, for change management, drafting concepts, linking ideas and issues together, framing a training session or seminar or as now, writing a book. They are incredibly flexible, a natural method to enable discussion, and a way to allay fear.

My use of mind maps and indeed cause and effect charts was developed as I had not discovered soft systems when I needed them. I have deliberately used the mind map in this chapter to demonstrate their flexibility in modelling difficult sets of information into a composition that does not need to be symmetrical or ordered and yet demonstrates many multi-task operations in parallel. It is unusual to discuss Systems Thinking and mind maps at the same time; however, I think that they are perfectly positioned within Visualising Transformation, as they are simple and adaptive.

In general I would recommend that any form of diagrammatic method that works for both you and the host be used freely. If you find an issue which you find difficult or impossible to model, consider a different style of model.

Endnotes

1 More correctly in this chapter this should be a systematic / scientific approach to change management.

2 There has been considerable debate about Systems Thinking, as applied to Deming/TPS. While it was originally wrong to do, it has been done, adopted and understood by a significant number of people. The positioning of this chapter in the book is a conscious one. Too much techy stuff at the front end would put people off the rest, causing too many lost opportunities to learn as a result. The debate can still go on via IDeA or the SSD website.

3 Ranks of Green belt, Black belt, Master black belt, Head of Six Sigma, retain a great deal of interest within Six Sigma, with too much emphasis for all to be trained to participate according to people who are more expert in other areas.

4 W Edwards Deming is revered in Japan, with a Deming prize being a great honour. Deming wrote extensively in his latter years, still learning and teaching even into his nineties. Deming, W E (1975) On probability as a basis for action, ***The American Statistician,*** 29(4), pp146-152 Deming, W E (1982) *Out of the Crisis: Quality, Productivity and Competitive Position* ISBN 0-521-30553-5

5 Walter Shewhart was a significant influence on Deming and others at the Bell telephone laboratories introducing the core SPC methodologies. Shewhart, W A (1931) *Economic Control of Quality of Manufactured Product* ISBN 0-87389-076-0 Shewhart, W A (1939) *Statistical Method from the Viewpoint of Quality Control* ISBN 0-486-65232-7

6 There is considerable reading for SPC, including: Oakland, J (2002) *Statistical Process Control* ISBN 0-7506-5766-9 Wheeler, D J (2000) *Normality and the Process-Behaviour Chart* ISBN 0-945320-56-6 Wheeler, D J & Chambers, D S (1992) *Understanding Statistical Process Control* ISBN 0-945320-13-2 Wheeler, Donald J. (1999). *Understanding Variation: The Key to Managing Chaos - 2nd Edition*. SPC Press, Inc. ISBN 0-945320-53-1.

7 TPS is extensively written about, with several versions of history. See: Jeffrey Liker (2003), *The Toyota Way: 14 Management Principles from the World's Greatest Manufacturer*, First edition, McGraw-Hill, ISBN 0-07-139231-9. Ohno, Taiichi (1995), *Toyota Production System: Beyond Large-scale Production*, Productivity Press Inc., ISBN 0-915299-14-3. Liker, J. (2006). *The Toyota Way Fieldbook*. New York, NY, USA: McGraw-Hill.

8 Womack, James P. and Jones, Daniel T. (2003), *Lean Thinking: Banish Waste and Create Wealth in Your Corporation, Revised and Updated*, HarperBusiness, ISBN 0-7432-4927-5. Womack, James P., Jones, Daniel T., and Roos, Daniel (1991), *The Machine That Changed the World: The Story of Lean Production*, HarperBusiness, ISBN 0-06-097417-6.

9 Last Planner is a trademark of the Lean Construction Institute www.leanconstruction.org

"Give me a place to stand with a lever and I will move the whole world"
ARCHIMEDES

Visualising Transformation is a system integrating a number of approaches from both traditional and scientific change management techniques to enable the host organisation to adopt characteristics which complement its current ethos, with a view to adopting and adapting to 'Transform' into a more effective efficient organisation in the future.

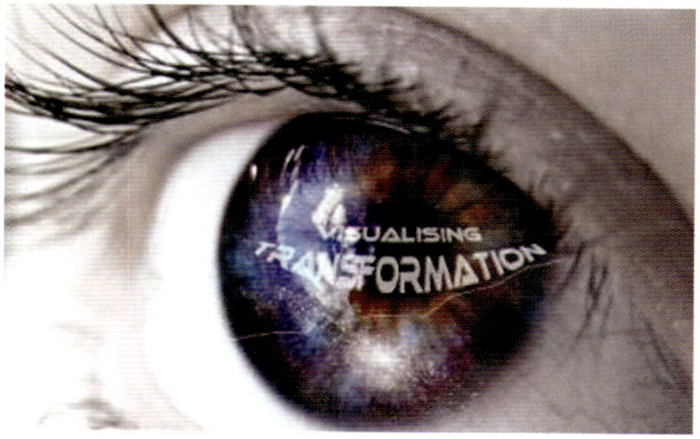

This book is written as a guide mainly for the public sector with a view to enabling other books to follow for other sectors.

Just in case you have a feeling of déjà vu, the picture and paragraph above are the same as in the introduction. This chapter asks you to do a number of things: To think through your journey, have you learned some new ideas? Can you look at data in a different way now to gain more insight? Have you started to rationalise the differences between data, information, knowledge and insight?

For many years I have said that my brain is like a large database, I store concepts, I separate knowledge from possible data, I remember sources of information attached to that information. I find linkages to disparate data, even when they are several months apart from one another and quickly find pairs of data that cannot possibly co-exist. I also carry out a rapid 'brain dump', bringing lots of ideas together quickly.

Hopefully the Ackoff pyramid will enable greater clarity for future conversations, so if after some wider training you are looking at the monthly accounts you could ascertain what the validity of the mix of information and data is when going through the accounts. *When my accountant produced 17 pages of numbers for a trial account, I circled about a dozen numbers and asked him to recheck them; invariably there were errors. He gradually learned to tune into the business, so that the numbers truly reflected what was happening operationally. As a result the errors reduced dramatically and we could operate within a ¼% margin of error. Having the accountant in the business helped enormously.*

There are well over a hundred graphs, tables and illustrations throughout this book. They were designed to capture interest, tell a story and create a hunger to use similar techniques, to perhaps learn more where you now work and definitely for where you could be next.

While the Check Plan *Appraise* Do cycle is at the heart of Visualising Transformation, it's not a literal, mechanistic process. It should be taken as a guide, effectively at any major stage of the whole thread of work. A quick sub-routine of CPAD can be run, for a quick win, or minor works evaluation. That's why the overview diagram on **page 149** shows the main cycle in motion with a series of minor cycles running at the same time.

Similarly the pair of diagrams below from chapter three show one unique thread placed alongside a number of other threads with a maze of interconnectivities. While this specifically shows a relationship to the project management board, the roles of project sponsors and lead officer for each Transformation thread can not be understated.

Where I have worked alongside some of the biggest consultants in Britain carrying out their version of 'Transformation', I'm horrified with the institutional damage they create via activity based concepts.

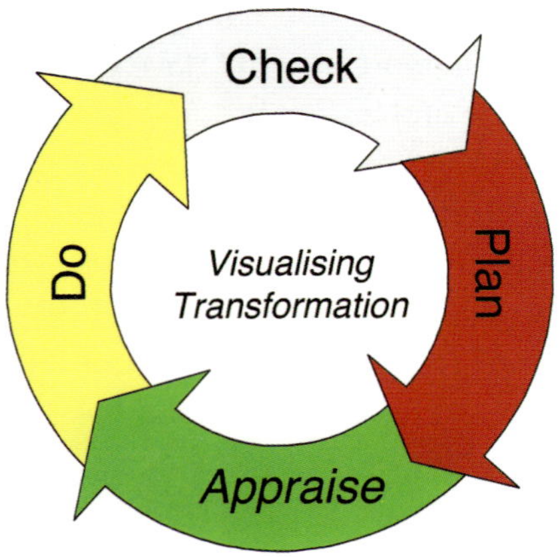

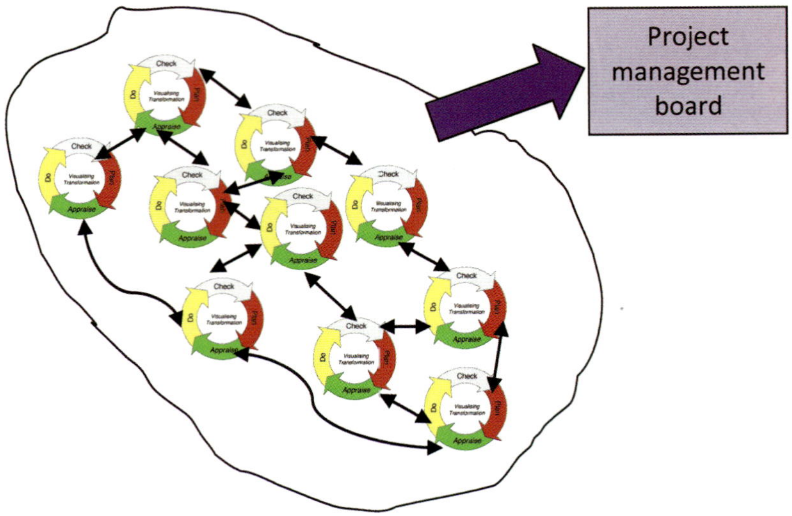

Where these are mixed with economy of scale and shared back office, I see the resources stripped out of the service areas and then a series of small savings extracted from say parking, to the demise of income.

I often hear about reviews where the prime aim is to deal with centralising debtor payments or simply to set up a call centre. All the analysis from the consultants shows that debt will be recovered more efficiently, that the customer experience will improve. Perhaps initially this will occur, but then secondary, totally unrelated issues will occur: From parking the number of tickets issued or fine income achieved will reduce, or in the call centre, the number of calls received per day will increase, or the turnover of staff in the call centre leads to a required grade increase to retain staff.

Most councils are centre-led since Best Value, LAA's and LSP's have predominated. Thus the majority of the internal voice heard by councillors and the executive is from finance and HR, plus the all-important performance team. The delivery side of the council is for individual cabinet members and back-benchers.

Thus most 'Transformations' are initiated by the people whose teams will have the least personal dis-benefit from those changes: Procure to Pay (P2P) will bolster central procurement and debtors. Often the problem of specifying to the procurer is just as difficult as writing a contract in the first place! These are carried out in the 'absolute knowledge' that repetition and batching work, or creating a shared back office will reduce the cost per widget made. I hope you will now challenge those concepts.

The big risk to the centre, from an E2E transformation, is that it will challenge the amount of hand-offs from one section to another. What value is there in 15 people doing 20% of a job when one person could do it all? If people are relegated to an automaton status doing the same small piece of work 300 times a day, do they have commitment to the job, do they enjoy work, can they add value?

The automaton aspect is what adds cost to employment, 'it's so boring you need to pay more to stay', or, 'the complaint handler has no richness of variety, they have complaint after complaint, so give up.' I recently was told about a large company, who have a specialist team to deal with serial nagging-complainers, the average period of employment in that team is four months. Why design a service to fail?

The widget industry leads to more failure demand and losses of income. Sometimes this takes time to be realised and the excuses machinery will roll in. The initial excuse will be, a new way of working will always create an initial loss of productivity; the next phase will be, 'we're so successful that more customers are calling us', the third phase will include that,' the service delivery unit is so bad it should be outsourced'.

If you hear any of this soon, or have heard it in the past, what version of the truth are you hearing? Was this additional budget pressure actually caused by the wrong design previously by the management? Is your organisation concentrating on centralist based services or the services that actually matter to your customers? I'll discuss car-park management from two perspectives, one as holistic management the other as incremental specialist management.

CAR PARK MANAGEMENT HIGH LEVEL DIAGRAM OF TWO PARADIGMS

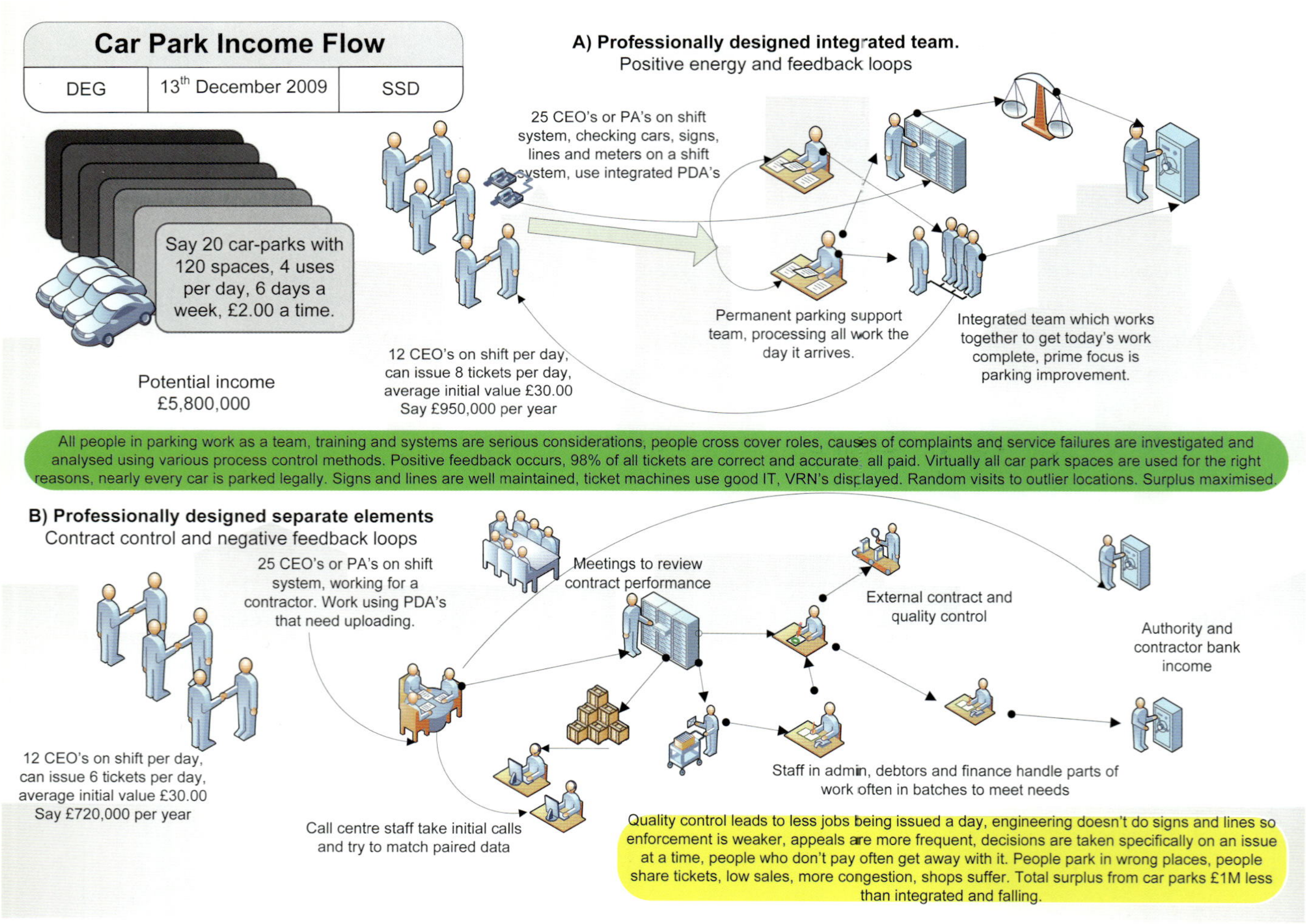

The top flow is based on an end–to–end holistic design, while the bottom flow is based on specialism designs.

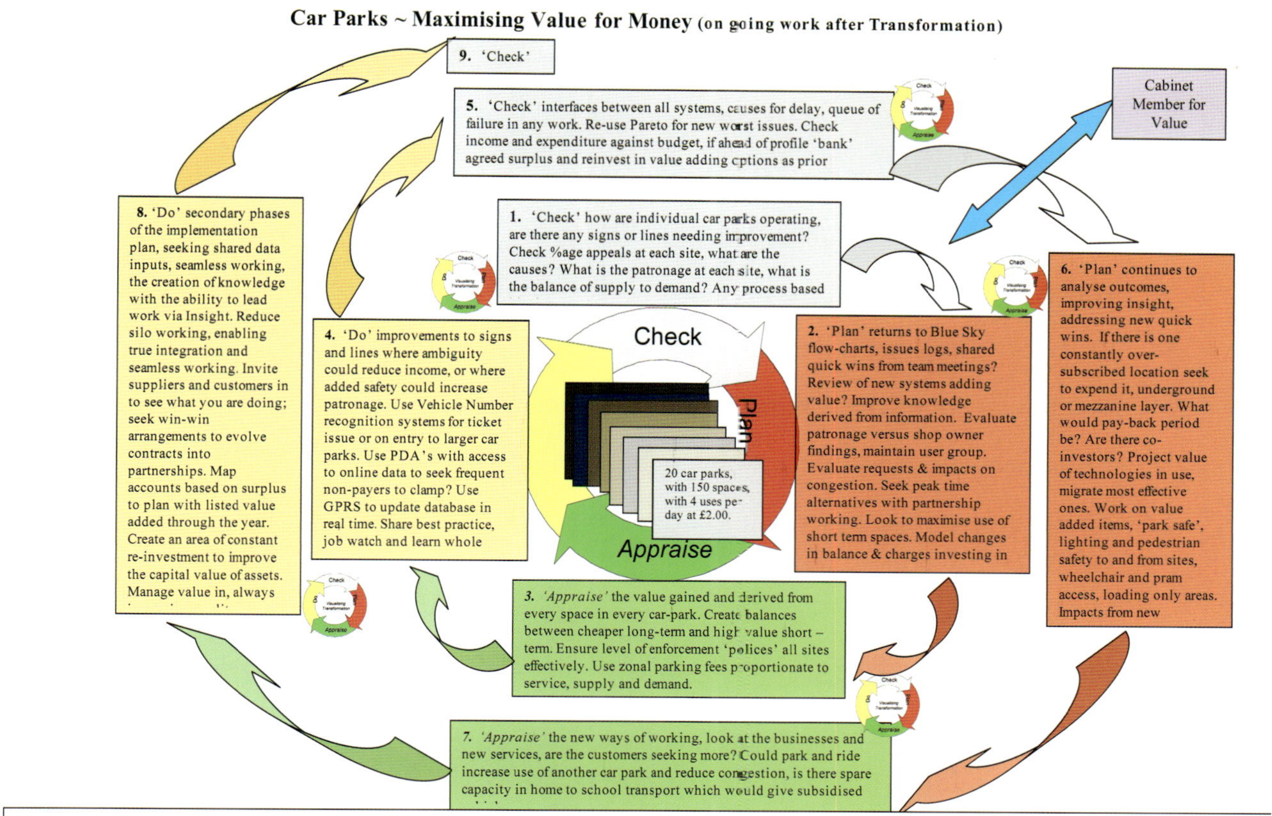

Visualising Transformation applied to Car Parking management. Potential income from car parks = £7.2M, patronage and non payers takes this down. Income from enforcement = possible £900K, errors or omissions may reduce this. The plan is to have the best quality of service provision at the maximum surplus for the council, with no sub-targets for any individual element. All parties work to a holistic plan, all work is done in real time. This is a whole team end to end service delivery. The whole system is self fulfilling with positive energy feedback. Support Service Direct

Within a positive energy system the starting budget derives from the original paradigm, which with a simple maximum position would show a budget of say £5.5M income with a £2.5M expenditure thus a surplus of £3M per annum. The first phase of CPAD would look at why appeals are successful, where income for a car park is low, where there are complaints and why those complaints are as they are? All parties in the work would have a voice and be actively listened to. If there are restricting forces to progress or barriers to improvement the leaders should challenge these areas to support the workers.

All staff will be cross trained to support one another; ideally all of work arriving today will be dealt with today. Any reported defects with signs, lines or machines will be checked the same day, or for outlying machines before 8.00 the next morning.

Patronage levels will be monitored as a sub-routine of income, showing profiled utilisation during the day, to understand relative demand. ASB will be monitored ensuring solutions in proportion to risk, evaluating the cost benefit to the site and risk. The 'fear of crime' aspect will be part of the reviews for ASB, lighting, CCTV and access routes to pedestrian destinations.

The reputation for car parks should be that they are:

- ✓ Clean, accessible, bright, tidy, free of graffiti
- ✓ Well managed, free of trips, good value for money
- ✓ Well maintained, faults are short lived, users are treated fairly
- ✓ Good to use for disabled, parents with small children, lone people
- ✓ Adding value to the community, the right facility in the right location
- ✓ A place where management is strong, people will use them as designed, always paying properly
- ✓ Not a safe place for thieves or vandals
- ✓ Going to be better next year than this.

The budget is allocated to the team and Cabinet member as a minimum of £3M surplus, with some basic rules for variance. If the surplus is forecast via advanced real time systems to exceed £3M, then 2/3rd of the surplus is fed into the revenue fund, and 1/3rd re-invested into car parks improvements.

A small car park surplus may include many of the following aspects:

- ▷ Car parks that are rarely inspected, are badly maintained and littered
- ▷ Car parks that have a high proportion of cars not paying for the service
- ▷ Signs and lines that need upgrading, causing uncertain customers, fines and appeals
- ▷ Car Park Attendants who don't care too much about adequate enforcement, or improvement
- ▷ Car parks that are sadly overdue maintenance, have regular machine failures.

The initial phase of Visualising Transformation will have addressed all the easy signs, lines, cleansing, IT and operational systems. This will create more 'value' activity per person per day and thus a step increase in income. The first step increase could be applied to: Software, new PCs, integrated PDAs, new ticket machines in the most neglected car parks, refurbishment from high use car parks to low use car parks, unless an easy improvement elsewhere is likely to increase revenues quickly.

The first phase improvement could easily be £400K extra surplus, £266K is retained by the revenue fund, and thus £133K is available for new machines or systems. As on-the-ground facilities improve, enforcement gets better, thus 'initially' fines issued per day increase, while appeals decrease, creating more fee income. As users get wise to improved enforcement, more parking tickets are purchased, and fewer fines are issued.

The ratio of fine income to car park income in this model is 1 to 8. Thus the income increases more dramatically as people pay for tickets, rather than risk fines.

Systems which work best:
Pay on exit, systems with car registrations on tickets, systems based on CCTV capture for time of entry and exit based on registration number.

Systems that have most issues:
Printed tickets with no registration numbers, light weight paper tickets which could blow off dash-boards, systems which tolerate people having eight tickets on display, systems which enable ticket swapping and locations needing no ticket for the first two hours parking.

Within the new broad design, the council would reduce controls on the budgets, empowering the cabinet member and parking team to act positively. Change of services would be expected and encouraged. Only major investment decisions would need further sanction.

There would be no need for stretch targets, Gershon savings or evaluations for additional capital bids against other services. As the service gravitates to maximum service delivery, it will be adding value which would be delighting customers, creating better town centre use, more shops to be open and opportunity to increase charges based on increased customer demand, as this will considerably help with their own income.

Very quickly the current paradigm could be:
Reduce investment in car parks equipment, replace over-age machines in another two years, accept loss of income due to machine failures and accept a loss of fine income due to inadequate lines. Reduce the chasing of unpaid fines as it costs £90 to chase £70 income. Reduce the number of Parking Attendants as fine income is reducing...

Which paradigm sounds like managing from a customer perspective and which gives better value for money?

In the new way of working, there will be no queues of work, nothing is batched and the public will expect issues to be resolved quickly and correctly. There will be no complex queue management systems, few hand-offs and a team of people who enjoy coming to work.

Consider a very early question in this book, 'How many minutes a day do you absolutely add value for customers?'

How will I measure success from this book?

I will consider it successful if:

- ✔ More people take a systems thinking based approach to work, perhaps taking a wider approach
- ✔ If an holistic view to service delivery genuinely is embraced more often
- ✔ Fragmenting organisation and fragmented work pieces become a thing of the past
- ✔ Enquiries through my website to a hundred or so cross-references in the book are often used
- ✔ The huge issues facing the public sector are predominantly addressed by adding value not cutting services
- ✔ Comments are raised to me, directly or via the IDeA network
- ✔ We get busier in this type of work
- ✔ This is adopted as a new international standard
- ✔ That the affects of the recession fade quickly, with no further unemployment.

I hope that you enjoyed this book and that it genuinely added value to you and your employer for the future, or if you are truly wedded to systems thinking and now Visualising Transformation, that you have already achieved several quick wins and have saved tens of thousands of pounds without meddling.

"Dave makes it so easy to understand the way forward, he takes amazingly difficult issues, to produce such simple ways forward"
PETER SLACK, DIRECTOR COMMUNITY SERVICES, TEESDALE D.C.

ABOUT THE AUTHOR

Dave trained as a Civil Engineer entering senior management at the age of 30, heading a wide ranging construction and maintenance department employing 200 staff. He was promoted to Director by the age of 35 heading an array of public sector services. His largest assignment saw him employing 2,500 staff with over a £100M budget.

Dave consciously started change management very early in his career, later discovering Deming and Continuous Improvement in 1992, developing additional ways to create positive change for services with a string of award winning, best in country services since then.

He has repeatedly transformed organisations, typically saving 14% of the total turnover for a whole department, while massively improving the speed and quality of customer services. These are generally technical based operations, including Highways, Housing, Waste, Parking, Street Scene, Transport, Facilities and Public Safety. He has also uniquely transformed recycling on many occasions, step improving recycling for no extra budget, including from 4 to 19% and from 38 to 68% with a considerable reduction in budget.

His previous book: *Quality or Politics/Politics or Quality* was the first addressing Systems Thinking in the public sector, this showed the delicate interactions between service improvement, political policy issues and the internal dynamics of working in the public sector. He has regularly presented concepts to learned organisations, with the longest running, most active, discussion threads on the IDeA website: http://www.idea.gov.uk/idk/forum/topics-index.do?forumId=10595955

Visualising Transformation™ is a new way of working designed by Dave Gaster, going beyond the normal boundaries of Systems Thinking, as it addresses Strategic and Operational development in parallel considering business opportunities even in a public sector area, adding far more value than simply cutting resources ever could.

ACKNOWLEDGEMENTS

This book has been created via an incredible amount of goodwill and the free sharing of information. It would have been impossible without the Deming Forum and Alliance of Deming Consultants. The ability to use the IDeA website for an open and frank exchange of thoughts, observations, research and case studies shows another way how modern technology can add value to society.

I must single out Nigel Clements and Geoff Elliott for their considerable support to gain insight, detail, correction and access to a whole new way of thinking. Your help has been phenomenal, thank you!

The availability of search engines such as Google and the on-line encyclopaedia called Wikipedia makes some work so much easier. Not all opinions in these areas are necessarily correct!

My immediate family of wife and three sons are so interesting to listen to; their experiences at work and socially bring a mixture of pleasure, to sending shudders down my spine. They work for some of the most admired companies in Britain, and yet the local management often ruin the ethos that has tried to be set. Far too often these businesses are concentrating on reducing costs, and in doing so, are reducing the value to their customers.

My parents live in Scotland, where a more progressive approach to supporting older, frail people at home is evident. The Scottish parliament appears a little less intrusive on day to day work, and more in tune with a systems thinking approach to service design.

My eldest son Daniel works with me, and is a fast developing BA. He notices the missed opportunities within traditional Lean interventions and does his best to add extra insight where people will listen. To him, Visualising Transformation is totally natural, it's the way that he has learned and worked.

Finally in this frame of mind the people who I have the privilege to work with and learn from have been phenomenal. I find that the vast majority of people who go to work have so much to say and give, if only the systems they work in would enable listening and receiving.

The book focuses on developing IT systems in many ways, frequently citing Microsoft systems such as Excel, Word, Access, PowerPoint, Outlook and Visio. I have used many other systems as well and have found my way round them to gain advantage. Two of my sons use Mac based systems, which enables a richness of choice and ability to address some options in a different way.

The advent of GIS and great report writing tools is heaven sent, don't under-estimate them.

REFERENCES

Ackoff, Russell L. (1999) Ackoff's Best: His Classic Writings on Management. Wiley. ISBN 0-471-31634-2

Checkland, Peter (1981) Systems Thinking, Systems Practice. Wiley. ISBN 0-471-27911-0

Clements, Nigel. PRISM training pack

Deming, W. Edwards (1966) Some Theory of Sampling. Dover Publications. ISBN 0-486-64684-X. OCLC 166526

Deming, W. Edwards (1986) Out of the Crisis. MIT Press. ISBN 0-911379-01-0. OCLC 13126265

Deming, W. Edwards (2000) The New Economics for Industry, Government, Education (2nd ed.). MIT Press. ISBN 0-262-54116-5. OCLC 44162616

Deming Forum. Circa 30 number A5 booklets

Gaster, Dave (2006) Quality or Politics, Nisbet Media. ISBN 0-9553000-0-2

Kohn, Alfie (1992) No Contest: The Case Against Competition; Revised edition. Mariner Books. ISBN 0-395-63125-4. OCLC 26255272

Kohn, Alfie (1999) Punished By Rewards: The Trouble with Gold Stars, Incentive Plans, A's, Praise, and Other Bribes. Mariner Books. ISBN 0-618-00181-6. OCLC 222755141

Mann, Nancy (1989). *Keys to Excellence: The Story of the Deming Philosophy – 3rd Edition*. Prestwick Books. ISBN 1-85251-097-8. OCLC 59892273

Neave, Henry R. (1990) The Deming Dimension. SPC Press, Inc. ISBN 0-945320-08-6. OCLC 22890202

Ohno, Taiichi (1995) Toyota Production System: Beyond Large-scale Production. Productivity Press Inc., ISBN 0-915299-14-3

Scholtes, Peter R. (1997) The Leader's Handbook: Making Things Happen, Getting Things Done. McGraw-Hill. ISBN 0-07-058028-6. OCLC 38097010

Seddon, John (2008) Systems Thinking in the Public Sector. Triarchy Press. ISBN 978-0-9550081-8-4

Seddon, John (2003) Freedom from Command and Control. Vanguard Press. ISBN 0 9546183 0 0

Senge, Peter M. (1990) The Fifth Discipline – The Art & Practice of The Learning Organization. Currency Doubleday. ISBN 0-385-26095-4

Shewhart, Walter A. (1939) Statistical Method from the Viewpoint of Quality Control. Dover Publications December 1, 1986. ISBN 0-486-65232-7. OCLC 13822053

Simcox, Julian. BaseLine® and Ackoff triangle

Tribus, Myron (1992) Quality First: Selected Papers on Quality and Productivity Improvement – 4th Edition. National Society of Professional Engineers. ISBN 99938-53-23-2

Walton, Mary (1986) The Deming Management Method. The Putnam Publishing Group. ISBN 0-399-55000-3. OCLC 13333772

Wheeler, Donald J. (1999) Understanding Variation: The Key to Managing Chaos – 2nd Edition. SPC Press Inc. ISBN 0-945320-53-1. OCLC 43697523

Wilson, Brian (2001) Soft Systems Methodology: Conceptual Model Building and its Contribution. Wiley. ISBN 0-471-89489-3

Womack, James P., Jones, Daniel T. and Roos, Daniel (1991) The Machine That Changed the World: The Story of Lean Production. HarperBusiness. ISBN 0-06-097417-6